4-Wheeler's Bible

Jim Allen

MBI Publishing Company

Dedication

As always, to Linda.

First published in 2002 by MBI Publishing Company, 380 Jackson Street, Suite 200, St. Paul, MN 55101-3885 USA

MBI Publishing Company books are also available at discounts in bulk quantity for industrial or sales-promotional use. For details write to Special Sales Manager at Motorbooks International Wholesalers & Distributors, 380 Jackson Street, Suite 200, St. Paul, MN 55101-3885 USA

Library of Congress Cataloging-in-Publication Data Available

ISBN 0-7603-1056-4

On the front cover:
Mindful of the transfer of weight to his rear tires, this Toyota driver keeps a close eye on the terrain ahead as he attempts a difficult uphill climb.

On the title page:
Four-wheeling is four-season fun, and each season presents its own challenges. These Rovers wend their way through barren, snow-covered mountains. The road is in pretty good shape here, but there's no guardrail to keep a mistake from becoming a long plummet downward.

On the back cover:
You don't need a hairy beast of a rig to enjoy four-wheel adventures. This Land Rover Discovery found its way to a very nice vantage point in ordinary, street-ready form.

Edited by Peter Bodensteiner
Designed by Stephanie Michaud
Layout by Bruce Leckie

Printed in China

About the Author

After training as a U.S. Army watercraft operator and serving as a marine engineer in the closing years of the Vietnam War, Jim Allen left the Army to pursue a career in auto repair. An ASE-certified Master Tech, Allen worked on everything from Abarths to Volkswagens, but ended up as a factory-trained Land Rover technician for nearly five years. After twenty years of twisting wrenches and ten years of part-time writing, he went full-time into the magazine biz, taking a sideline job with Land Rover North America as an off-highway-driving instructor. He began recreational four-wheeling in 1975, when he purchased a military surplus Dodge. A succession of 4x4s has followed that tired old GI truck. Allen is the author of almost 1,500 magazine articles and six books on four-wheeling topics. He lives on a 45-acre farm in northwestern Ohio.

Contents

PREFACE

Welcome to the *Four-Wheeler's Bible*. I hope you'll enjoy this armchair trip as a companion to the real thing. More to the point, I hope what you read and see here will enhance your enjoyment of the world of four-wheeling. You won't be rinsing any grit out of your hair after taking this paper journey, but if it inspires you to more frequent and enjoyable real trips, I will be content.

Besides being a four-wheeler of more than 27 years' experience, I had the opportunity to teach the four-wheeling arts for one of the world's great four-wheel-drive manufacturers, Land Rover. That company has a stunning program for teaching these skills, both to owners and to their own employees. In a bit more than three years, I taught thousands of people in assorted situations and venues. It was a rewarding experience personally, but it also offered an opportunity to see the areas where many people have problems. Combining that experience with years of four-wheeling and observing people on the trail, I ended up with some ideas on how and what to teach.

Much of the motivation for this book came from seeing some of my favorite four-wheeling spots closed. With the ranks of the four-wheeling public swollen to highest-ever numbers, our impact must be measured and minimized. Some people say the only way to do this is by locking us out. Many others say that by adopting land-friendly techniques and responsible behavior, four-wheelers can accomplish the same thing. While there is a destructive element in our midst determined to ignore common sense, the majority of us are willing to work to keep what we have. Newcomers can benefit from learning the right way to do things, and the rest of us can always use a refresher course. My hope is that this book serves both purposes.

—Jim Allen
Western Colorado, Winter 2002

ACKNOWLEDGMENTS

A great many people helped in the writing of this book. Some didn't even know they were doing it! Over a 27-year period, that's a lot of people. To every four-wheeler who aced an obstacle with exceptional skill and made me nod my head in respect, I say thanks. To every person who walked up with an idea on how to tackle the problem that was overwhelming my Right Guard and my patience, a humble thank you. To the people who stripped their rig of parts to get mine going again, I say thanks. To every student driver who came up with a brilliant line over an obstacle I thought was figured out, thank you for the lesson in humility. To the gearheads who teach by fine example, many thanks. Thanks to all the 'wheelers who drove in front of my hungry camera, only to be gobbled up by the celluloid for all time—especially those of you who were having a bad day at that moment.

There are also a number of people who were directly involved in this book. I'll start with some of my four-wheeling role models. Thanks to Tom Collins, one of the best 'wheelers on the planet and a great team leader. And the same to the rest of the "old gang" at Land Rover—J.P. Slavin, Lea Magee, Tim Hensley, and Mark McDonald; as well as the "new gang" additions, Bob Burns, Don Floyd, Jim Swett, Jim West, Fred Monsees, and Mike Hopwood. They were good times!

Bill Burke, instructor extraordinaire, thanks for the help under very tough circumstances. Thanks, Don Haines and Chris Overacker, for helping to set up and endure the seemingly endless photo sessions. Ken Brubaker came through with some photos at the right time; thanks, Ken! Randy Lyman, the "Diffgod" himself, enhanced my understanding of axles at a critical time. Steve Watson was always a willing ear and an agile brain to bounce deep technical concepts from to see where they landed. Thanks to John Radloff for educating me on the ham radio world. I may yet take that test! Jun Yoshioka, thanks for setting me straight on the math. Tom Telford, thanks for the first insights into engineering practice. Tom Wood, thanks for making sure I was properly versed in the world of driveshafts. To everyone else whose name has slipped from my feeble memory's grasp, a final word of thanks.

Introduction

Four-wheeling has become a wildly popular pastime. It combines an enjoyment of the outdoors with what has become an American obsession—the motor vehicle. To some, the four-wheel-drive vehicle is the means to an end. It delivers them to the spots they want to enjoy on foot, bike, snowmobile, ATV, skis, or horseback. To others, it's the end itself. The challenge of mastering terrain and vehicle is the motivation. Either way, the better a driver masters the skills needed to surmount the obstacles, the safer and more enjoyable the trip.

Four-wheeling encompasses elements beyond driving skill. Vehicle preparation and modifications play a big part as well. The choices in these areas can be mind-boggling, and my technical experience and deep involvement in four-wheeling may offer you some useful insight and perspective. Included are enough technical details and straightforward advice

from manufacturers and experts to get you started, at least. Because of the wide-angle scope of this book, I've had to assume a little technical knowledge on your part. You may be above or below the arbitrary mark I set, but other books and a number of great magazines can help fill you in on the technical part of 4x4 buildups. I would also refer you to two of my other books—*Jeep 4x4 Performance Handbook* and *Chevy and GMC Truck Performance Handbook*—for more information on this topic. In some ways, they are very universal, so they may be worth a look even if you don't drive a rig wearing one of those nameplates.

Four-wheel-drive vehicles can also go beyond the grit-in-their-teeth crowd. This technology is used to enhance traction and safety on the highway, particularly in areas of severe winter weather. Comparing the all-wheel-drive cars and SUVs designed for street use to off-highway-capable four-wheel-drive rigs is like comparing apples and oranges. Each type has its place and use, and each has advantages

and disadvantages. The problem is that you can't substitute oranges in an apple pie and you can't put apples in an Orange Crush soft drink. This book will keep the apples in the pie and the oranges in the Crush, but bear in mind that it's slanted toward off-highway driving and the vehicles capable of that. We won't be dealing much with all-wheel-drive cars or SUVs and their use on the highway.

This book is a clearinghouse of information and technique that will be most useful to novice and middle-level four-wheelers. By the time you get into the advanced category, you will have figured things out your own, or through the school of hard knocks. Knowing that even the most grizzled gear grinder is always looking for a new edge, however, I imagine they might find something of use here too.

Finally, I hope that you can integrate all the do's and don'ts into a mental program that runs in the background and doesn't take away from your deep enjoyment of experiencing the outdoors in your 4x4. Happy trails!

CHAPTER 1

ZEN AND THE ART OF FOUR-WHEELING

Attitude and Emergencies

Where does it go? Seeing what's over the next ridge or around the next bend is part of what draws us into the outback. A 4x4 can be both the means to an end, or the end itself. Some of us use our rigs to carry us to the truly remote areas where we can enjoy the outdoors outside the vehicle. For others, the vehicle is a vital part of the enjoyment. Either way, knowing the ins and outs will carry you up this trail in safety and fully able to enjoy the experience.

To be a successful four-wheeler, you'll need to acquire the necessary tools and equipment. At the top of that list are good judgment and common sense. Everything else stems from these attributes, including the fun part of the hobby. We'll call the combination of these things "attitude." Most of us would agree that it's more fun to be a successful, thinking driver than it is to be a disaster area on wheels. It's also cheaper!

Imagine yourself as the captain of that little four-wheel-drive landship. Just like any commander, your choices dictate the fate of the ship and the people aboard. Ask yourself if you'd rather be the skipper of the *Titanic*, haunted forever by one major error in judgment, or a captain who finishes a career without the notoriety of a major disaster.

Inevitably, all of us have moments when our best judgment fails us. Overall, these times are mercifully few, and we hope they occur when we are strapped into a recliner and not the driver's seat. Other than sheer fate and human error, there are two influences beyond abject carelessness that can cause lapses of judgment out there on the trail. One is

universal and the other limited to the male of species.

ADRENALINE POISONING

The excitement and healthy fear of a new or tricky situation may induce a shot of adrenaline. Without the physical exertions of fight or flight, a shot of adrenaline in a relatively inactive human body is like racing a car engine at 5,000 rpm in the garage! Beyond lapses of judgment, other notable symptoms can occur, including deterioration of motor skills, freezing up, tunnel vision, and an odd perception that the world has slowed down. This last symptom is very common and results in drivers who tend to drive too

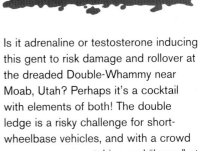

the dirt

Adrenaline Poisoning: Nature intended adrenaline (a.k.a. epinephrine) to be our bodies' supercharger in times of danger. It gives us the strength to fight harder or to run faster. Unfortunately, it also seems to shut down a good deal of our higher brain functions.

Is it adrenaline or testosterone inducing this gent to risk damage and rollover at the dreaded Double-Whammy near Moab, Utah? Perhaps it's a cocktail with elements of both! The double ledge is a risky challenge for short-wheelbase vehicles, and with a crowd watching and "honor" at stake, it's easy to let the moment overcome good judgment. It takes a high level of skill and finesse to get a Wrangler up the "Whammy." When facing a challenge such as this for the first time, watch and analyze others before making your attempts. Give it three or four shots, and if unsuccessful, back off to let your adrenaline disperse. You can always try it again later, whether that's in 15 minutes or next year.

The Camel Trophy was an international adventure/competition held annually from 1980 to 1998 in many out-of-the-way corners of the world. The core of the event was getting essentially stock vehicles through thousands of miles of barely navigable terrain. Vehicles such as this Land Rover Discovery endured a lifetime of hardship on just one event that often measured daily mileage in single digits. The key to getting through at all was good driving, judgment, and, as in this obvious predicament, recovery skills–though such participants as Fred Hoess, shown here in the 1996 Kalimantan event, were often challenged as athletes. Training and experience got them through areas where even the stout Land Rovers were overwhelmed.

fast. Adrenaline poisoning temporarily takes the fine edge off our capabilities when we can least afford to lose them. Time, oxygen, and exercise tend to cancel out the bad effects of adrenaline. Often a few deep breaths and a moment of pause are enough to regain equilibrium. A short rest or some walking may also help to slow you down.

TESTOSTERONE POISONING

This is a little tongue-in-cheek, but it's my way of describing the sometimes-inexplicable actions in groups of men facing a challenge. In the effort to outdo the other guy, we are vulnerable to taking unnecessary chances with our equipment and our safety. I suppose it's an offshoot of our animal instinct to attract mates by showing our manly prowess. Unfortunately, we do it even when there are no females around. Wherever it comes from, men, resist!

THE CAMEL CREDO

From 1980 to 1998, an annual international four-wheel-drive adventure/competition created a new definition for the term "tough four-wheeling." It

was known as the Camel Trophy. The locations varied, but the common element was the extreme four-wheeling and endurance challenges contestants faced over a 1,000-mile (or more) excursion across almost trackless terrain in some very remote part of the world. Sometimes the daily mileage was counted in single digits … and that could be for a full 24-hour day of work!

The teams trained in their own countries with coordinators who were past participants or acknowledged experts. Land Rover supplied the identically prepared competition and support vehicles for all but the first and last events, and their experienced instructors aided in developing the driver-training program. In the long years of practice, someone in that organization distilled four-wheeling into one sentence. If you only remember one thing from this book, remember this….

As slowly as possible, as fast as necessary.

This is the essence of four-wheeling. Recreational four-wheeling is not a race and the single most common mistake is to drive too fast. Part of that is the result of the "speeded-up" effect of adrenaline poisoning we talked about earlier. The second part of the Camel Credo, "as fast as necessary,"

recognizes that there are times when a more aggressive driving style is needed.

THE LEARNING CURVE

Whether you are starting from scratch or going up from one level of difficulty to another, you will be faced with failures and mistakes that seem outrageously stupid in retrospect. The

trail will soon become a familiar and comfortable environment and your skill level will increase with practice.

As you learn, choosing trails becomes an important way to further your skills and to stay within your current skill level. How can you determine the degree of difficulty of a given trail? Often you can't. If you start up a trail that exceeds your limits, simply turn back when the trip gets too hairy.

The learning curve includes gradually increasing the level of difficulty as your skill and comfort levels increase. You will naturally develop to a level where you wish to stop.

TREAD LIGHTLY

The upswing of 4x4 popularity has drastically increased the numbers of vehicles on public and private lands. This can have a very negative impact on these areas if we don't all do our part. Unfortunately, there is a small but very destructive element in

our midst that not only doesn't do its part, but goes out of its way to tear things up. Each of these destructive acts supplies ammunition to environmental groups with dedicated lawyers and lobbyists who seek to close more areas on our ever-shrinking list of four-wheeling sites. The rules for treading lightly are simple, common sense, and will not hinder your ability to have fun.

Stay on the Established Trail

Never go cross-country and avoid obviously unauthorized bypasses or spur trails. Bypasses happen when people veer off the trail to avoid an obstacle. Before long, that bypass is avoided by another bypass and soon you have a 50-foot swath of torn-up ground. Most four-wheelers like a challenge! When a tough obstacle comes, take your lumps.

Unauthorized trails happen in a similar way, when someone blazes a trail and later travelers encounter it and want to see where it goes. Given enough time, it can become a fairly established-looking trail.

Avoid spurs that are obviously not authorized routes. If in doubt, avoid it altogether. Maps are not always helpful, as authorized routes sometimes mysteriously "disappear" from maps. Conspiracy theorists in the four-wheeling groups accuse government agencies of deliberately doing this as a precursor to closing a trail.

This is what happens when drivers bypass a wet spot on the trail. First, the trail gets wider, visible to the right of the Bum-V. Eventually, a whole new road is created (far right). Instead of a 10- or 12-foot swath through this mountain meadow, you now have 40 feet, and with wet weather ahead, it will probably grow even wider. This is what helps get trails closed.

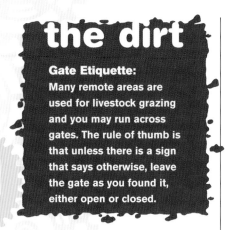

the dirt

Gate Etiquette:
Many remote areas are used for livestock grazing and you may run across gates. The rule of thumb is that unless there is a sign that says otherwise, leave the gate as you found it, either open or closed.

Vehicular Hemorrhages:
Never leave pools of coolant. Its sweet odor attracts animals to drink and the coolant will kill them.

Ride 'Em Cowboy:
Horses are flight animals and some are easily frightened by loud machinery. Give riders a wide berth so their horses don't rear or bolt.

Haul Out Your Trash

While you're at it, take the time to haul out a little of someone else's litter. Always leave your campsite or lunch stop area better than you found it. Many four-wheelers stop to pick up trash they observe on or near the trail. In fact, some groups compete to see who hauls out the most. The logic is simple: reduce the mess, reduce the reasons why other people want to keep four-wheelers out.

Be Kind to the Trail

An unpaved road is susceptible to damage. Avoid actions that chew it up unnecessarily, such as tire spinning and rooster tails in wet conditions. Certain unpaved roads are best not driven when exceedingly wet. If you do tear up a section of trail in the normal course of travel, a little shovel work could save it from future erosion.

Vehicular Hemorrhages

It's not uncommon in the harder-core four-wheeling realms to have a vehicle problem that involves fluid leakage. Collect what you can in any sort of container or soak it up with rags. After repairs, it's your duty to clean up as much as you can. Oil-soaked dirt can be bagged and taken home; oily rocks can be wiped up with rags, or soaked up with dirt that can be hauled off. Brake fluid and coolant can be rinsed with water and diluted. By taking even the most moderate measures, you can prevent the contamination of streams and the ground and the poisoning of wild critters.

Hikers, Bikers, and Critters Get the Right-of-Way

Give hikers and mountain bikers the right-of-way. Your exhaust and dust can lessen their enjoyment of the outdoors. Remember that they don't have a window to roll up! Responsible four-wheelers will stop and let people and people-powered machines pass. Ditto for people on horseback. If the area is remote and the climate is warm, I may also ask hikers and bikers if they have enough water and

maybe even offer them a cold drink if I have some to spare. Finally, let wild critters and livestock pass with a minimum of disruption.

Respect Private Property

Don't drive past "private property" or "no trespassing" signs. Access to private property is at the pleasure of the owner, so don't abuse the privilege if you have it. When you are crossing private property on a public right-of-way, don't assume that the property on either side of the road is free to access. Often, owners will allow you to recreate on their land if you ask for permission.

Respect History and Natural Wonders

If every visitor to a historical or natural wonder picked up a souvenir, there'd be nothing left for anyone to look at. Don't be a vulture. Look, pick up, and examine if you must, but leave it there.

TRAIL ETIQUETTE

Beyond treating our land with respect, a certain four-wheeling trail etiquette has evolved in the 50 or so years of the sport. Learning these informal but common-sense courtesies will allow you to fit in with any group of four-wheelers.

Bring a Vehicle in Good Condition

Nothing will get you on the fecal list faster than ruining a group's trip with an avoidable breakdown. Your companions are obligated by common decency to offer aid and not leave you stranded alone in the wilderness. Most four-wheelers will strip their own rig of parts to get you going again. But if it's obvious that your breakdown was easily avoidable by maintenance or some pre-trip repairs, you can look forward to some unpleasant looks, rather edgy jibes, and a reputation you'll have to work hard to overcome. Bring the food, fuel, and sundries you need for the trip. Don't be known as the mooch.

Towing Points and Gear

Life gets tough for everyone when you get stuck or disabled and don't have proper recovery points. We'll get into this in some depth later, but trail etiquette dictates at least one solidly mounted recovery point front and rear. Even better, have a good tow/recovery strap and a couple of shackles in your kit.

trail as well. I've seen cats, ferrets, parrots, cockatiels, and one huge iguana riding gleefully in their owner's 4x4s.

Trail Improvements

Every vehicle is different, so it stands to reason that some rigs might need to pile a few rocks here or there to create clearance while others may not. The people with better-equipped

Make it easy for folks to help. Having a safe recovery point at each end of your rig, whether it be bone stock or highly modified, is both common sense and a trail etiquette item.

Animals

Dogs and other animals can make great four-wheeling companions and are commonly seen on the trail. Always remember that your animal reflects on you. A friendly, well-mannered pooch can make you a lot of friends. A dog that has to mark every tire on the run and sniff every crotch can have the opposite effect. Overly protective animals that may lunge at or even bite people walking close to their owner's rigs will not earn high marks, either. You may see other domesticated critters on the

rigs find it annoying to encounter a path that's been made too easy. It's customary that if you have to make more than just a few modifications to an obstacle, you undo your road

Whether your nonhuman traveling companion is reptile or canine, it's your responsibility to keep them under control. This good-natured critter was particularly well-behaved, earning mondo popularity points for its owner. I won't show you pics of the pooch that bit the sun shade off my camera or the one that urinated on my camera bag.

building for the next person or group. If the area looks like most, if not all, of the vehicles passing through need the trail mods, you are doing the next person a favor to leave your improvements in place.

WHEN ALL ELSE FAILS, READ THE MANUAL

The manual for your 4x4 truck or SUV is chock full of good information on the operation of controls, vehicle specifications, and often some pretty good driving tips. Take the time to familiarize yourself with this little book. The main points of interest are the operation of the controls and vital specifications, such as fording depth, approach, departure, and ramp breakover angles; tire pressures; and service specifications. It will be the most specific information available for your rig.

SAFETY

Four-wheeling is very safe overall. Certainly your odds are better on the trail than they are in rush hour. Unlike the daily commute, what happens on the trail mostly comes down to the driver and most of that is within his or her control. Drive well and safely, and nothing bad happens.

One safety consideration many new 4x4 owners fail to grasp before purchasing an SUV or pickup is how differently these vehicles handle from an ordinary car. That's not to say that a properly driven four-wheel-drive vehicle is inherently unsafe, despite what you may have seen on the TV news shows. The very attributes that make them perform on the trail, however, detract from their highway prowess. Driving a 4x4 as an everyday transporter should be an informed choice. You need to drive any 4x4 with more respect and with a finer touch. They are not sports cars!

It's much more fun and safer to travel in a group, though a group this large can test your patience. You always travel as slowly as the slowest member of the group—but then the whole idea is to enjoy your time in the slow lane.

Another cardinal rule is to avoid traveling alone in remote areas. The dangers of this are obvious. Out there, a breakdown, illness, or injury is more difficult to deal with and potentially more dangerous. It's safer and more fun to go in groups of two or more.

Vehicle maintenance is a safety item. Breaking down in a remote area is a potentially fatal problem. A rig that has been regularly serviced and checked usually does not break down, because problems are caught early. That's not to say that problems will never happen to a well-maintained 4x4; the odds are just reduced to a more acceptable level.

As mentioned before, vehicle damage is a possibility that gets more probable as the degree of terrain difficulty increases. OK, so once you've got your rig intact enough to limp back; you're home free, right? Wrong-o! Temporary repairs involving tires, suspension, steering, drivetrain, or the fuel system should be dealt with in a permanent manner before you take the highway home. Until that happens, you crawl along at a safe pace. More than a few

four-wheelers have made corncob repairs on the trail and blithely headed home, only to "crash and burn" back on the highway.

Emergency Gear

I regard emergency items as insurance. Paying out the money and investing the time is often a sort of cosmic "get-out-of-jail-free" card. On the other hand, it only takes one potentially dangerous incident for which you were totally prepared for that equipment to earn "paid in full" status. I have found my own emergency equipment more an aid to others than myself. That's how things sometimes seem to work, but I don't tempt fate and invite the universe to bite me in the butt.

Fire Extinguishers

Since the day after I had to beat out an engine fire with a neighbor's doormat, I have had a fire extinguisher in all my vehicles. From that day in 1975, I have never had another fire, though I have emptied my extinguisher three times to save other rigs. Fire's

The ultimate limp! With a broken rear axle shaft (c-clip type) and no spare, the owner of this Wrangler was faced with a grim dilemma. Leave the rig out in the boondocks for the better part of a day, possibly to be picked clean before he could get back; spend the night with the rig until help and parts returned; or nurse it back to a spot where it could be hauled onto a trailer. With the help of enterprising friends, he was able to nurse the rig along on three wheels after some special preparation. The vehicle was driven about 10 miles over tough terrain this way. A truck and a trailer waited on an easier section of trail to bring him to civilization for proper repairs. This is not an advisable solution in every case, but it shows that ingenuity and persistence can solve almost any problem.

An old joke, but it does give me the chance to illustrate a point. To some, four-wheeling is like an addictive drug and they spend every waking moment and all spare (and some not-so-spare) cash on their rig. It's your time on Earth and your money, but there are other things in life. Especially if a family is involved, maintain perspective. Don't let your spouse be a 4x4 widow or your kids 4x4 orphans.

destructive and life-threatening potential is obvious—making a fire extinguisher mandatory gear.

There are many different types of fire extinguishers, some of which are not practical for vehicle use. The most common and inexpensive extinguisher is the dry chemical type. These are divided into two general categories: the standard "department store," or stored-pressure, variety; and cartridge-operated designs.

In the first type, the dry chemical is stored in a pressurized container. The chief advantages of this type are low cost and compact size. Disadvantages are the relatively vulnerable container and the possibility of the unit losing pressure over time.

In the cartridge-operated extinguisher, the chemical is stored in one container and a small, separate, nitrogen-charged container provides the pressure when actuated. These extinguishers are very efficient but expensive

to buy and maintain. They are bulky but more effective than a stored pressure extinguisher. They are also more durable in harsh environments.

Fire extinguishers are rated A, B, C, and D, for different types of fires. Class A fires are of combustible materials such as wood and paper that can be extinguished with water and with certain (but not all) dry chemicals. Class B fires involve flammable liquids or vapors, and Class C fires are electrical in nature. Both B and C classes require smothering by a substance that will not spread the fire or conduct electricity (using water on high-voltage electrical fires can get you electrocuted). Class D fires occur with materials such as magnesium, titanium, sodium, and zirconium. Putting out these difficult fires requires very specialized equipment that is beyond the scope of our discussion.

Looking at the classifications, Class B and C come to mind for vehicles,

A First Aid Kit

Here is a common sense kit that includes most of what a person may need off-road. It does not cover every eventuality, but it is usable within the realm of most people's first aid knowledge. If you have any medical training, add to the list as your experience dictates. I strongly suggest that all frequent four-wheelers take a Red Cross CPR and First Aid class.

Pain
aspirin
ibuprofen

Stomach
antidiarrheals (Immodium, Pepto Bismol)
antacids
Ipecac (for inducing vomiting)

Antiseptic
alcohol swabs
alcohol (liquid, in plastic bottle)
hydrogen peroxide

Bandages
selection of Band-Aids
sterile pads, nonstick (Telfa),
    assorted sizes
tape
sterile gauze roll
Sterislips (for closing wounds)
large sterile dressings
elastic wrap (Ace) bandages

Tools
fine tweezers
scissors
splint (inflatable)
cervical collar
cold pack (for sprains and burns)
face shield or mask (for rescue breathing)
compact first aid manual
tourniquet
sterile latex gloves
sturdy case for first aid kit

Skin
sunblock
calamine lotion
hand cleaner
Oak & Ivy Armor (for appropriate areas)
hydrocortisone cream
antibacterial ointment
sterile latex gloves

but consider that you may need fire suppression for other things, such as a campfire that gets out of control or a brush fire started by a catalytic converter. In this overall situation, an ABC extinguisher has you covered for everything. The difference is in the chemicals used. The B- and C-rated units use plain old sodium bicarbonate (baking soda), which is white in color. The ABC units use monoammonium phosphate, which is a good smother agent, and is yellow in color.

Mount your extinguisher in a place that is easily accessible and readily visible. Fires demand immediate attention, and the person who needs to find and retrieve your extinguisher won't necessarily be you. Check the gauges regularly and service them every couple of years. Not only can the pressurized charge leak slowly, but the powder inside can become compacted and you may not get a full charge when you need it.

You can go to a discount store and buy a cheap, nonserviceable, one-shot extinguisher. These units are better than throwing dirt, but since some of their vital parts are made of plastic, they may not hold up well in a rough-and-tumble four-wheeler. For a few

more dollars, you can get an extinguisher with metal parts. These can be serviced over and over and are essentially lifetime units, as long as the containers are not dented.

First Aid

Although a first-aid kit may be most important to a four-wheeler who is farther away from medical help, people have died beside the freeway for the lack of a simple first-aid kit and the knowledge needed to use it. A first-aid kit of some type is a must for any well-equipped 4x4. How elaborate you get depends a lot on your planned destinations. Obviously, crossing the Sahara will require more preparation than a highway day trip, but some basics should be in every first-aid kit.

The first items would fall under the heading of prescription drugs. If anyone in your party has special needs in that area, it's appropriate to ensure that that person has sufficient medication for the time away from home, plus a little extra in case of a delay. An obvious example is insulin, but the rule applies to any necessary medication. I heard a story about a diabetic man who got stranded in the outback by bad weather without enough medication. Only the heroic efforts of some very determined rescuers saved the man's life.

Most medical situations are minor. A headache, diarrhea, indigestion, or altitude sickness can take the fun out of a trip, so it makes sense to have some remedies around for these minor ailments. Too much fun can also result in minor cuts and abrasions, so anti-

You can buy first aid kits in any form, from a few Band-Aids in a box to something that beats many Third World hospitals. You need not go to elaborate extremes if you are an occasional day-tripper. But if you like the really offbeat locales, think about a high-end kit. Look at the suggested first aid kit contents in the nearby sidebar for some ideas on what to carry.

The days when we could go cross country are long gone. Even when I snapped the photo 17 years ago, this was considered poor practice. Though cross-country jaunts weren't strictly illegal everywhere back then, those of us with a long history in four-wheeling probably have some actions in our past to regret. Back then, it didn't seem like a big deal. There were plenty of places to four-wheel. Today, with our available four-wheeling areas reduced by half (my educated guess), we are fighting for the right to continue using motor vehicles in remote areas, and we can't afford even one incident of straying off the trail.

septic and small bandages are in order. Sprains are not unusual in outdoor frolicking, so elastic-wrap bandages can be handy. Skin lotions, sunblock, bug repellent, and a poison oak or ivy protectant (in the areas where it abounds) are all common-sense items.

When you get into more major injuries or illnesses, the focus shifts to your knowledge of first aid. Even if you're not trained in this area, there may be someone around who is, and having the right stuff on hand could mean life or death for an injured person. You have the option of taking first-aid courses as well. The Red Cross, for one, offers both basic first aid and CPR classes in most larger towns.

Cargo Tie-Downs

Have you ever been beaned in the back of the head on a steep downhill by some small bit of cargo that came adrift? Perhaps you can't remember because of the resulting brain injury? Imagine your overloaded toolbox hitting you in the head. It might be the last thing you imagine! You can buy nifty, flush-mounted tie-downs for the cargo area. You can also head down to the wrecking yard or surplus store and find something that works. The main goal is to get your heavy gear secured.

Rollover Protection

An open-topped rig should have at least a minimal roll bar. Since the 1970s, open-topped rigs have come so

16

equipped. Harder-core 'wheelers often make improvements to the basic setup for increased protection. Hardtopped rigs sometimes will have internal protection built in. Modern hardtops come with some built-in protection that is adequate in most situations. Older hardtops may actually be more at risk, despite their reputations of being built tougher in the "good-ol'-days."

My recommendation for all open-topped rigs is to have at least one bar. If the rig is used in upper-medium to difficult terrain, I recommend a full-cage setup. Hardtops are pretty safe overall, so the addition of a bar or cage is not generally necessary. The few hardtopped rigs that operate in the hard-core realms often have cages built into them.

Survival

Most of us don't go so far into the boondocks that dying of thirst or hunger is a significant danger, yet a few people die in just these circumstances every year. The root cause is usually going out alone and unprepared. Weather is often a primary issue as well. Heading alone into the mountains with a snowstorm imminent, for example, is asking for trouble. In a similar vein, people have headed to remote desert spots alone, gotten stuck or broken down, and died. Extreme conditions of hot or cold cause people to suffer the most and die the quickest. In most other areas, you can live for more than two days without food, shelter, or water.

There are many survival books on the market devoted totally to the subject. These typically advise you to stay with the vehicle in adverse weather, unless there are compelling reasons to do otherwise. The vehicle will provide at least some measure of shelter and comfort and, depending on its color

and that of the surroundings, may be easier for rescuers to spot than a person alone. Weigh those considerations against the distance to help, a *known* route to help, the weather conditions, how well you are prepared (health, clothing, shoes, supplies, and so on), and the potential of help finding you in short order. Compelling reasons to take more risks would be if you are in a vulnerable position somehow or you have an injured person who needs aid (you shouldn't leave an injured person alone in most cases).

The first line of defense is to not put yourself into these dire situations. Travel in a group. The second defense is knowledge. People have died of exposure because they didn't know how to replace a fuse or perform the most rudimentary recovery operation. People have been stranded by what they forgot. I ran across a family stuck for the better part of a day with a well-equipped rig because they had left the winch control at home. And last, a common-sense array of survival gear can give you the basics to last until help arrives.

A small bag or pack with a few survival items appropriate to the area can be a lifesaver. In winter, appropriate clothing, including a warm hat, gloves, and winter boots, a sleeping bag, high-energy food, and water are all it takes to keep you from doing a Popsicle imitation. In the desert, water and more water is what you need, as well as shade (a tarp or sun shade is better than the vehicle, which soaks up heat), and a flashlight for signaling and working at night. You have two or three signal mirrors on the vehicle. There's more to know, of course, but these are the basics. Carry more if you deem it necessary, but at least *think* about potential survival situations every time you hit the dirt and make a few simple preparations.

CHAPTER 2

GET A GRIP

Traction at work! The grip those four tires have on terra firma, whatever sort of terra firma, is what makes the trail a go or no-go situation.

Traction 101

HERE WE'LL COVER:

The types of four-wheel drive
•
The meaning of traction
•
Different types of differentials
•
Using these systems on the road and trail

Half the battle in learning to four-wheel well is understanding the dynamics of your vehicle and translating that knowledge into effective driving technique. It's a complex equation, but when you boil it down, there are only two elements your 4x4 needs to perform in the dirt: traction and clearance. How much or how little of these two elements a vehicle possesses will dictate its trail performance.

WHAT IS FOUR-WHEEL DRIVE?

Four-wheel drive doubles the amount of traction available to an ordinary two-wheel-drive rig by providing a second driving axle. What is traction? After looking through several dictionaries and engineering texts, I learned that traction can be defined a few different ways. For the purposes of our Traction 101 discussion, let's call it the transformation of engine torque into vehicular motion. Most of that transformation occurs where the tires meet the ground. Therefore, the tire's grip on the ground surface plays a big part in the traction equation, as does the number of gripping tires that have power applied.

The basic and perennial four-wheel-drive system consists of three components. First is the transfer case, which splits the power from the engine to drive the other two components, the front and rear axles. The transfer case may also contain a selectable gearing-down mechanism called low range,

which drops the overall gear ratio. This gearing step-down is used to provide increased engine torque multiplication or engine braking capabilities needed for steeper terrain.

Part-Time Four-Wheel Drive

For most of four-wheel drive's history, part-time systems have been the norm. Until recently, the means to shift from two-wheel to four-wheel drive was a mechanical lever. These days, the lever has been replaced in many vehicles by a push-button or selector switch setup that actuates an electric servo motor that does the actual shifting.

Before Arthur Warn made free-wheeling hubs popular in the late 1940s, the front axles of four-wheel-drive vehicles would spin along with the tires, causing extra drag and reducing fuel economy. Warn's invention uncoupled the axles from the hubs,

the dirt

Part-time Systems:
The main advantage of a part-time system is that the vehicle drives like a "normal" 4x2 until the extra traction capability is needed for rough terrain. Driving only two wheels burns less fuel and reduces tire and mechanical wear and tear, especially on dry pavement.

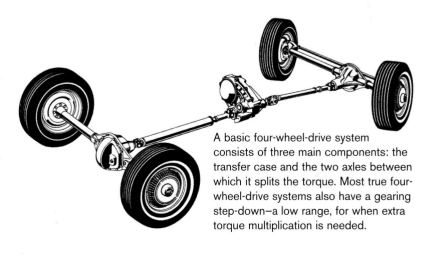

A basic four-wheel-drive system consists of three main components: the transfer case and the two axles between which it splits the torque. Most true four-wheel-drive systems also have a gearing step-down—a low range, for when extra torque multiplication is needed.

THE POWER PATH

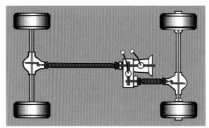

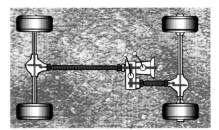

Part-time four-wheel drive in two-wheel drive. Power is delivered through the trans, t-case, and to the ring gear. On this high-traction surface, the power can use both axles.

Part-time four-wheel drive in four-wheel drive. On this high-tractive surface, both the front and rear diffs are delivering power equally to all four wheels.

Part-time four-wheel drive on a low-tractive surface. You can see that the power has taken the path of least resistance and has gone to one tire on each axle. Which side it will take depends on which tire has the best traction. It could be opposite, like this, or both on one side or the other.

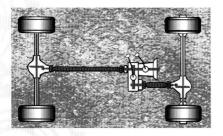

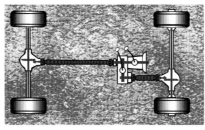

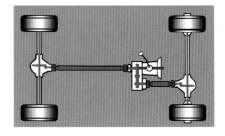

Shown here is a part-time system in four-wheel drive with a rear locker. In this configuration, you've got three tires pulling.

Shown here is a part-time system with true four-wheel drive, meaning lockers in both axles. All four tires are pulling in this configuration.

Shown here is a full-time system with the center diff unlocked. On hard pavement, it can deliver power to the front or rear and allows some difference of speed front to rear. With open diffs, the same thing happens at the axles.

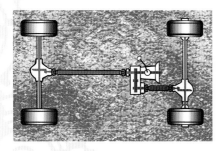

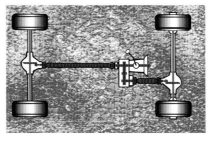

This is what happens when a low-traction situation is encountered with the center differential unlocked. Power may take the path of least resistance. . . to one tire! It could be any of the four.

With the center diff locked, the full-time unit becomes just like a part-time rig in four-wheel drive.

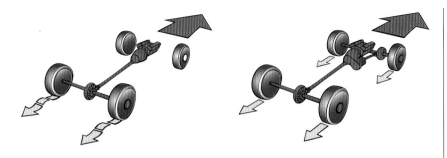

Four-wheel drive provides twice the grip, or at least the potential for twice the grip. True four-wheel drive requires locking differentials in both axles, but a highly tractive surface equally applied to all four wheels does almost as well.

allowing the wheels to spin separately from the axle shafts. When needed, the axles could be recoupled. This simple manual device has been refined over the years to include automatic units that lock when four-wheel drive is engaged. Typically, a part-time four-wheel-drive vehicle gains 2 to 5 miles per gallon by the addition of free-wheeling hubs. Virtually all recent 4x4s with part-time systems come from the factory with freewheeling hubs of some type, or a Center Axle Disconnect (CAD).

A CAD complicates the installation of a limited slip or automatic locker later on. CADs have been fitted to many mid-1980 and newer Jeeps, and IFS trucks/SUVs from General Motors starting in 1983.

Full-Time Four-Wheel Drive

Full-time four-wheel drive was actually the norm until the development of the part-time transfer case by Timken for a production Dodge military truck in 1934. The modern era of full-time systems began in 1973, when AMC Jeep introduced the Borg-Warner 1339 transfer case in the Wagoneer and J-Series trucks and called it Quadra-Trac. From there, full-time systems have developed into a very common element in the 4x4 arena, especially for SUVs.

Full-time systems continuously supply torque to the front and rear axles, but because front and rear wheel speeds differ in turns, a differential device is needed in the transfer case to

allow the front and rear driveshafts to turn at different speeds. In most 4x4s, this center differential can be locked when a true 50/50 torque split is needed in rough terrain. Some full-time systems use a manual lock and others use an automatic lock or limited slip. Automatic locking has been accomplished in various ways, from the crude clutch packs of the first-generation Quadra-Trac system, to the silky smooth viscous couplings of today. The four-bys without center locks are usually in the cars and light trucks with all-wheel drive.

The advantages of full-time systems are user-friendliness and improved traction on the highway, especially in inclement weather. The disadvantages can include a loss of fuel economy from barely noticeable to significant, increased tire wear (low to moderate), some quirky road feel issues and vibration, and increased maintenance and repair costs. The most modern systems are nearly seamless in operation and minimize the negatives.

Automatic Four-Wheel Drive

Some of the newest SUVs and trucks have automatic four-wheel-drive systems that operate in two-wheel drive until slippage is sensed at the rear axle (via the same wheel-speed sensors used for the anti-lock brakes). They then shift into a four-wheel-drive mode automatically until the need has passed. These units can usually be locked into a two-wheel-drive mode or four-wheel drive, but the "auto" feature makes it a no-brainer when conditions change rapidly. These systems are designed mostly for inclement weather in highway situations.

All-Wheel Drive vs. Four-Wheel Drive

The term "All-Wheel Drive" goes way back, but has lately been applied to vehicles that use a four-wheel-drive system designed more for improved roadholding and inclement weather traction rather than for off-highway pursuits. The Olds Bravada, assorted Subaru and Mitsubishi models, certain Porsches, Audi's Quattro line, certain SUVs, and even minivans have all-wheel-drive systems designed primarily for the street. What's the difference?

The first major difference between all-wheel and four-wheel-drive systems is that all-wheel drives do not have a low range in the transfer case. Some do not even have a transfer case in the traditional sense of the word. Also, many of them do not have a means of locking the transfer case (if they have one) to supply a 50/50 torque split front and rear. They usually rely on sophisticated torque or wheel-speed sensing devices that can determine which tire has grip and will direct power there.

Certain newer SUVs, such as the Honda CR-V, Ford Escape, Toyota RAV4, Geo Sidekick/Vitara, Kia Sportage, Land Rover Freelander, GMC Yukon Denali, Subaru Forester, and a few others, fit between the street-oriented all-wheel-drive rigs and the true off-highway machines. While they lack a low range, they partially make up for it by being more robust and having a bit more clearance. Some are able to lock into a true 50/50 torque split at the transfer case and are generally capable of dealing with true off-highway terrain from the easy stuff into the lower area of moderate terrain. They often combine their trail traits with a healthy dose of sophistication. Some, like the new Land Rover Freelander, even use four-wheel traction-control systems.

WHERE DID FOUR-WHEEL DRIVE COME FROM?

Four-wheel drive has existed in various forms since 1824, when the Burstall and Hill steam-powered four-wheel-drive coach was built in England during the early days of steam power. Largely forgotten by history, it was a small part of the entrepreneurial development process that led to the steam locomotive.

More four-wheel-drive and a spate of other automotive ideas followed as the motorized era gained momentum at the end of the nineteenth and beginning of the twentieth centuries. Some of these early four-wheel-drive systems were successful, but most were not. The idea persisted because the automobile predated a system of paved roads. Early inventors recognized that driving all four wheels would improve traction on the primitive roads of the time, but the technology for doing so proved elusive. Developing a front axle that could steer the vehicle effectively while delivering torque to the wheels was a difficult part of the problem. Splitting the torque front and rear, via a transfer case, was relatively easy in comparison.

Wisconsin machinist and inventor Otto Zachow summed up the logic for four-wheel drive in 1907, exclaiming, "Who ever heard of a mule who walked on two legs?!" After laboriously recovering his 1906 two-wheel-drive Reo from an accidental "tour" of a ravine, Zachow was sufficiently annoyed to design, patent, and produce a four-wheel-drive system with his friend and partner, William Besserdich.

Zachow and Besserdich's labor provided the building blocks for the big-truck four-wheel-drive dynasty that remains in business to this day, the FWD Corporation. FWD owned the design patents for what is now the standard four-wheel-drive layout until World War I, when they surrendered the patents to the U.S. government to

the dirt

All-Wheel Drive:
Many all-wheel-drive systems work quite well, providing seamless traction in a variety of low-grip driving situations, but they often lack the robust qualities needed for serious trail work.

the dirt

Four-By First:
In 1908, Otto Zachow and William Besserdich were the first in America to produce a four-wheel-drive vehicle with a steerable driving front axle and a four-wheel-drive system of the general design we still use today.

aid the war effort. They were not the first with the idea, however.

The very first application of a four-wheel-drive system similar to what we use today appeared in the Dutch-built Spyker race car of 1903. It was a one-off, but a few similar cars were built later. The system was built primarily for roadholding on the dirt roads of early Europe. We Americans like to think that four-wheel drive begins and ends here, but various European and Asian nations have pursued the technology with at least as much vigor over the past hundred years.

Early four-wheel-drive systems were most common in commercial or military use, where the extra cost could be justified. This slowed development of the technology on the civilian side and left most of the major breakthroughs to military designers. Fortunately, most of those breakthroughs trickled down to the civilian markets.

Speaking of the military, you'll see the terms "4x4" and "4x2" bandied about here and elsewhere. They began as military nomenclature to describe the wheel and drive configurations of military vehicles. The first number signifies the number of wheels on the vehicle and the second the number of those that are powered. You could have a 4x4 (four wheels, all powered),

4x2 (four wheels, two powered), 6x4 (six wheels, four powered), 6x6 (six wheels, all driven), and so on, in any number of combinations.

THE BATTLE FOR TRACTION

Traction is the battle between engine torque, via the drivetrain, and the grip of the tire onto the ground. It's a complex equation that is infinitely variable when looked at under a microscope, but it's largely predictable with a broader view. Many factors contribute to traction, or detract from it.

Ground Conditions

The first major traction-controlling factor is the ground surface. Two primary attributes determine the traction the ground can provide: surface strength and shear strength. Surface strength supports, or fails to support, the weight of the vehicle. In the latter situation, the tire sinks into the soft ground. Snow and mud are two well-known ground conditions that offer low surface strength.

The second attribute affecting traction is the shear strength of the ground surface. Shear strength controls how much grip is available to the tires. If shear strength is low, the surface tears away and the tire slips.

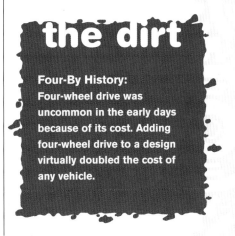

the dirt

Four-By History:
Four-wheel drive was uncommon in the early days because of its cost. Adding four-wheel drive to a design virtually doubled the cost of any vehicle.

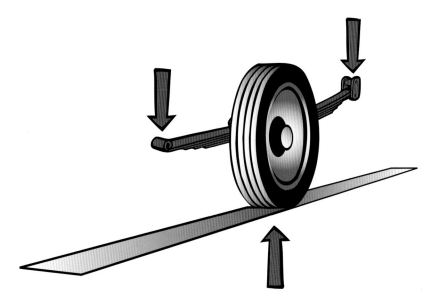

Weight plus tire footprint plus ground surface equals grip. Part of what creates traction, or grip, is ground pressure. Ground pressure is a combination of weight and the tire footprint. More weight or a smaller footprint equals more ground pressure and vice versa. High ground pressure works for you on hard ground by increasing grip, but it works against you on soft ground by letting you sink into the surface.

Torque plus grip equals traction. Torque multiplication takes what the engine produces, multiplies it by the transmission gear ratios, the transfer case gear ratios, and the axle ratios and turns it into motion. How much grip the tire can generate is the controlling factor of how much of that torque can be turned into forward motion. When a tire cannot generate the required grip, one cure is to reduce the torque load to the tire by decreasing the throttle application, or reducing the torque multiplication by shifting up a gear.

Pavement, concrete, solid rock, and other similar surfaces have high shear strength, while sand, dirt, gravel, mud, and so on, have low shear strength.

The available traction of any ground surface is expressed as a coefficient that combines the grip of the tire and the ground condition. Perfect traction is expressed as 1.0. Pavement runs from 0.60–0.80 for "normal" tires of a type used for most 4x4s and 0.9–plus for high-performance street tires. The coefficient for ice is about 0.15–0.20, depending on the tire. Mud ranges from 0.2–0.4, and dirt has a high of about 0.5. The traction coefficient is infinitely variable, depending on the combination of tire and ground condition. You may see it expressed as an absolute, such as mud with a .4 coefficient, but such a number is really an average that combines an "average" tire with "average" mud.

Tires

Of all the vehicular elements involved in the traction equation, tires are the biggest controlling factor. Tire grip varies according to the ground condition and the design of the tires. Tread pattern and the composition of the rubber are the primary variables in tire design. On hard surfaces, the rubber compound plays the bigger part. On hard, dry surfaces, the rubber compound provides 75 to 80 percent of the grip. The softer the rubber, the better the grip.

Rubber compounds vary in softness according to design. Softer compounds grip better on hard surfaces, but wear faster. Finding the right combination is the tire manufacturer's eternal battle. Performance tires, either for street cars or 4x4s, are often biased toward the softer, more grippy compounds, but a good tread design can give harder, longer-lasting tire compounds a chance to compete with softer rubber.

Grip on a hard surface comes down to the weight on the tire and the shear strength of the ground. Within a certain range, more weight equals more traction, but more weight also *requires* more traction, so the equations spiral upward in that case. Mud tires do well in rocks because they have so many voids that increase the ground pressure on each of the little blocks of tread. Many a rig has been pulled up an otherwise impossible climb by one knob of tread that has glued itself to a rock by a concentration of weight.

On soft surfaces, tread design plays the major part in creating the overall traction capability of the tire—as much as 75 percent—with the cleated edges of the tread working much like paddles in water to provide traction. In the soft-ground environment, flotation comes into play. The tire's ability to stay *above* the ground is vital. To start with, the farther the tire sinks, the greater the drag; more traction is needed to overcome it.

Floatation is a product of tire size, or, more precisely, the size of the tire's footprint on the ground in relation to the vehicle weight. With a larger footprint, vehicle weight is spread out over a larger section of ground. Ground pressure is measured in pounds per square inch (psi), and a lower number means better floatation. Take a set of 235/75R-15 tires on a vehicle that weighs 4,500 pounds. At 35 psi, these tires have a footprint of approximately 6.5x6 inches, or about 39 square inches per tire, multiplied by four tires. Assuming a 50/50 weight distribution (not likely in any front-engine vehicle), that's a ground pressure of 28.8

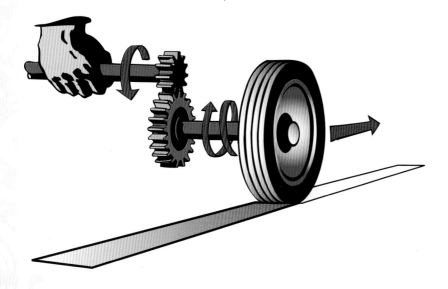

pounds per square inch (4500 ÷ (39 x 4) = 28.846). If you lower the tire pressure of those 235s, the footprint increases to 61.2 square inches per tire, and ground pressure decreases to 18.4 psi. If you upgrade to 33x12.50-15 tires, their 35-psi-inflation footprint, 20.4 psi, offers almost the same ground pressure as the aired-down 235/75R-15. When aired down to 15 psi, the upgraded tires have a ground pressure of 13.7 psi, less than half that of the fully inflated smaller tire. These changes in ground pressure numbers from tire pressure or size may mean the difference between being *on* or *in* terra firma!

Last, bear in mind that the above calculations do not take into account the tire voids. A mud tire, for example, may only put 70 percent of its footprint directly onto the ground. The rest is open voids in the tread. An all-terrain tire might put 85 percent of its tread in direct contact with the ground. But once the mud tire sinks into the ground a little, the voids fill and the flotation increases.

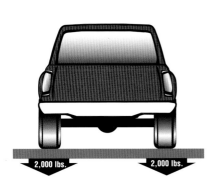

Here is a typical distribution of weight on a full-sized SUV on level ground. The front tires almost always carry more weight, unless the vehicle is carrying a load in the cargo area. We're assuming a 5,000-pound total weight for this SUV.

Climbing throws some of the front weight to the rear. How much depends on the steepness of the climb. Longer-wheelbase rigs transfer far less weight at any given angle than short-wheelbase rigs.

Descents can be spookier with vehicles that are very nose-heavy, because even more weight will transfer from the already light rear and can severely reduce traction there.

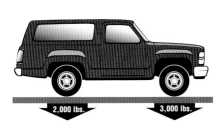

Side-to-side weight can also vary, even at one end or the other. The driver's side is almost always heavier, even on level ground and at the rear.

Figure on having more weight on the driver's side when it's at the low end of a sidehill.

When the axle is articulated, the compressed side will be carrying most of the weight, which could allow the low-side tire to slip due to lack of ground pressure.

Vehicle Weight

The heavier the vehicle, the more tire grip is required to maintain traction. It will also need more engine torque and suitable gearing. It's relatively easy to find and fit the big tires that can supply enough grip to make a light or moderate-weight vehicle perform well, but as weight increases, it gets tougher. Really big tires are available, but the modifications needed to fit them can be complicated.

Weight Transfer

Traction also changes according to weight transfer. When you climb, weight is transferred from the front to the rear. The opposite is true when you descend. Similarly, on side slopes, weight will transfer from the uphill to the downhill side. When the suspension is articulated, that is, when one tire is at the upper end of suspension travel and the other tire is at the lower end of suspension travel, the upper tire is bearing most of the weight.

The actual amount of weight transfer is dependent on many factors, including the angle of the slope and the center of gravity of the vehicle. In general, a longer-wheelbase rig will transfer a bit less weight than a short-wheelbase rig. At about 25 degrees of slope (a fairly mild climb), upslope-to-downslope weight transfer will be 5 to 10 percent.

Tire grip on a hard surface is partially dependent upon weight or, more precisely, ground pressure. More weight, or ground pressure, will result in increased grip, but it's not proportional to the weight change. Adding 25 percent more weight will not necessarily result in 25 percent more grip. In many cases, grip will be reduced because the extra weight may exceed the tires' ultimate grip. Similarly, reducing the weight on a tire will decrease traction, but not in proportion to the weight loss. Each tire has a weight range, at a given tire pressure, when the grip will remain relatively constant. Above or below that range, grip will be reduced. Unfortunately, that range is difficult to plot because of the many variances in tire design and construction. It becomes a "seat-o-the-pants" determination that each driver learns by feel. There are things you can predict, including the following:

- A smaller-tire footprint will lose grip sooner than a larger one.
- Your rear tires may slip on a climb due to overloading and the fronts may slip due to underloading.
- Vice versa on a descent.
- An articulated axle will usually slip first on the low, least-loaded tire.
- If you are cross-axled (axles articulated opposite each other), both or either of the low tires will be the first to slip.

Torque Multiplication vs. Grip

The grip offered by any tire or any ground surface can be overcome by torque. Even the best tire or tractive surface can be overcome by enough torque. Torque from your engine is multiplied by the drivetrain before it's delivered to the tire. If the engine makes 100 lbs-ft at a given rpm and has a 4:1 first-gear ratio, a 2:1 transfer-case low range, and a 4:1 axle ratio, the torque delivered to the wheels will be 3,200 lbs-ft (100 x 4 x 2 x 4 = 3,200). That torque is pitted against the four tires' ability to grip as well as the ground's resistance shear. The moral here is that in some conditions you must reduce the torque delivery to the tires to maintain traction. This can mean using less throttle, using a higher gear to reduce multiplication, or by substituting vehicle momentum, which will allow use of a higher gear and reduce the need for grip.

WHAT'S THE DIFF?

The differential is the heart of the axle and of many full-time four wheel-drive transfer cases. It's a relatively simple device that has a complicated job to perform. The simple part is that it has to deliver torque to the wheels to provide motive power. It gets complicated when the vehicle turns. Then, the inner and outer wheels will rotate at different speeds, with the inner wheel slowing down and the outer wheel speeding up—because the outer wheel has more distance to travel around the turn. This difference in speeds also occurs between the front and rear axles in a full-time four-wheel-drive system. Something has to give, and a system without a differential will lose traction on one tire during the turn, causing excessive tire wear, handling problems, increased steering effort, and stress on the drive-train components.

Open Differentials–The Path of Least Resistance

The so-called "open" differential is the standard type that's been used in motor vehicles since the dawn of the motorized era. The open diff works

The pinion gear (in red) takes the torque from the driveshaft and delivers it to the ring gear (in yellow) and two things happen. First, it turns that torque 90 degrees and delivers it to the tires through the differential and axles. (The differential seen in the other pictures nearby lives in the center of the ring gear.) Second, the ring and pinion combine to create the axle gear ratio. The number of teeth on the ring gear divided by the number of teeth on the pinion gear equals the gear ratio. If there are 37 ring gear teeth and 9 pinion teeth, the ratio is 4.11:1. This means that the pinion gear rotates 4 and 11/100th times for each revolution of the axle. This multiplies the torque by the high number of the gear ratio, but reduces the output speed by the same amount.

Right: In a low-traction situation, the torque will take the path of least resistance. In this case, the green axle is in soft stuff and the white axle is on more solid ground. The white axle and side gear are stationary and the carrier (black) is rotating around it. Because the spider gears are locked to the carrier, they are turning around the stationary white side gear and forcing the green gear to rotate and spin the loose tire.

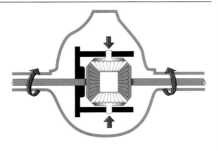

The open differential delivers torque equally to both axles (green) when the traction is equal on both sides and the vehicle is going straight. In this situation, the diff carrier (black) is turning at the same speed as the ring gear, as are the side gears (green) and the spider gears (white).

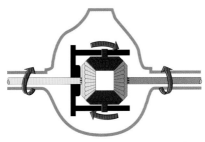

Above: In a turning situation, one axle speeds up (green) and the other slows down (yellow). The speed changes are proportional to each other, according to the number of teeth in the side and spider gears. The carrier (black) is turning at the speed of the ring gear and the side and spider gears are turning independently within it.

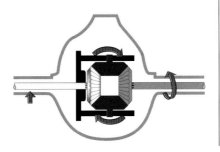

the dirt

Limited Slip Theory:
The locking factor indicates, in a percentage, how much of the input torque can be applied to only one axle.

ROCK TALK

Bias Ratio:
The bias ratio indicates how much torque the differential can transfer to the high-traction wheel, relative to the amount of torque the low-traction side can support.

Shown here is a typical clutch-type limited slip, in this case a Spicer Powr-Lok. This is an extra-stout unit with a four-pinion differential. This unit can be "loaded" to increase the bias ratio.

1-Case halves
2-Side gear
3-Spider (differential pinion) gear
4-Pinion cross-shaft
5-Spacer ring
6-Steel plates
7-Friction discs
8-Case bolt
Courtesy the Spicer Axle Division of the Dana Corporation

best when there is roughly equal traction available to both tires. As the difference in traction increases, the torque through the open diff tries to take the path of least resistance, transferring it to the tire with the least amount of traction. It boils down to this: if you have one wheel on pavement and the other wheel in goo, torque will go to the one in the goo.

Full-time four-wheel-drive systems with center differentials face the same problem times three. With the center diff unlocked, you can put three tires on pavement and one in goo, and the torque will go to the one in the goo, regardless of where that one tire is located. That's why full-time rigs intended for trail work have a lockable center differential.

The Limited Slip Differential

The limited slip (LS) differential operates more or less like an open diff in everyday use. But in low-traction situations, it may transfer some torque to the wheel with the most traction. The two most common types of LS are the clutch type and gear type.

Clutch-Type Limited Slips

The most common clutch-type LS diffs have a set of normal differential gears but with clutch packs that are preloaded to provide resistance at each axle. In effect, they provide a "brake" to discourage the torque from taking the path of least resistance. The clutch packs are preloaded to a precisely calibrated "breakaway torque," meaning

that as the traction differential between the tires increases, the torque will eventually overcome the clutch pack resistance on the low-traction side and begin to slip.

There are a couple of ways to express the amount of torque that a limited slip can transfer to a single wheel. It can be expressed as a locking factor (in percent) or as a bias ratio (x:1). A totally locked differential has a 100-percent locking factor because all of the available torque can be applied to the high-traction tire. An open differential has a 0-percent locking factor because the high-traction side can receive only as much torque as the low-traction side can hold. Actually, because of the friction of the mechanical parts in the diff, not even open diffs are quite as low as 0-percent, but they can get pretty close. Seldom do you see limited slips with locking factors near or above 80 percent because they are so close to complete lockup that they are nearly intractable on the street.

Bias ratio is how most manufacturers describe the performance characteristics of their limited-slip differentials. A 4:1 bias ratio (60 percent locking factor) would allow four times more torque to be supplied to the high-traction side than the low-traction side. If the low-traction tire can support 100 lbs-ft, then the differential can deliver up to 400 lbs-ft to the opposite side. The amount of torque the low-traction side can absorb includes the preload or braking action built into the LS. A nearby chart illustrates how locking factor and bias ratios correlate.

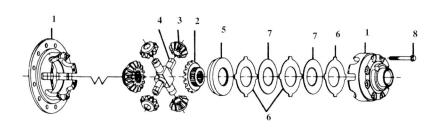

28

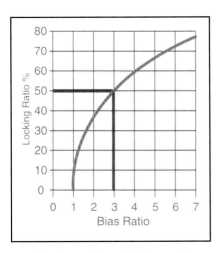

Clutch-type limited slips can be set "loose" or "tight," referring to the difference in the locking factor built in. These range from about 25 percent on up, with the lower ratios being the milder units. Standard-equipment limited-slips are built deliberately loose (25 to 50 percent) to make sure they will reach breakaway torque easily in a turn, and the smoother they do that, the better, in the opinion of the OE manufacturers. Their downfall is that they can be easily overcome in trail situations where a great difference in traction exists between the tires. This can occur when a tire lifts in extreme terrain, for example, or when there is a great deal of weight on one tire and little on the other. A tight clutch-type unit will operate better when the differences in traction are greater side to side, but it may exhibit some adverse characteristics on the street, just like a true locker, inducing harsh breakaway (or none at all) in turns on the street.

Clutch-type limited slips usually use plate-type clutches or cone clutches. The cone types are generally a bit less expensive than the plate types. Because the cones have a metal-to-metal contact with the case halves, the cone units can be more expensive to overhaul. The plate types are very sensitive to lubricants and need special limited-slip additives to work smoothly. In fact, if your limited slip chatters, it could be due to the lack of that special additive. Eventually, it will destroy itself without the additive. Cone clutches are not as sensitive to lubricants, but they also can chatter.

Just like any product with a friction material (brakes, clutches, and so on), the LS clutches wear and gradually get looser with time. The harder they are worked, the faster this happens.

Gear-Type Limited Slips

There are gear-type limited slip units that do essentially the same thing as the clutch units, but work quite differently. They do not have differential gears or clutches, but a case full of small gears. These gears provide resistance just like the clutches. In one type, the TracTech TruTrac, small worm-type pinion gears provide resistance via the pressure angle of the gears on the pinion, which forces them against the case and increases resistance. This provides a "brake" and the unit begins to transfer some torque to the other side. Locking factors can be changed according to the number of pinions in the unit and by varying the pressure angles (how the gears mesh) on the teeth of the worm gears. The TruTrac models use bias ratios between 2:1 and 3.5:1 (36- to 55-percent locking factor), depending on the application.

The Torsen unit (short for Torque-Sensing) is similar in concept to the TruTrac, in that it uses gears and friction to provide the braking action needed to create a favorable torque bias. There are several versions of the unit, including the original Type 1 and a later Type 2, plus a few variations built for specialty markets. The Type 1 is offered in bias ratios of between 2.5:1 and 5.0:1, while the milder Type 2 is available in ratios from 1.4:1 to 3:1.

Both the Torsen and the TruTrac require a small application of the brake pedal to be totally effective when there is a large difference in traction side to side. While the gear-type units are generally more seamless on the street than the clutch types, they are more expensive and less positive in their operation without some brake pedal manipulation by the driver. For the most part, the gear-type LS units are life-of-the-vehicle products, and their purchase price reflects this.

the dirt

Limited Slip Working Life: By the time a rig hits 100,000 miles, the average clutch limited slip has turned into an open diff. An exception would be Eaton's relatively new carbon-disc LS units, which use a space-age textured Pyrolytic carbon material that is essentially a forever product.

the dirt

Limited Slip Finesse: Unlike an automatic locker, you can't finesse a tight limited slip into letting loose and behaving. Most people think that a gear-type limited slip is smoother than a clutch type with the same locking factor.

Using Limited Slips

Limited-slip driving techniques vary somewhat depending on whether you have a tight or loose unit, or a gear or clutch unit. On the street, the loose unit will be nearly, if not completely, transparent. Driving with the tighter clutch units, with a locking factor much above 60 percent (4:1 bias ratio), you may experience some barking of the tires or unusual handling. These tendencies will increase with the locking factor.

On the trail, you can finesse a limited slip into locking up tighter by applying a little brake. This is true of both gear- and clutch-type limited slips. The idea is to supply a little extra braking to the unloaded tire and transfer a little more torque to the other one. You can use either the foot brake or the parking brake. In a situation where you've lost traction all around, the foot brake will help, whether your front axle is open or equipped with an LS. If it's primarily the rear slipping, using the parking brake is the best method (assuming it actuates the rear brakes) because it doesn't add braking resistance to the front tires and thereby increase the vehicle's overall traction needs. A partial application of the parking brake for the duration of the difficult situation may be all you need. If it doesn't work with the parking brake applied halfway, odds are good that giving it more parking brake won't work, either.

Locking Differentials

All sorts of traction-aiding differentials have been tossed under the heading of "locker." This is not totally accurate, as you will learn. The "true" lockers are best looked at individually.

Automatic Lockers

Automatic lockers will deliver 100-percent torque to either wheel and, under light loads and equal traction, they will mimic an open diff. They may exhibit some handling quirks on the street, and this will vary from one type to another. Most use a dog clutch arrangement that engages when it senses a difference in wheel speed while torque is being applied.

Many people use an automatic locker in front-axle applications, but these drivers must sometimes unlock a hub or disengage the front axle to make a tight turn. An automatic locker is generally not much more expensive than a limited slip (in some cases they are less expensive), but they are preferred by the harder-core crowd who are willing to sacrifice some on-road user-friendliness for better traction.

Automatic lockers can be divided into those that replace the carrier and the "plug-in" units that use the OE carrier but replace the spider and side gears. The latter setup has the advantage of being easy to install and inexpensive. On the downside, it relies on the OE carrier for its basic strength. A good carrier combined with the plug-in locker ends up being a stout unit, but a weak carrier can make it a weak unit overall. The lockers with replacement carriers are stronger overall, but are more expensive and more difficult to install.

The Lock Right and the No-Slip are plug-in lockers from Power Trax, and the E-Z Locker and Gearless Locker are plug-ins from TracTech. The Detroit (or No-Spin) Locker from TracTech is an integrated carrier automatic locker.

On-Demand Lockers

On-demand lockers achieve 100-percent lockup by various means, but they are all driver-controlled. They can be operated hydraulically, by a cable, via air or vacuum, or even electrically. The beauty is that until they are actuated, they operate as a normal open diff. This gives you 100-percent traction when you need it, with no side effects. This makes them ideal for full-time four-wheel-drive rigs, or in front-axle applications. They are the most expensive and the most complicated type of locker.

The two brands you will see in the United States are the ARB Air Locker and the Ox cable locker. The Air Locker has been around many years and has applications to fit most rigs. The Ox came on the market just a

the dirt

True Lockers:
A true locking differential has a 100-percent locking factor—in other words, it will supply all the torque to either wheel.

the dirt

On-Demand Lockers:
An on-demand locker is ideal for front or rear axles and safe with full-time systems. Because they are manually operated, pilot error becomes an issue but, then again, many pilots feel they can "out-think" an automatic locker.

short time ago and has just a couple of applications, with more planned or on the drawing board. A few other brands are available outside the United States.

Variable Bias Lockers

Back in the 1980s, Eaton, most famous for building the GM "Posi-Traction" limited slips, built an automatic locker that has often been called the "Gov-Lok," though Eaton does not advocate that term. It came as an option on a variety of GM trucks and SUVs. A new version, the Command Traxx, is similar in operation and is available on recent GM trucks as an option. Equipped with clutch packs, it has a very loose limited-slip capability, but it also uses a complex flyweight governor device that senses differences in wheel speed. With a 100- to 150-rpm difference in wheel speed, the flyweight setup ratchets against the clutch packs to apply increased clamping pressure, effectively locking them up solid. When wheel speed equalizes, the unit releases the clutches and unlocks itself. The flyweight releases the locker at around 25 miles per hour to prevent handling problems.

Using Automatic Lockers

The on-demand lockers operate as an open diff when disengaged, so they do not offer any adverse symptoms on the street. With most of the automatics, you will need to adopt a new style of driving to avoid the worst of the clicking and clacking, barking tires, and unusual handling characteristics. This information should forearm you, and not steer you away from any type of locker. I use a Detroit Locker in the rear of my own rig (more for trail than street) and think the compromises made in driving style are more than worth the utility and awesome strength of the unit on the trail. As I've mentioned before, informed choices are the best ones.

Because the automatic lockers operate via differences in wheel speed, every time you make a turn, the dog clutch–type units (Detroit Locker, E-Z Locker, Lock-Right) may make a ratcheting noise. This is

because the teeth of the dog clutches of the outer sections are snapping past the teeth of the inner section according to the differing speed of the wheels. Don't worry; the noise is not harmful, though it sounds like it is. In fact, I once heard a locker manufacturer's representative call this noise "free advertising." The Power Trax No-Slip is reputedly an exception to the "ratcheting rule" because it contains a synchronizer system. The "SofLocker" version of the Detroit is also considerably quieter than its earlier iteration. The TracTech Gearless locker is a very quiet unit.

Lockers will go from ratcheting to lockup as soon as more than a tiny bit of power is applied. If it locks, that's when our second adverse characteristic starts. The tires bark because they are locked together at the same speed. The locker doesn't allow one tire to speed up and one to slow down, as is normal for an open diff in a turn. Something's gotta give, so the tires let out a few barks as they slip. At that moment, you have lost some traction.

Suddenly applying throttle while going around a long, sweeping turn at speed can result in momentary locking. The same thing can happen when you suddenly lift off the throttle—you can get a momentary wiggle of the tail. Fortunately, the lockers usually release quickly on deceleration. If you continue to use power in a turn at higher speeds, you can get into trouble in slippery conditions.

So what's the answer to tricky lockers on the street? The installation or owner's manual for the particular unit will outline the cautions specific to that locker, but here are some general tips. One primary key is not to apply power, or much power, in a turn. Try to coast around the corner or use only very light throttle. Obviously, making a turn from a dead stop cannot be done without use of the throttle, but you can minimize the bad effects by going light on the accelerator. If the unit locks up at an inopportune moment, a partial lifting of the throttle (reducing the torque load) is usually enough to

The Lock-Right from Power Trax is a plug-in locker that fits inside the vehicle's original carrier and is one of the easiest lockers to install. The two round pieces on top are the couplers that attach to the axles. Below them are the two driver halves; the center pin fits between them (note the slot on the right driver) just as the pin would fit through the spider gears on a normal diff. The slots on the drivers are slightly egg-shaped so that torque will push the two halves apart and tightly lock the unit. The springs in the foreground lightly push the driver halves apart, but allow them to ratchet when the vehicle is turning.

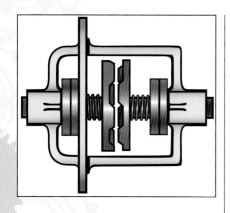

The most common types of automatic lockers use variations of this idea. Dog clutches are splined to each axle and they can ratchet past each other when the vehicle turns (top). When traction is needed, they lock together (below). What's missing in this illustration is the driver unit. With a Detroit Locker, a central driver unit would be pinned to the case in four places and sandwiched between the clutches that are splined to the axles. With the Power Trax and E-Z Locker, there is a single drive pin and a pair of drivers on either side. There are various methods used to encourage the unit to ratchet in turns or to lock when torque is applied.

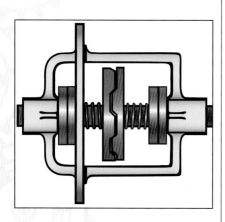

"finesse" it into releasing. The adverse effects are variable according to the particular combination of vehicle characteristics. Long-wheelbase, heavy vehicles seem less affected than shorter, lighter rigs.

On the trail, the automatic locker becomes your best buddy. It provides instant traction when you need it. Since traction here is almost always less than on pavement, the unit will feel quiet and docile. Some of the aforementioned handling quirks may occasionally be an issue in low-traction situations, such as on a snowy dirt road. There are very few other issues with an automatic locker on the trail. Occasionally, it may lock up and make tight maneuvering difficult.

If you have an automatic locker up front, your first trip probably taught you what to do. If the unit engages, it's nearly impossible to maneuver, and it's very hard on the front axle shaft universal joints when you have the wheels cranked over hard. Sometimes, releasing the bind on the drivetrain by going to neutral or backing up will get you through the turn. Most often, you can simply unlock one hub to make the turn. If your vehicle is equipped with a twin-stick transfer case (either OE or aftermarket), use it to momentarily disengage the front axle.

Using On-Demand Lockers

As previously mentioned, on-demand lockers are virtually transparent on the street. A general caution: make sure they don't get accidentally engaged on the pavement in day-to-day use. Locate the controls so they cannot be accidentally activated by a curious kid pulling a "what does this do, Daddy," while you are cruising down the highway.

With the ARB Air Locker, I further recommend that you install a master isolating switch between the ignition power source wire and the main relay. A switch like this effectively kills the system when it's switched off. This will make sense when you see the ARB harness or wiring diagram. The switch is an easy retrofit if yours was not wired this way originally. Just

about any type of locker can be protected from accidental application with some ingenuity. I would recommend the effort if you have kids or a vehicle that is driven by a number of people, some of whom may not be familiar with all the controls.

The ideal method is to engage the locker just before you need it. Read the terrain and hit the button or work the lever just prior to assaulting the obstacle. If you misread the terrain and find the locker isn't needed, you may disengage it at any time. The bigger problems come if you misread the other way and find the locker is needed partway through an obstacle. It's OK to engage the locker in the middle of the obstacle, but don't do it while wildly spinning the tires or with the drivetrain under a severe load. In either situation, the locker may refuse to engage fully, or it may break due to shock loading. Bear in mind that the unit may not immediately engage or disengage if it's under torque. The on-demand locker can be useful on the street in snow and ice, mostly to get you moving. Once the vehicle is in motion, however, be sure to disengage it, or the severe handling changes a fully locked rear axle imparts may send you into the nearest snowbank.

You won't often need a front on-demand locker, but it can mean the difference between making it or not on some very hard obstacles. A locker up front will induce many odd handling characteristics, so it's not something you'll need on the street. Trying to turn with the unit locked is very hard on front axles, particularly front-axle U-joints or CV joints. For these reasons, you will find that the on-demand front locker is generally used only for brief periods. Bear in mind that if you have the drivetrain in a bind or with a torque load on the front axle, the locker may not immediately disengage, so you may be forced to back up or roll in neutral to coax disengagement.

Traction Control Systems

Electronic Traction Control (ETC) appears on some newer SUVs in the upper price ranges. ETC is a slick adaptation of the ABS system that, with a little extra programming, uses the same equipment to do a completely different job. When the wheel speed sensors read a large differential in wheel speed on one axle, the ETC system will partially engage the brake on the faster wheel, assuming it is the low-traction side. As discussed in the open diff section above, this will force the differential to transfer torque to the opposite wheel, which is presumed to have more traction. The system works reasonably well, but in my experience, it is usually a little slow to engage. You may have to induce a little more wheelspin than you think is prudent before it fully engages. Each system is different and you will need to experiment to determine the best techniques for each one. Both Mercedes and Land Rover four-wheel drives use an ETC system.

AM General provided a variation on both ETC and limited-slip differentials by combining them. They joined low bias-ratio Torsen Type 2 diffs with an ETC. The earlier-generation Hummer and its military counterpart had been using the Torsen Type 1 diffs from the outset, but many drivers had problems with the brake modulation techniques necessary to maximize trail performance. The new design uses the ABS system to apply brakes to the spinning tire. This provides additional "braking" on the low-traction side to transfer more torque to the high-traction side.

Something Else

In 1999, Jeep introduced a major remake of the Grand Cherokee. The WJ, as it came to be known, offered a four-wheel-drive system developed by Dana Spicer that was awesome in scope and the "smartest" four-wheel-drive system yet offered on an SUV. It deserves some words here, because I don't think this is the last time you'll see it applied.

The system incorporates two new products: the NV-247 Quadra-Trac II transfer case and Vari-Lok axles. Both axles and the transfer case incorporate hydraulic gerotor pumps that are used in a similar fashion. (Gerotor is short for generated-rotor, an advanced type of internal rotary pump.) Starting with the transfer case, under normal driving conditions, the Quadra-Trac II transfers most torque to the rear wheels. If a front wheel loses traction, the speed variation between the front and rear driveshafts actuates the gerotor pump, which applies hydraulic pressure to a multi-disc clutch pack that couples the rear transfer case output to the front. Hydraulic pressure varies according to the speed difference between the front and rear outputs. The greater the difference, the tighter the lockup, until it reaches nearly 100 percent. The NV-247 transfer case also has a 2.72:1 low range and can be locked to provide a 50/50 front-to-rear torque split. This system is reputed to respond faster and more transparently than any of the others offered in SUVs.

The Vari-Lok differential also contains a gerotor pump that operates between the two axle shafts. Differences in wheel speed from side to side operate the pump, which pressurizes a clutch pack that couples the two axles together. Again, the greater the difference in wheel speed, the tighter the coupling. The system operates so quickly that it can be used on both the front and rear axles. Jeep claims the Quadra-Trac II and Vari-Lok are "virtually" transparent to the driver, but some customers disagree. In tight turning and parking maneuvers, some drivers have reported that the Vari-Lok axles partially engage, which produces minor tire barking or steering wheel bucking. Still, it's a system that offers serious traction and makes the Grand Cherokee a great "out-o-the-box" trail performer.

the dirt

Locker Finesse:
When your automatic locker locks up, you can finesse release by unloading the drivetrain. Do this by gently reversing or going into neutral briefly and letting the vehicle roll a few feet.

the dirt

Front Locker Reluctance:
The most obvious vehicle quirk with the front locker engaged is an unwillingness to turn. The vehicle will want to travel in a straight line.

the dirt

Traction Control Finesse:
Some traction control systems will shut down after certain periods in operation to keep the brakes cool. Others have brake overheat warnings.

CHAPTER 3

CHOOSE YER WEAPON

Choosing Your 4x4

During the few years they were available in the United States (1994–1997), the Land Rover Defender 90 earned high marks. The North American version is one of the best stock performers on the planet. It came with relatively big tires, a stout aluminum V-8, a five-speed manual or four-speed auto (on 1997s only), a flexible coil spring suspension, and four-wheel disc brakes. It's very stout and modification-friendly. On the downside, you can buy two used Jeep Wranglers for the price of one used D90.

HERE WE'LL COVER:

The basic categories of 4x4 vehicles
•
Choosing the best vehicle for your needs
•
Criteria used to judge 4x4 vehicles
•
How (or whether to) try to balance the demands of street and trail performance

If you put the best driver in the worst vehicle and the worst driver in the best vehicle, most of the time the better driver will get farther up the trail. Put the best driver in the best vehicle, and the sky is the limit. The vehicle you choose—whether you plan to keep it stock or make modifications—can enhance or detract from your 4x4 fun. I won't address personal likes and dislikes here, but will talk about the characteristics that make a better trail machine or a better basis for a buildup. I'll also get heavily into machines that do the best job of bridging the street/trail gap.

WHERE DO YOU FIT?

Four-wheel-drive technology is used in many different ways. Many four-wheel-drive vehicles are utilized solely as foul-weather transport in areas where the weather makes travel difficult. Others are used on unimproved roads and in remote areas. Some are used solely as recreational trail vehicles. The first step is to find out where you fit.

As stated in the introduction, we are dealing with vehicles that have off-highway capabilities, at least beyond a minimal level. Your choice may limit one aspect or another, so an honest evaluation of your needs is important.

THE RESPONSIBLE CHOICE

The characteristics that make a vehicle perform best on the trail may detract from its performance, comfort, or safety on the highway. For that reason, don't make the jump into a four-wheel drive or a modified four-wheel drive lightly. Become familiar with the pluses and minuses for each vehicle you consider owning, or modification you consider making, and make a choice that best suits your needs and concerns.

SUV safety seems to be making the evening news more and more these days. My personal opinion is that much of this is overblown and the result of investigative reporters looking for another notch in their pistol grips, or news directors looking for "if it bleeds it leads" headline stories. Still,

the dirt

All-Wheel Drives:
For day-to-day use and inclement weather only, all-wheel-drive cars and SUVs are a better choice. With their lower center of gravity and superior handling, they will always outperform the off-highway-capable rigs on the highway, in good or poor weather. If you plan to venture off the paved roads, then the advantage turns to the four-wheel drives built for that purpose.

Off-highway legend Ned Bacon's buggy sorta looks like a Jeep, but it's not. It's a hand-built rig with components selected for maximum trail performance. It's missing even the most elementary comfort items. While there are only a few rigs that could follow this rig in tough terrain, if Ned had to drive it on the highway, he wouldn't get around as much as he does.

At the other side of the Great Divide is this stock Jimmy four-door SUV that's stymied by a mild trail challeng. On the other hand, this owner wouldn't hesitate to drive this rig on a 3,000-mile jaunt to Florida.

TRAIL ENDERS

4x4 Safety:
A four-wheel-drive vehicle, whether it be SUV or truck, is not a sports car, and even the safest car is not idiot-proof. These vehicles are not inherently unsafe, but they are less forgiving of driver error than the ordinary car.

The Samurai is one of the formerly unsung heroes of the short-wheelbase (SWB) crowd. It has recently come into great favor and has a good aftermarket following. Its size enables it to fit just about anywhere and because it's a basic, straightforward design, it lends itself to modifications. Comfort isn't its strong suit, but it's no worse than many other SWB utility rigs.

there is a core of truth in the fact that SUVs and trucks do not handle as well as many cars. No kidding! Off-highway driving instructors have been telling people that for decades.

The SUV or truck requires the driver to be more alert and more aware of the vehicle's performance characteristics. That's a responsibility you assume when you choose a four-wheel-drive truck or SUV. The most common driver errors involve speed or inattention, and these same errors kill many car drivers as well. The answer to many concerns is simply to slow down and pay more attention. Adjust your street driving to the capabilities of the vehicle.

THE GREAT DIVIDE

The things that make a great daily driver are diametrically opposed to the things that make a great trail machine. For this reason you can't have a vehicle that does both things extremely well. There are many four-wheel drives that bridge the "great divide" well, but there are always compromises. How much that affects you depends on your appetites. For some of us, it means a less trail-capable but more streetable four-wheel drive, and for others it means having a "regular" vehicle for day-to-day use and a trail machine for those days in the dirt.

How far your built-up rig can go into the trail-capable category and retain a healthy measure of street safety is debatable and subject to the general type of vehicle. To the safety mavens, no modification is acceptable. To others, virtually everything goes. A clear-headed adult with good judgment can almost always come to a *modus vivendi*. Even a built-up rig can be safe when driven safely, and a relatively mild and "safe" 4x4 can be a deathtrap with an idiot at the wheel.

TYPES OF 4X4S

There is a huge range of 4x4 vehicles available. And what you can't buy

Shown here is the 4x4 that started the recreational 'wheeling craze. The Jeep flatfender is eternal and a cornerstone of the hobby. Though its numbers are in decline, it's still a part of the four-wheeling scene. Lots of buildup material is still available, though unaltered older CJs are in the collector's category.

off the shelf, you can modify or build. Ever hear the saying, "Great trail Jeeps are built, not bought?" Change the brand name and you could talk about any 4x4 that way. What follows is a general list of types and their pluses and minuses.

Classic 4x4s

This list would include anything from the aforementioned 1824 Burstall and Hill steam coach to vehicles into the early 1980s, when technology began to better bridge the gap between the strictly workhorse rigs and the true dual-purpose machines. Into the 1970s, nearly all 4x4s were slow, uncomfortable, and almost brutal in terms of driver comfort. In some cases, trail performance was good, or at least adequate, though modern technology has eclipsed these machines. You can buy better stock trail performance in modern machines, but nothing new has the sheer *class* of an old Jeep flatfender, a vintage Dodge Power Wagon, or an early Ford Bronco. You may want to own a classic rig as a restored piece of history. Many owners will combine the old shell with

the dirt

Trail Monsters:
If your vehicle begins to creep farther and farther into that "trail monster" category as you add to it, consider relegating it to "trail use only" status and use a more suitable vehicle for day-to-day transportation or hauling your precious family around town. You may even wisely consider trailering it to and from the trail.

One of the best bridges over the Great Divide is the Jeep Grand Cherokee. A mild lift, a tire upgrade, and lockers turn it into a force to be reckoned with. Best of all, it retains the "Grand" part of its personality.

This older Range Rover is tackling one of the most difficult trails in Western Colorado: the notorious 21 Road. It just goes to prove the old adage about having your cake and eating it too. Note the armor up front, the rocker protection, and the rear quarter panel guards. These make the expensive aluminum bodywork safe from all but the worst encounters. This protection is the key element in any SUV's successful trail forays into the harder-core realms. More vulnerable than a utilitarian rig, machines such as this one are also expensive to repair when they are damaged.

modern machinery to make a rig that looks old and drives like new. Certain older rigs will also provide a great basis for a ground-up rebuild into a dedicated trail rig. In whatever form a classic 4x4 takes, it will require a higher level of commitment than a newer rig.

results are a vehicle that can be a handful, both on and off the highway. Consider SWB rigs the sports cars of the four-wheeling world. They can offer levels of trail performance unmatched by anything else, but they require more skill and judgment, and offer greater risks.

SUVs

Sport utility vehicles are the current 4x4 craze. They offer the comfort, convenience, and capacity once found in the American station wagon, but add four-wheel drive and off-highway capability as well as a measure of increased performance in inclement weather. They vary in off-highway performance from what is almost a joke to superb. They vary in highway comfort and performance from bare bones, barely acceptable, to comfort that rivals the best luxury cars. Some feature performance to rival a sports or muscle car. Cost is almost always the determining factor in the particular attributes of an SUV. SUVs come in two- and four-door varieties, with four-doors growing ever more prevalent. Some SUVs are quite capable on the trail, but the major liability of all brands and types is their vulnerability to damage. While it isn't a given that damage will occur, especially with good driving, a mistake will almost always be more costly in an SUV. The truck-platform-based SUVs are almost always tougher and more capable on the trail, but less carlike on the street.

Short Wheelbase

Short-wheelbase (SWB, under 100 inches) 4x4s are fast going the way of the dinosaur. Only a few SWB models are sold these days. Part of this is due to their lack of carrying capacity and part is due to the higher level of driver skill required—and the resulting increase in manufacturer liability. When a short wheelbase is combined with a higher center of gravity, the

Your best bet in an SWB builder is the 1987–1995 Wrangler YJ. They are solid platforms for a buildup at any level. They can be made into relatively comfortable daily drivers and still retain a high level of trail prowess. At the other end of the spectrum, they can be turned into radical trail machines with few peers.

Pickups

Pickups are almost as popular as SUVs. They offer the occasional hauling utility many people need or desire and they can tow various toys to and from favorite playgrounds. Most pickups do quite well on the trail and are stout enough for most trails. Their major detriments come in two forms: size and ride quality. Trucks are built to carry weight and volume, so by necessity they have to be big enough and have a high-enough spring rate to handle the load. As you will learn, size may limit where you can go, but the stiff truck spring will make the bumps of the trail a brutal torture. The stiff springs also resist articulation. This effect increases with the weight rating of the truck. A half-ton truck may be acceptable, but take a 3/4 or 1-ton on

make, look at the vehicle's characteristics to determine which one has the general features you want and need. The attributes listed below are shown more or less in order of importance.

Clearance

This would include ground clearance under the diffs, clearance of vital chassis components, front and rear overhang (which limit approach and departure angles), and body clearance. Axle and chassis ground clearance should

a bumpy road and you may be spitting out teeth if you drive at more than a crawl. Lower tire pressures (assuming no load) can partially negate this effect, as can certain modifications, but if you plan to four-wheel a pickup, especially a higher-GVW (Gross Vehicle Weight) unit, wear your kidney belt and mouthpiece (just kidding!).

be listed in the manufacturer's spec sheets, as well as approach, departure, and ramp breakover angles. Body clearance is an eyeball measurement. A long rear overhang with vulnerable rear quarter panels, for example, facilitates minor body damage, if not impaired capabilities, so a vehicle with a "short tail" might be a better choice.

The ubiquitous Suburban does surprisingly well on the trail with a few modifications. Because it starts out as a very trucklike machine, the mods don't become a major detriment. This older Sub made quite a reputation for itself around Moab a few years ago. There's room in this rig for everyone and everything.

The short full-sized SUVs of past years, such as the Blazer, Bronco, and Trailblazer, offer a decent compromise between size and capacity. Using truck chassis and drivetrains, they have a good deal of buildup potential without major sacrifices in day-to-day drivability.

CHOOSING A 4X4

When you go looking for a 4x4, a number of attributes are important to obtaining the best trail performance. Your first choices are going to be strictly personal, such as truck or SUV, cargo or passenger capacity, price, color and level of accoutrements. I will not be so foolish as to enter into the minefield of personal choice. Rather, I will deal with certain general attributes that are comparable vehicle to vehicle and let you make the ultimate choice. Bearing in mind the level of on-road sacrifices you are willing to

The 1984–2001 Jeep Cherokee is a bargain machine with lots of potential in stock or built-up forms. They are a little short of fenderwell space, requiring more lift for bigger tires. They are very well addressed by the aftermarket suppliers, so mild to wild buildups are possible. They have good trail dimensions.

Electronic Traction Control:
Electronic traction control (ETC) comes in various forms and while it's certainly better than nothing, but don't depend on it as the end-all-be-all, despite the advertising hyperbole you may see and hear.

Tire Upgrades:
Along with fenderwell clearance, drivetrain strength must be considered as well as the suspension's suitability to being lifted, which is almost always a part of a serious tire upgrade.

Even the ultralong pickups can do some trail work. This one is bone stock and traversing a moderately difficult trail. The key element is maneuvering room. The serious detriment to long-wheelbase trucks is ramp breakover angles. They need really big tires and lifts to get clearance under their vulnerable mid-sections, and this can create other problems and costs.

Limited Slip Diffs/Locking Diffs/Traction Control

While lockers and limited slips are available from the aftermarket for most four-wheel-drive vehicles, some come from the factory. In general, the factory limited slips are of marginal value and generally very loose. You might be better off having an after-market unit installed. The few factory rigs that come with electrically actuated locking diffs, such as the Toyota Tacoma and Land Cruiser models, are a notable exception.

Big Tires

"Big" is relative when it comes to factory 4x4s. For SUVs, a 31-inch-tall, 10-inch-wide tire is about the biggest readily available; pickups are some-times equipped with larger tires. In general, the rigs with the largest tires will offer the best traction in factory trim, but consider this feature as only a part of the equation. What may be more important in the long run is how big a tire may be fitted to a particular vehicle later, with or without modifi-cations. Some rigs have a fair amount of built-in capacity for larger tires, while others do not. For example, a pickup can usually accommodate a larger tire upgrade than can an SUV.

Low Gearing

Low gearing comes in the form of axle gearing and transmission and transfer case gearing. The former can be altered, while the latter is generally

changeable only by swapping. Across the board, automatic transmissions will offer the most flexibility on the street and trail. Most manual trans-missions, with the exception of certain truck units with an extra low "granny" first gear, have close-ratio gearboxes with relatively tall first and second gear ratios. This leads to stalling, clutch abuse, and higher-than-prudent speeds on the trail. Most rigs have at least a couple of optional ratios. Again, "low" is relative, but by choosing the lowest available factory axle gear ratio, you are both enhancing the vehicle's trail performance (perhaps with an accom-panying slight-to-moderate decrease in freeway fuel economy) and allowing the gearing leeway necessary for a tire upgrade. Most factory-optional ratios are on the mild side, say from 3.07 to 3.54:1 or 3.54 to 3.73:1. In some cases, you must order an equipment package of some sort, such as a trailer-towing package, to get the lower gears. If you are buying a used vehicle, the axle ratio is not a choice, but you can look for a particular rig with the low-est available ratio. A gearing swap is the same price (expensive!) regardless of whether you are swapping from 3.07:1 to 3.73: 1 or from 3.07 to 4.56:1. If you plan to keep your rig on the mild side but just need a slightly lower ratio for a tire upgrade or for better 'wheeling on the stock tires, it's more cost-effective to find a vehi-cle with the right ratios. If you plan a more serious buildup, the axle

Rigs that get too far into the trail category are often brought to the trailhead by truck or trailer. This vintage Ford F-600 was resurrected to become a prime mover for a built-up flatfender. Most rigs aren't this stylish. Usually a car trailer is towed behind a pickup or motorhome.

the dirt

Gearing:
Regardless of transmission type, axle gearing is the most easily alterable factory element in the drivetrain.

the dirt

On Weight:
A two-door SUV is generally lighter than a four-door. A half-ton pickup is lighter than a three-quarter- or 1-ton pickup. Power windows, seats, and so on will add several hundred pounds. More fuel equals more weight, so the larger-capacity fuel tank may be a liability unless you need the extra range.

ratio change will probably be a part of the plan.

Size and Weight

Smaller, lighter vehicles will always do better on the trail. Size is variable according to the terrain. If you 'wheel in more open areas, the larger rigs are less a liability. Weight is something else. The more weight, the more traction is needed to haul the vehicle over rough terrain, irrespective of size. The moral here is to travel as light as possible, minimize the amount of extra "iron" you attach to the vehicle in the form of accessories, and, if you are buying a vehicle, choose one with the least amount of extra bric-a-brac.

Modification Potential

Some four-wheel-drive vehicles are very modification-friendly; others are not. With some rigs, even the slightest mods are difficult due to the basic design and structure. With others, it's simply a lack of popularity. The availability of aftermarket buildup products is market driven, so it's a good idea to see how much is available for a particular rig before you buy it. Custom fabrication and adaptation require much more labor and cash.

Independent Front Suspension vs. Solid Axle

Solid-front axle-four-wheel drive has been the perennial favorite of the OE manufacturer, but lately it has been giving way to independent front suspension (IFS). These designs do not have to be particularly fragile—the Hummer has a stout IFS setup—but a solid axle can generally be made stouter for less money. The solid-axle setup is also more easily modified and better served by the aftermarket industry.

From the performance side, IFS systems do not articulate as a solid axle

ROCK TALK

IFS vs. Solid Axle:
Independent Front Suspension, or IFS, uses half-shafts instead of a solid axle, so each wheel can move up and down on its own. IFS provides for nice handling on the street and it saves weight. On the downside, it's generally more fragile than a solid axle, with many more parts to fail or break.

The Toyota 4-Runner is an SUV with legions of buyers and outright fanatics. This comes from a combination of innate performance and quality at a good market price. They have also proven to be a good basis for a buildup over their nearly 18 years of production.

This midsized pickup represents a good compromise between size and utility. Its owner has pushed this older Ranger a lot farther into the trail realm by modifying it with a Dana 44 front-axle swap and a 302 V-8. This truck is awesome in capability but remains relatively streetable. Had the owner opted, it could have been even more streetable.

The Toyota Land Cruiser is a legend in trail circles. It was imported in relatively small numbers from 1958 to 1983 and is now relatively uncommon and fast entering classic status. It is an extremely stout basis for a buildup, however, and has a following that makes up for small numbers by rabid fanaticism. As to comfort, they were in the same category as contemporary rigs, meaning downright Spartan by today's standard.

does, so they are more prone to lifting tires in more difficult terrain (hence losing the traction of one or both tires). Also, because each side operates independently, ground clearance can be a problem. If, for example, you put one tire onto a rock to avoid an obstacle, instead of that lifting the entire vehicle clear, the suspension compresses and actually lowers the center toward the ground, decreasing clearance.

In terms of trail performance on a stock, or nearly stock, vehicle for easy to moderate trails, both systems can work well enough, though the complexity and fragility issues will come into play for the IFS. As IFS systems become more prevalent, the aftermarket is providing more products to beef them up, as well as IFS-to-solid-axle conversion kits.

These conversions are labor-and cost-intensive, but can radically improve trail performance and durability.

Engine Power and Torque

More power is the American way and a tradition. As a result, many rigs are ordered with more engine than they need, or modified to produce more power than they need. First you need to understand the difference between power and torque. Horsepower is work times speed and is the element that boosts you up from 50 to 80 miles per hour to pass a semi. Torque is force times distance; it helps you climb that 40 degree slope and launches your vehicle from a dead stop.

How much is adequate? It's all related to engine torque versus the weight of the vehicle. If you take the rated engine torque and divide it into the curb weight, you will get the torque-to-weight ratio. Anything much over 20:1 is generally inadequate. The upper teens are acceptable, the middle teens are good, the lower teens are great, and under 10:1 is probably overkill.

Since its debut in 1993, the AM General Hummer has been the tough guy on the American 4x4 block. Now distributed by GM, the Hummer H1 will soon be joined by a more conventional H2 version built on GM running gear. Overall, the H1 Hummer is probably the most capable off-the-shelf 4x4 built in America, but you could buy and modify a stable of other rigs for what they cost.

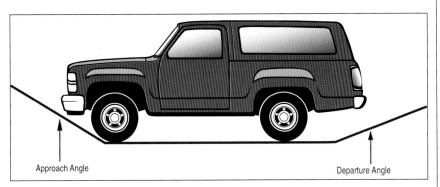

Approach Angle   Departure Angle

Approach and departure angles are part of the clearance equation. A vehicle with steep angles will perform better, because it can approach a steeper climb without some part besides the tires making contact. Departure angles are important for climbing as well as for the transition part of a descent. Lift and taller tires both increase these angles.

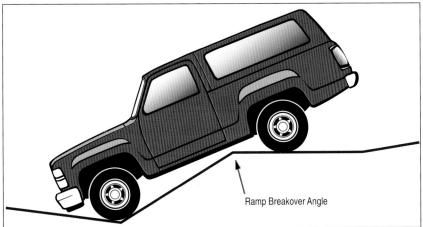

Ramp Breakover Angle

Ramp breakover angle is also important. The transitions from a flat area to a descent and from a climb to flat ground are common hanging-up points for rigs with a poor ramp breakover angle.

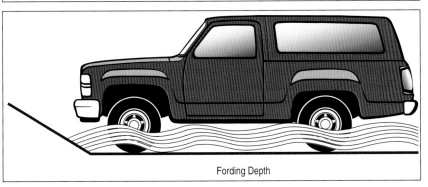

Fording Depth

It's harder to get fording depth info these days, and when it's given, it's usually similar to what is shown here, the level of the hubs. The more modern rigs tend to be very water shy for many good reasons.

CHAPTER 4

WHAT DOES THAT LEVER DO?

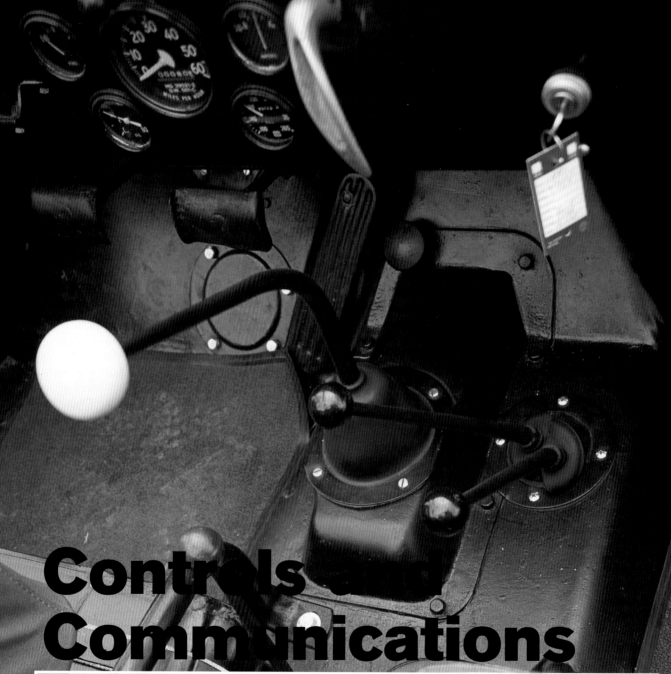

Controls and Communications

There are enough sticks here to inspire lever envy, or perhaps lever aversion. This 1947 CJ-2A Jeep features not only the floor shift for the main three-speed transmission, but the twin sticks of the old Model 18 Spicer transfer case. The left lever engages the front output to power the front axle. Forward is disengaged and back is engaged. The right lever engages the range box, with forward being low, center neutral, and back high. This operation is typical of many vintage rigs. If three levers aren't enough, the fourth lever between the seats operates a Power Take-Off unit to run farm machinery. Optionally, this rig could also have had a fifth lever for an overdrive unit. All of these controls offer great flexibility, but you need to know the wherefores and the whys to make full use of the capabilities they offer.

You can't do much with a tool unless you know how to use it. A 4x4 is a tool that is often taken for granted because, in essence, it operates pretty much like an ordinary car. The familiar controls are all in the right places, but there are a few extra ones that can really throw you a curve. When you hit the trail, a whole new set of rules applies and things don't work quite the same as they do on the street. This section covers the items you will find on virtually every standard four-wheel drive, though not every item covered here will be on every vehicle.

Communications on the trail is both a convenience and a potential lifesaver. From the convenience side, a simple, inexpensive CB radio allows you to converse with trail buddies, warn of impending problems, and summon help. Ditto for the little FRS (Family Radio System) handhelds. You can move up into the Single Sideband (SSB) radios or even mobile ham radios (VHF/UHF/HF), if you need longer-range commo. Don't forget the ubiquitous cell phone, either. All of these options add a measure of fun and safety.

THE STEERING WHEEL

I can hear some of you already! "Get serious! The steering wheel needs special instruction?" The short answer is, yes.

Ten and Two

The best positions for your hands on the steering wheel are at the typical 10 o'clock and 2 o'clock positions. This gives you plenty of leverage and control. When actually steering, use the "push and slide" method rather than the cross-arm method you see race drivers use. Push and slide keeps your hands more or less in the 10 and 2 position and you steer by using one hand to push, the other to pull within a steering-wheel rotation of about 80 degrees. You then grip with one hand, and slide the other for a new purchase, alternating hands.

Thumbs 'n' Things

The other steering wheel caveat is to keep your thumbs outside the inner rim of the steering wheel. Regardless of power steering, in certain situations

Casual Driving:
The one-hand-casually-draped-on-the-steering-wheel driving style doesn't cut it on the trail. The irregular surfaces and bumps can easily yank the wheel out of a casual grip.

Shown here is the old ten and two, with a twist. Keep those thumbs outside the rim of the steering wheel. Power steering and steering dampers have all but ended the days when steering kickback would yank the wheel out of your hand, but it still happens. If one of the wildly spinning spokes happened to catch your thumb, ouch! That's one part of the "good old days" I don't miss!

Left-foot braking is the accepted technique for automatics and even low-geared manuals. It may take some time to train that "atrophied" left foot, but it will save lots of hassles and right-foot tap dancing on the pedals.

the steering wheel can suddenly kick back, and if your thumb happens to be in the way of a steering wheel spoke, a serious ouch will result. It happens infrequently these days, with the advent of power steering and steering dampers, but one incident is usually a cure for *ever* inserting your thumbs inside the rim again, street or trail.

Death Grip

After reading the above, it might seem appropriate to have a death grip on the wheel the next time you hit the trail! Just the opposite is true. Loosen up and lighten up, but be ready to exert the force needed, when it's needed.

You Drive

Severe articulation may cause the suspension to exert a certain amount of force on the steering wheel. For example, on some rigs, when the left wheel droops to its bottom position, it tends to pull the steering wheel right. When faced with that experience the first time, many people just let it happen, some to the point of letting the wheel spin wildly like the wheel of the SS *Minnow* on *Gilligan's Island.* Hold that steering wheel in the position you want it.

THE BRAKE PEDAL

The brake pedal has been anointed by long-time street drivers as the magic cure for all problems. Even on the street, that's not really true, but on the trail it's even less so. The brake pedal can actually get you into trouble. In many ways, braking traction is the same as driving traction. You either have tire grip or your don't. If you are trying to climb a steep, slippery slope and don't have the traction, you just say, "Oh, well," and back down. If you are coming down that hill, apply too much brake and lose traction, your words will be much stronger as you slide out of control.

Light Foot

A light and sensitive foot is best. Two braking methods are known to work well. The first is to simply be attuned to tire grip. Apply a little brake until you hear or feel tires starting to slide on the ground surface (it almost always will be the unloaded rear tires first on a downhill). You either reduce pressure on the brake pedal or remove your foot altogether. The other method is cadence braking, which is a gentle, continuous on-off, on-off application of the brakes, never applying enough pressure to lock the tires.

Left Foot

Left-foot braking is a useful tool for the trail, especially with automatics. If you're not used to using that foot, it can take some practice to train it for the job, but the benefits are a much smoother technique and better performance overall. In certain situations, such as rock crawling, you might even use the throttle and brake simultaneously. Hold just a bit of throttle and vary brake pressure to keep speed controlled going up and down the sides of the rocks.

THE THROTTLE

Also known as the gas pedal, the accelerator pedal, the foot-feed, the go-pedal, the hammer, and other terms, the throttle is a vital control to master. The most common mistakes involve too much throttle, though timidity is also common. Analogous to the Three Bears story, there's too much, too little, and just right. The problem with just right is that it changes according to the obstacle. In most cases, just a little is just right, but sometimes you need the opposite approach. The trick is to know when and where to put the hammer down.

Use of the accelerator pedal is so variable that I can give only a few generalities. First, work the level of throttle up gradually. Start off with small amounts and work your way up as needed. Second, it matters where on the pedal you place your foot. With a foot suspended over the pedal with no side support, your tiring ankle and calf may be subject to uncontrolled applications of throttle due to bumps or bouncing. A foot wedged against the transmission tunnel will be much more stable and controlled, and less subject to fatigue.

THE TRANSMISSION AND TRANSFER CASE

Gear selection is one of the most important parts of four-wheeling. Gear selection is especially important if you drive a manual transmission vehicle, because you often have to select the gear without a chance to change your mind partway through.

To maximize grip on a climb, you want as little torque multiplication as possible. This is critical on low-traction climbs. That means as little throttle as possible and as high a gear as possible without lugging the engine. Choose a gearing and throttle combo that keeps the engine in a useful torque range, the speed of the vehicle as slow as possible—while still utilizing some momentum—and the torque multiplication under control. That combo will vary greatly across the many vehicles out there.

Going down is the opposite. Use the lowest possible gear to let engine braking slow the descent. Let the hill be your guide. Second low may be OK for a mild slope or if you have very deep gears. On descents with low traction, you may find a situation analogous to excessive braking where the tires will slip, especially the rear. In this case, you can shift up, or increase the speed of the vehicle with the throttle. More on that in the next chapter.

The Automatic Transmission

Though ages old, there are still strong debates in the four-wheeling world over the automatic's place on the trail. But frankly it's all moot. Drive what you like, though in most cases, for most people, the auto is superior.

Gear selection with the automatic is easy: let the transmission do it! With three-speed autos, keep the unit in "D" or "3," and for four-speed autos, use "3." The trans will select the correct gear for the terrain or obstacle. This rule is flexible according to conditions. There's nothing wrong with using "2" if speeds are slow enough and you are doing a lot of shifting down to "1." If you want or need to avoid an automatic upshift or downshift, such as on a hill where you need a fair bit of throttle and you don't want the unit to suddenly downshift, you can select a particular gear. Some rigs have a lockout button that will hold the vehicle in the preselected gear. Avoid using that overdrive gear—usually "D" on four-speed autos—on the trail while in low range. It's not the strongest set of gears in your transmission.

The biggest performance difference between the automatic and the manual is engine braking on descents. With a mechanical lockup, the manual has the advantage in slowing the vehicle more on descents. Low gears or a low-rpm stall torque converter will help the automatic, but that fluid coupling simply does not allow a 100 percent lockup. The manual transmission may not require use of the footbrakes on a steep downhill, but the auto almost always needs a judicious foot on the brake pedal.

With an autobox, you can get away with somewhat taller gearing

Shown here is the typical three-speed automatic shifter. A four-speed auto might differ in having a "3" position below "D." In the case of this three-speed, most of your wheeling would be done in "D." A four-speed auto would use "3." At very slow speeds, it would be acceptable to use "2," especially if you were doing a lot of shifting down to "1."

Manual Transmission Tips:
It's not always safe or advisable to shift a manual transmission partway up a climb. You also have to be smooth. A herky-jerky driving style transmits severe shock loads to the drivetrain, breaking parts much more often on manual transmission 4x4s than automatics.

Starting in gear is a useful tactic in many venues, but it's not always possible in modern rigs because the clutch must be depressed before the starter circuit will operate. Toyota is one manufacturer that offers a momentary bypass switch so you can start the vehicle in gear when needed. This is a feature that you can wire in yourself on nearly any rig.

the dirt

Trail Gearing:
If you find yourself having to slip the clutch constantly to avoid stalling in tough terrain, you probably need lower gearing.

because, in effect, the torque converter is a variable-ratio first gear. The mechanical first-gear ratios of most automatics, 2.4-3:1, don't sound impressive until you multiply it by the torque converter ratio, typically 2.0–2.5:1. This ratio, combined with the mechanical ratios, gives you the effect of a lower ratio. That "ratio" changes with engine speed. You might have a 2.5:1 converter ratio (times the mechanical ratio) at 850 rpm, but by 1,000 rpm, it's down to about 1.5:1 and by 1,500 rpm, the converter is locked up at nearly 1:1.

The Manual Transmission and Clutch

Driving a manual transmission rig requires you to be decisive. Often, you have to choose the right gear for the job without an opportunity for a second chance.

If you drive a manual, get in the habit of gently letting the drivetrain wind up its slack before putting the hammer down. Above all, don't ride the clutch. Except for the actual moment of the shift, keep your left foot flat on the floor—if it's not on the brake. There are some screaming emergency situations where you might slip the clutch, such as a sputtering engine ready to die in the middle of a fast-moving stream taking you to Newark. Otherwise, don't.

On hills, being uncoupled from the engine means that you are one step closer to being out of control. Exceptions are those dead-slow conditions where you have to creep off a rock. Obviously, most rigs aren't geared low enough to do that and the driver has to rely 100 percent on the brakes.

Starting in Gear

It's often difficult or impossible to start a stalled engine on a slope and start moving again in the same manner as you would on level ground. You need 3 feet to do it right (see the Parking Brake section farther on for more tips). It can also be a little hairy, because declutching the engine from the drivetrain deprives you of the most

efficient means of descent control. Going down a hill backward tends to unload the front (steering) wheels due to weight transfer. Application of the brakes in this situation tends to make the front tires lock up, and you immediately lose some, or all, steering control.

It's often safer and more practical to leave the clutch out, and simply turn the key to restart the engine. Whether your engine will, in fact, restart depends on the steepness of the hill, how well the engine runs, overall gearing, and the strength of your starter and battery. Is it inherently hard on the starter to do this? Yes, but not overtly so unless it's a very regular occurrence. If it's clear that your vehicle will not restart in this manner, don't beat the poor horse to death; instead, perform a failed climb procedure as outlined in the next chapter.

Bypassing the Clutch Pedal Starter Lock-Out

Nearly all of the newer manual-transmission–equipped 4x4s have a switch on the clutch pedal that prevents the vehicle from starting unless the pedal is depressed. The idea is to prevent you from accidentally starting the vehicle in gear and taking out the back wall of your garage. Since it's sometimes advisable to start the vehicle in gear on the trail with the clutch out, and the switch prevents this, some owners will bypass it by connecting the two wires on the switch together. This is a choice you have to make, and a responsibility you will assume if you think this modification is needed for your style of four-wheeling. The most serious danger is that you will forget—or another driver may not realize—what you have done and accidentally start the vehicle in gear. At least one manufacturer, Toyota, has the needs of four-wheelers in mind and offers a dash-mounted momentary bypass switch so the vehicle can be started in gear. This is an optional modification you could make. By wiring in a momentary switch (meaning that the switch is spring loaded and you have to hold it

Single-stick transfer cases were the big improvement in four-wheel drive of the 1950s and they are still made today. The shift pattern is usually in a line front to back. Note the position of neutral. This unit is in a mid-1980s Ford pickup, but is typical of many other single-stick t-cases.

The best of the electrically shifted transfer cases offer a neutral position. This GM truck also has an "Auto" setting that can be used when traction problems are imminent. When the system senses rear-wheel slippage (via the ABS wheel speed sensors), it engages four-wheel drive.

THE TRANSFER CASE CONTROLS

Engage four-wheel-high as soon as you get to the point where you wouldn't drive the family car, and use low range on uneven terrain or if the going gets tough. Simple! Many drivers prefer using low range from the start because they are more prepared for the unexpected and have better engine braking.

If you drive a vehicle with full-time four-wheel drive and a manually locked center differential, lock that center diff when the going gets tough or if you are using low range. Engage the center differential lock only when the vehicle is nearly stationary or when the drivetrain is not under a big load.

Many full-time transfer cases have viscous couplings or other devices that automatically engage when a major traction differential is sensed between the front and rear tires. Bear in mind that they also unlock automatically and can do so at inopportune times. You just need to be sensitive and give the unit time to adjust to varying conditions.

"Shift on the fly" is an overused term that implies that you can shift the transfer case at any speed—not completely true. You can shift into or out of four-wheel-high at nearly any speed, but not into low range. Shifting into low is best done with the vehicle stopped or just barely rolling.

I always double-check once I've put the vehicle in gear, by backing off on the throttle and giving the shift lever another shove. If your rig has a t-case shifted by a servo, the unit will continue to try to fully engage the gears, so merely backing off for a second may allow them to finish the job if the gears didn't completely engage. If your rig pops out of gear, which all rigs may do occasionally, go back into neutral and drop the t-case back into gear. If this becomes a continual problem, you may have an internal transfer case or a linkage problem.

THE PARKING BRAKE

Also commonly called the "emergency" brake, the parking brake has many uses on the trail, not the least of which is parking. Unlike the street, where "Park" on the automatic trans or leaving the manual trans in gear is often considered sufficient to keep the vehicle from rolling away, the more acute grades on the trail make parking brake use mandatory.

The automatic trans has a "parking pawl" that locks it in place when you put the gear selection lever in Park. If

in), you could have the bypass when you need it without the worry of accidentally starting in gear on the street.

Sticks and Buttons: Transfer Case Controls

Transfer case controls have evolved substantially from the days when drivers had one or two sticks coming up through the floor. Most t-cases are electronically shifted these days. The driver activates a simple switch or button and a servo motor does the shifting at the transfer case. This is both good and bad from a four-wheeling perspective.

The good part is user-friendliness. No reaching down and jerking on a recalcitrant stick with both hands. These modern designs are often shift-on-the-fly systems that can be operated at substantial road speeds. There are also "smart" systems with automatic features that will shift into four-wheel drive when sensors detect slippage at the rear wheel. This does not include the almost seamless full-time system now available.

The concerns with the push-button systems are mainly related to reliability in tough environments. With a lever, the stick has a direct, or nearly direct, connection with the gears in the transfer case. When you pull it into four-low, you know it's in four-low. That isn't always

true of the servo types, where electrical circuits and motors can fail due to dirt or water intrusion or simply from normal wear. These failures correspond to how the vehicle is used and they will fail more often in harsh environments. Some manufacturers offer an emergency method of shifting the t-case, usually in the form of a large Allen wrench. Your owner's manual will detail this.

Some manufacturers still offer a choice of manually or electrically shifted transfer cases, but these choices are few and far between. If you plan on being a regular on the trail, my advice is to go with a manually shifted t-case, the simple and reliable choice. Beyond that rare choice, look for units that offer a neutral position. Many systems do not have a neutral button, so if the time comes to tow your rig you will be restricted to short distances or risk transmission or transfer case damage. A true neutral position allows much more leeway in towing without having to undergo the onerous process of removing driveshafts.

the dirt

Stuck in Park:
If your transmission gets jammed in Park, try to get another vehicle to pull you slightly uphill. This will take the weight off the pawl and should allow you to shift.

the dirt

Trail Parking:
Leave a manual transmission vehicle in first gear on an uphill lie, and reverse gear if the vehicle is aimed downhill.

you park on a grade and let the pawl hold the entire weight, you might find it impossible to get out of park. To avoid this dilemma, apply the parking brake first, and then put the shift lever into Park. That way the parking brakes take the load, and the park pawl becomes the backup device.

With manual transmissions, a vehicle held in place only by the gearbox and engine will still move if the hill is steep enough: the engine will simply turn over. Locking the wheels with the parking brake will prevent this.

The parking brake can be used to great advantage with manual trans rigs, especially with the Euro-style, lever-type units that mount between the seats. Starting on a hill is the ages-old predicament for stick shifters. Some people start in gear, though this is not possible for all rigs all the time. Others master a heel-and-toe approach that would make Mr. Bojangles proud. But the easiest method is to use the parking brake.

Here's how:
- While holding the vehicle with the foot brake, shift the vehicle into the appropriate gear.

- With the right hand, pull the parking brake up hard, keeping the button pressed in so the lever doesn't lock. Assuming the hill is not super steep and your parking brake is properly adjusted, it should hold the vehicle.
- Release the foot brake and use that foot on the accelerator pedal.
- As you engage the clutch and apply throttle, the clutch will begin taking the weight of the vehicle and you can gradually release the parking brake.

As you have probably figured, this trick will not work with rigs that have foot-actuated parking brakes. If you had the extra foot, you wouldn't need the parking brake.

Some four-wheelers with open differentials will use the parking brake as a poor-man's traction control. In situations where all the torque is going to a slipping or unloaded rear tire, applying some parking brake can help stop or slow that spinning tire and force the diff to transfer some torque to the wheel with traction. This applies only to vehicles that have parking brakes

that actuate on the rear wheels. Rigs such as older Jeeps, Toyotas, and older-to-current Land Rovers with transfer case–mounted parking brakes will gain nothing.

As with almost everything in the four-wheeling world, there are a few caveats to parking brake use. Dedicated snow bashers will sometimes avoid using the parking brake because as the vehicle rapidly cools to ambient temperature, the melted snow on or in the brakes can freeze solid and lock the mechanism. I remember seeing one hapless four-wheeler urinating on his brakes after a snow trip lunch break to free them up so he could continue. Ahem! Similar problems can happen in mud and water, though it's usually a case of repeated dunkings and neglect afterward. People who run in water and mud with regularity will need to clean out their brakes often to ensure proper operation.

FREEWHEELING HUBS

Many 4x4s these days are full-time systems, which have no freewheeling hubs at all. Some part-time systems use a Center Axle Disconnect, or CAD, also eliminating hubs from the equation. Many others use automatic locking hubs that engage when four-wheel drive is selected. If you have manual hubs, lock them in when you hit the dirt. Pretty simple.

TRACTION CONTROL

As mentioned in the previous chapter, some 4x4s use an electronic traction control system that utilizes

the anti-lock brakes to slow the spinning tire and transfer some torque to the tire with the most traction. They operate automatically, but sometimes are slow to engage. Sometimes they need more wheelspin than you might initially think necessary. You'll soon get a feel for the conditions and situations that fool your ETC. These systems work well in mild to moderate situations, but some of them have a built-in timer that temporarily shuts the system down to prevent the brakes from being overheated. Fate usually decrees this to happen at the moment

The parking brake is an important control for secure parking at any angle, but especially so for manual transmission–equipped rigs. A hand-operated brake makes starting on a grade easier. The best setups are the Euro-style brakes (left). The type that pulls out of the dash (center) can also be used effectively. The important consideration is that they can be used with one hand and used without locking. The foot-operated brake is useless. If you had the third foot, you wouldn't need the brake at all!

Parking Brake Operation:
Parking brakes can freeze up in cold climates or from repeated exposure to water and mud without proper cleanup afterward.

Automatic Hubs:
There are a few caveats to certain automatic hubs. Some will disconnect on steep descents under the right circumstances. When they get old and gummy, sometimes they won't engage at all.

You won't find this control on many factory rigs. A rear diff lock is a real asset and makes any OE rig capable of greater trail prowess. This feature comes on many Toyota trucks when the TRD (Toyota Racing Development) option is ordered.

you need it most. Traction control may interfere with certain types of aftermarket lockers

ANTI-LOCK BRAKES

Anti-lock brakes are great on the highway. For most drivers, they shorten stopping distances and improve control. Double ditto on slippery pavement, but sometimes they can complicate four-wheeling. Anti-lock brake systems (ABS) come in two-channel (with anti-lock capability on only two wheels, usually the rear) or four-channel (operating on all four wheels) designs. The system operates via wheel speed sensors, an electronic control unit, and a complicated set of electric valves in the hydraulic part of the brake system. The ABS system's goal is to keep wheel speed equal and keep the wheels rolling (remember, on pavement, a skidding tire delivers little traction). It prevents wheel lockup by momentarily releasing hydraulic brake pressure at the wheel. By constantly monitoring wheel speeds, the control unit can regulate wheel speed and lockup at each wheel individually using these electronically controlled valves, and do it well enough to compensate for all sorts of divergent road surface conditions. The response time is measured in milliseconds and the ABS system usually offers arrow-true stopping.

Some ABS systems are disengaged when the vehicle is put into low range. Others may have an on-off switch. Every system has a threshold speed below which the ABS is inoperative. This speed varies according to the vehicle type, but it ranges from about 3 to 6 miles per hour. I have not done a survey of every four-channel ABS system available on 4x4s, but I know that some systems may be able to distinguish between road or trail situations and adjust that threshold speed somewhat.

The problems come in the more difficult realms of the four-wheeling world, where there is a completely different set of forces at work. Here are some situations where an ABS system can cause problems.

Weight Transfer Situations

One primary example is a failed climb. Because brake bias is to the front, when backing down on a failed climb, the front tires tend to lock up first due to weight transfer. You may be carefully modulating the brake pedal to avoid lockup, but if you accidentally let a wheel lock momentarily, or even if the front wheels slow down significantly compared to the rear, the ABS system may sense the difference in wheel speed front to rear and start releasing the rear brakes. Since this is your primary set of brakes for the duration of the failed climb, the vehicle speeds up. You mash harder on the pedal to no avail. About all you can do at that point is try to maintain control. Going down frontways can cause a similar problem. The key here is to keep the speed below the ABS system's threshold speed, which may or may not be possible.

Lifted Tires

Lifted tires can cause the ABS system to read differences in wheel speed and engage. For example, say you are coming off a rock and fully articulated. If you have an open diff on the wheel that's lifted, the ABS system may sense a different wheel speed one side to another and kick in while you are easing off a rock. Again, staying below the threshold speed is the key.

Ground Conditions

There are times when a locked-up wheel will stop you faster than a continuously rolling one. For example, a locked-up wheel will create a plowing effect in gravel, loose shale, or sand, and it piles up material in front of the tires. You could call it a "dynamic wheel block," and it works well. To avoid having the ABS system prevent this phenomenon, you need to stay below the speed threshold.

Read the Manual

Since the ABS system is built-in, and few, if any, have an "off" switch, it

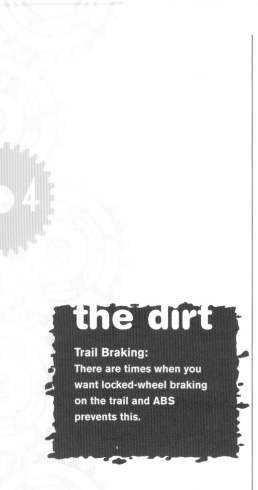

the dirt

Trail Braking:
There are times when you want locked-wheel braking on the trail and ABS prevents this.

behooves you to read the section of your owner's manual that details how the system works. Knowing what it's designed to do will allow you to adjust your driving style to account for it.

COMMUNICATIONS

There are basically four levels of communications available. They start with CB (Citizens Band), then jump to SSB (Single Sideband), UHF/VHF (Ultra High Frequen-cy/Very High Frequency, and finally HF (High Frequency). There are some divisions within these groups, but they are listed in order of the buy-in costs and knowledge required. A fifth level would be the cell phone, which has actually become a useful device, even in some very remote areas.

A Word on FCC Licensing and Legalities

The Federal Communications Commission (FCC) licenses access to transmissions over radio waves. The only exempt bands are the Citizens Band, a narrow range of frequencies on the AM band, the FRS (Family Radio System) broadcasting on low-power FM, and certain bands of the SSB. Beyond these, an Amateur Radio or "ham" license is required and they come at different levels for different types and complexities of radio, with the tests reflecting the amount of knowledge required.

You don't need an FCC license to buy an FCC-regulated radio, or to turn it on and listen, but a license is required to press that mike button and talk. If you used a regulated radio in a life-or-death emergency without being licensed, it's likely you'd get a pass, both from the government and from the ham radio community. Otherwise, watch out!

Amateur Radio licenses come in several basic categories: the *Technician Class, General Class,* and *Amateur Extra Class.* There are a couple of other divisions and some old categories for which no new licenses are being issued. The technician-class test

consists of 35 questions and you must get 26 questions right to pass. To get a general-class license, you must also pass the 35-question test, as well as a five word-per-minute Morse code test. If you want the amateur extra-class license, you have to pass an additional 50-question test. The basic level entitles the operator to use equipment in a certain frequency range, with access to more frequencies as you move up the license levels.

CB Radios

CB radios can be anything from a cheap handheld to a fancy dash-mounted unit with lots of bells and whistles. CBs use an FCC-allotted band of AM (amplitude modulation) frequencies, sometimes called "Double Sideband." No license is required for a CB operator. By law, CBs of any type are limited to a 4-watt output. This provides a useful communications range of about 2 to 5 miles, basically within the unit's natural ground wave effect (a radius around the antenna) with a good antenna and perfect conditions. On a really good day, with an outstanding setup, 25-mile two-way conversations are possible. The CB's AM radio waves can "skip" off the atmosphere, and in very rare circumstances when the right atmospheric conditions exist, you can actually have a conversation with someone very far away. Technically, it's illegal to have a conversation with someone more than 150 miles away on the CB.

CBs' limited range may make them impractical for use in all emergency situations, especially for a lone vehicle in a remote area. In some cases, there may be enough people within range to form a communications chain and relay an emergency message to the right authority. Often, the cure in an emergency situation might be to summon a person who's only a short distance away, from your own traveling group, perhaps. Another option is to dispatch a member of your group to a point where he or she can summon help, or at least pass a message.

The CB Radio 10-Code

10-1 Signal Weak
10-2 Signal Strong
10-3 Stop Transmitting
10-4 OK
10-5 Relay To
10-6 Busy
10-7 Out of Service
10-8 In Service
10-9 Say Again
10-10 Negative
10-11 On Duty
10-12 Stand By
10-13 Existing Conditions
10-14 Have Message
10-15 Message Delivered
10-16 Reply to Message
10-17 En Route
10-18 Urgent
10-19 In Contact
10-20 Location
10-21 Call by Phone
10-22 Disregard
10-23 Arrived at Scene
10-24 Assignment Complete
10-25 Meet
10-26 ETA
10-27 License Information
10-28 Ownership Information
10-29 Records Check
10-30 Danger
10-31 Pick Up
10-32 Units Needed
10-33 Need Help Fast
10-34 Time
10-100 Potty Break

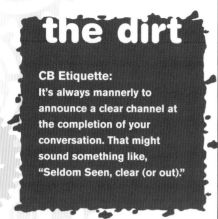

The main use of a CB in the four-wheeling realm is for fun and information. The running CB commentary heard in a group of four-wheelers on a trail run is better than any TV show.

Using the CB

Many CBers have a "handle," or radio nickname. Pick whatever you like, or use your actual name if you prefer. The handle is better because there may be lots of Janes, Bills, Bobs, Wendys, and so on. Odds are that you can come up with a handle that suits your personality and is less common than your name. Handles are unofficial, so you're not stuck with your first pick.

CB etiquette calls for not hogging the channel, using brevity in your messages, and avoiding bad language. The airwaves are first come/first serve. That means a person using the channel in your range gets to finish before you get your chance. In an emergency, feel free to break right in and demand a clear channel.

When you want to contact someone, you follow a standard form about like this: "Buffalo Hunter, this is Seldom Seen." Wait a moment and if there is no reply, try again a few times. If you don't make contact, get on one last time and say, "Negative contact Buffalo Hunter, Seldom Seen clear (or out)." The reason for this is that there may be others waiting to use the channel and by clearing, you are opening the channel.

If you need to use a channel that has some traffic, normal etiquette is to allow the speakers some time to complete their conversation. If they are overly windy, wait for a lull and jump in with, "Break One-One" (or "Break" and whatever channel you are on). This is a hint that you need to use the channel and could they please give you a "break" and wrap up the talk. Most often, one of them will reply, "Go, breaker," and you will be allowed to conduct your business. They may ask for a moment to complete their conversation and then give a postponed "Go breaker," or announce a clear channel.

Some ex-military people have a certain radio procedure ingrained, which includes the phonetic alphabet (Alpha, Bravo, Charlie, Delta, Echo, and so on), saying "over" after each completed sentence, and using "Roger" and "Wilco" (Will Comply) as affirmatives. That's OK but not necessary. The "10-Code" (see page 53) is a police code that has long been a part of CB use. This is not necessary either, but it's cool and many four-wheelers use the codes that apply. It wouldn't hurt to know the common 10-codes so that you understand what you're hearing.

Use of CB Controls

Every CB is different, but there is much commonality in the controls. Some of what follows is universal and some is optional and appears only on the higher-line units.

Microphone- The "mike" is simple, with a "grille" area into which you speak and a transmit button (a.k.a. the PTT [Push to Talk] switch). Hold the mike about 2 inches from your mouth, press the transmit button, and speak normally. Release the button when you finish speaking. There is usually an LED indicator on the face of the radio that goes red when transmitting. The unit cannot transmit and receive at the same time, so you need to release the mike button to listen.

Channel Selector- Modern CBs use 40 channels; older units had 23.

Squelch- This control tunes out noise. Generally, you will turn the squelch down (counterclockwise) until you hear hissing and then slowly turn back until the noise disappears. More squelch (quieter) tends to limit the range of incoming transmissions. If someone is at extreme range, you may have to live with the squelch way down and try to hear over the static.

S/RF Meter- This is a small meter that indicates the strength of both the incoming and outgoing signals, usually on a scale of 1 through 9. The higher number indicates the more powerful signal. Many radios have this feature.

Local/DX- This switch controls receiver sensitivity. On local, the unit will hear only the stronger nearby stations but will hear them more clearly and without as much background noise. On DX, the radio will hear all stations, weak or strong, to the accompaniment of more background noise.

ANL- This is a noise limiter that helps to tune out extraneous external noise, such as the crackling from ignition systems or whines from alternators. It does tend to reduce the clarity of reception, so it's usually off until needed. If your CB is troubled by noise from the vehicle in which it's mounted, there are various filters that can be installed to insulate the radio from them.

RF Gain- This is a manual control for reception sensitivity. Set at maximum, it will pick up very weak signals, but will also be subject to bleedover interference from other channels on either side of the one selected.

CB Radio Choices

The beginning range of choices is the handheld units. Though all CBs will have a four-watt output, the handheld's short antennas as well as low and short-term battery power puts them at a disadvantage. With these units, a 12-volt power adapter/charger becomes an important accessory. They can be very handy on a slow trail for helping guide vehicles though tough obstacles or where people are walking around. The higher-priced units are better performers.

A mounted transceiver is the best overall choice. There are many out there, from under $100 to nearly $1,000. It all comes down to the quality of the components and the features. Some units will allow your CB to be used as a mini PA system. You can also make microphone upgrades to clarify or amplify your voice. A few CBs incorporate an SSB transceiver.

Among options, the weather channel is the most useful. This channel gives you the opportunity to monitor weather changes that could be inconvenient or even deadly.

Antenna Choices

With your output limited to 4 watts, your antenna choice becomes of paramount importance to good range. Handhelds are at the bottom of the food chain in this area and are usually limited to a mile or so with their tiny antennas. Many can be temporarily converted to work on an outside vehicle antenna. This equipment makes a worthwhile supplemental purchase.

Bear in mind that the radio and antenna must be matched, or tuned, to the vehicle via an SWR (standing wave ratio) meter. Each vehicle is slightly different, so adjustments made after installation are akin to a performance tune-up on your engine. It's a relatively simple process and SWR meters are not expensive, so it can be a do-it-yourself task, or one you reserve for a pro. The primary adjustment is tuning the length of the antenna. This can be done by physically shortening or lengthening the antenna or, in the case of a loaded coil antenna, making an adjustment via a tuning screw on the antenna, or by "bobbing" the antenna to the right length. Sometimes the length of the coaxial cable connecting the radio to the antenna is important. On a new installation, making the adjustments is vital to performance, as a severely out-of-tune radio can suffer component damage.

Antennas work best when they have a sizable ground plane, which is a "capture" or "mirror" area below the antenna. The ideal size is 18x18 feet, but in a vehicle, the best you will find is a few square feet of metal roof. That's the best place to mount a CB antenna. If you have a ragtop, do the best you can. The person who tunes your radio might be able to find the next best spot. It varies from vehicle to vehicle. One specialist I spoke with told me that two identical vehicles can be completely different in this regard.

This may not seem to be the ideal spot for a CB antenna, but the SWR meter liked it. The body is fiberglass, so the ground plane effect is somewhat limited. This was helped by the addition of a big stainless-steel toolbox in the bed nearby.

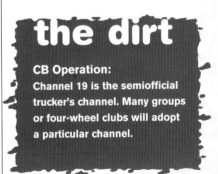

the dirt

CB Operation:
Channel 19 is the semiofficial trucker's channel. Many groups or four-wheel clubs will adopt a particular channel.

These very compact VHF and UHF units can reach stations across the nation as long as they are within line-of-sight and range of a repeater. Repeaters are common in many parts of the country, even in more remote areas, but terrain or natural obstacles can block transmissions. An FCC license is required for these units. The sophisticated equipment in the background is a sure sign of a dedicated ham operator.

This repeater directory gives licensed operators the codes for repeaters all over the United States—it's necessary when you go traveling. It will give you the locations for the repeaters so that you can determine what your communications capability will be wherever you go.

Magnetic mounts on roofs are popular, as are clamp-on mounts on the sideview mirrors, bumper mounts, and windshield frame mounts. Some folks don't even mind putting a hole in the side of the body and mount a bracket there.

There are many types of antennas, from 108-inch whips to short, loaded antennas. Obviously the loaded units are easiest to deal with, but a taller antenna reaches out farther. A tall antenna offers a better ground wave effect and therefore a longer effective range. A loaded antenna contains extra coils of wire inside that simulate a longer antenna. Fiberglass or carbon fiber antenna bodies are used, with the wire inside. Some are metal.

The antenna is connected to the radio via coaxial cable. There is definitely a quality difference between department-store cable and professional-quality stuff. This material can mean the difference between really good range and being able to shout farther than your CB can transmit.

In conclusion, the taller antenna has a greater range, but physical limitations may well dictate a short, loaded antenna.

External Speakers

In a loud or open-topped vehicle, hearing your CB may be difficult. Almost all units have a small, built-in speaker, but often an external speaker is necessary to hear over the whine of tires. These are specially designed to make the human voice sound louder

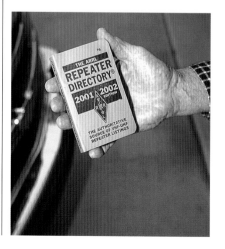

and clearer. Almost all CBs have a jack for this speaker. Many also have a jack for a low-power PA-type speaker. This can be very useful for the trail, but take care using it in street traffic, as they are illegal in some locales.

Single Sideband

SSB radios are a variation of the AM technology used with CBs. I've avoided radio theory up to now, and I won't get into the technical differences here. SSB opens up more channels and offers quite a bit more range—the right setups can reach hundreds of miles. Some SSB frequencies require an FCC license, but some do not. Radios that combine CB and SSB are available, and these units have the "legal" SSB frequencies that do not require a license. SSB transmits at 12 watts, and is also more efficient (some sources say 16 times more efficient), resulting in a much longer range. SSB is the logical choice for four-wheelers wanting to reach out farther in case of an emergency. According to some Amateur Radio people, the available channels may not be well monitored in some areas.

Ham: VHF/UHF

UHF and VHF are part of the FM (frequency modulation) band used for TV and high-quality radio, but a certain batch of frequencies is allotted to Amateur Radio. These are the most popular of the Amateur Radio frequencies. They have some limitations because FM is line-of-sight. That means when a mountain or other obstacle is in the way, the signal stops. Your experiences with TV reception prior to cable may be the best example of line-of-sight radio wave problems.

What's happened over the years with Amateur Radio is that tens of thousands of repeaters have been set up all over the country. All but the most remote areas now have repeaters. A repeater is a radio that takes your transmission and rebroadcasts it to another repeater, and another. The repeaters are individually coded, requiring a special code to be entered

on the radio to trigger it. Each one has a special code and you need to know the code for the repeater nearest you to make it work. The repeater codes are available for sale in booklets and the proceeds go to maintain the repeaters. Repeater maintenance and setup is most often done on a volunteer basis by the legions of hams and ham associations around the country.

If a repeater is available, you can speak to someone almost anywhere. In fact, you can even get a phone line if your set (and the repeater) has what's called a "patch." You can dial up and make a phone call, just like a cell phone. That includes a 911 call or just a call to let the spouse know you'll be late and to hold dinner. If no repeater is available, then your transmission is limited to line-of sight. UHF/VHF is very well monitored and help is available 24 hours a day. Some VHF/UHF units are handhelds, but if a repeater is within its more limited range, you can still speak to someone on the other side of the country

Ham: HF

The HF bands, also commonly known as short wave, are part of the AM band and can reach all over the world. Power output is very high, in the thousands of watts, though most mobile stations are in the hundreds of watts or less. An upper-end FCC license is required for this type of unit. They do not need repeaters and you will find this realm well monitored. Many hams with upper-end licenses

often have equipment that has SSB, FM, and HF combined.

Family Radio Systems

FRS radios have become popular and useful family tools, enabling members to stay in contact at crowded events, on hikes, or wherever they are separated but in the same general vicinity. Their low power output, 0.5 watts, limits range to under 2 miles in the best conditions. Unlike CBs, which operate on AM frequencies, the FRS units use FM and voice clarity is better, but they are strictly line-of-sight. Many have a feature that transmits a sub-audible tone that only another FRS unit tuned to the same tone can read. This offers "private channel" communications, even when others are using FRS units on the same frequency. FRS radios could be used by four-wheeling families to stay in touch when some of them are out of the vehicle on a slow-moving trail. No license is required for FRS units.

Cell Phones

It's surprising how many remote places have cell phone service, and equally surprising how many less remote places don't. There's no guarantee that your cell will work in the boonies, but bring it anyway. Also bring an extra, charged battery and a 12-volt adapter. In a serious situation, you don't want the battery dying before all the important words are spoken. Among the lessons of September 11 was the value of a cell phone.

You don't need to have a cockpit similar to a Boeing 747 jumbo jet to have UHF/VHF and high-wattage HF capability in your vehicle. The control heads of longtime ham John Radloff's mobile setup are compact, with UHF/VHF on the left and HF in the center. The actual units are housed in a box in the cargo compartment. This compartment is ventilated with small 12-volt fans, as the units can generate heat. Antenna needs are modest as well, with one of the two in view through the windshield.

CHAPTER 5

SOLID FOUNDATIONS

Essential Skills of Stock and Technique

High mountain shelf roads, such as this one in Central Colorado, are within the realm of almost any stock 4x4 and even many all-wheel-drive rigs. Some drivers find them intimidating at first. In this case, the trail is a fairly smooth dirt and gravel road that would be a "no worries" jaunt if it weren't for the 3,000-foot drop on one side. With plenty of room to negotiate this section, only abject stupidity by the driver or an act of God comparable to the great flood would pose a danger.

HERE WE'LL COVER:

Reading the terrain and picking a line of attack

•

Using spotters for help in tricky situations

•

***How to use momentum to carry you through
low-traction areas***

•

***Traversing hairy angles, obstacles,
and surface conditions***

Some years back, a four-wheeling friend from Britain came for a visit and, no big surprise, we went 'wheeling in some of the toughest nearby terrain. Andy has a good deal of experience, but between having to drive on the "wrong" side of the vehicle and the fact that my full-sized Blazer was bigger than anything he had ever four-wheeled, it took some time for him to get oriented. As he situated himself behind the wheel and looked over the vast expanse of the Blazer's hood (or should I say bonnet!), he exclaimed, "It's like looking out over the flight deck of the bloody *Nimitz*!" Andy's example illustrates the need for all of us to fine-tune our four-wheeling "whiskers" to get a feel for the vehicle.

Whiskers? Have you ever wondered about those long whiskers on a cat's face? These are the feline equivalent of sensors. With them, the cat can determine how big a gap he can crawl through. The four-wheeling equivalent is when the driver has a feel or sense of his rig in tight quarters. This comes from practice, but rather than practicing by peeling the sheet metal off the passenger side of your shiny 4x4, take some time for a walk around. The goals are to commit the layout of the vehicle to memory and develop a feel for where the less directly visible parts of the vehicle are at all times.

With practice, a driver can develop this into an almost instinctive sense.

COMMON SENSE

Many people lament the apparent death of common sense. It's not dead, but it sometimes hides behind people unwilling to admit to stupid mistakes. I'm relying on you to apply common sense to any formula you read here. Common sense comes from paying attention. Properly secure your vehicle every time you step out to evaluate the terrain, for example. Don't get so lost in the thrills of 'wheeling that you forget to realize that a vehicle will roll away if not secured by the parking brake or in Park. (See the previous chapter for more on using the parking brake.) That's why I'm not going to burden

the dirt

Technique:
If what you are doing isn't
working, try something different!

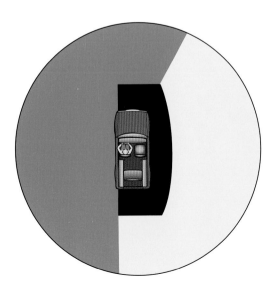

The driver's point of view (POV) has many areas where vision is restricted or outright blocked. This graphic represents the driver's POV in a typical SUV. Any compact, doorless, open-topped rig such as a Jeep utility would offer better visibility. The green areas indicate the best visibility. Yellow indicates restricted areas and black denotes areas where the driver's view is completely blocked or shadowed. Because the driver can hang his head out the window, the entire driver's side of the vehicle is in the green area.

The front and rear wheels take different paths in a turn. In tight maneuvering situations, you must take this into account. Consider it both when you select your approach and in the turn itself. Swing as wide as possible and don't make your final cut until the rear wheels are about even with the object you are maneuvering around, and then cut hard.

either of us by constantly mentioning the basic common sense items in my descriptions of techniques.

DRIVER POV: READING TERRAIN

The driver's point of view (POV) is obstructed in many ways. The long hood means you cannot see the ground 10 feet or more in front of your vehicle. Vision to the rear is even more obstructed. You can see well enough on the driver's side (and toward the front) by hanging your head out the window, but vision is obstructed on the passenger's side.

The nearby illustration on page 59 shows the driver's POV, where vision is best restricted, or completely blocked. In effect, you are blind to certain areas, not the least of which is right in front of you. The defense is to memorize the terrain as you approach. Many novice drivers stretch their necks like E.T., trying to look over the hood and see the ground directly in front of the vehicle. The end result is that their POV is restricted to a very narrow arc and they are merely reacting to changing terrain as it appears inside that narrow arc, rather than preparing well in advance.

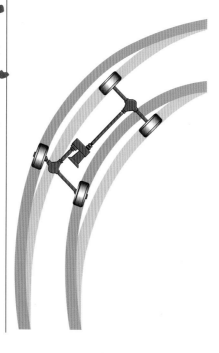

The better approach is a scanning technique where you observe the general terrain features as far up the trail as you can see and then scan back to 20 or 30 feet ahead of the vehicle and memorize the terrain features. You then have plenty of time to react and get set up to tackle obstacles. It's a continual scan that increases in intensity with the terrain difficulty or complexity.

DRIVER POV: PICKING LINES

A "line" is an approach and path over or through an obstacle that allows the vehicle to surmount the obstacle without damage. One hopes the line picked is the "best" line, but to paraphrase an old pilot's adage about landings, any line that gets you up and over without damage or injury is a good line. Picking lines comes very naturally to some people and with more difficulty to others. Rest assured, even those with the least amount of innate ability can learn to do it well enough: the trouble for us that it's a very difficult skill to teach in a book.

Watching an experienced driver is a great way to learn the art of picking lines. Comparing his line, and the end results of that line, with the one you charted in your head can be a very useful exercise.

A well-known British off-highway driving instructor, who spent at least 40 years teaching people the fine art of four-wheeling, has a colorful saying when it comes to lines. "Pick the high ground," Don Green is fond of saying, "just like John Wayne." This alludes to one of the absolutes in picking lines, which is to pick a path for your tires that keeps the undercarriage clear and unobstructed. You will also seek to keep the vehicle as level as possible. As you learned in chapter 2, an unloaded tire from a vehicle at a severe angle, or a tire in the air, is not providing traction. Drivers must also look for the spots with the best surface for maximum traction. That may be only one axle at a time on good ground, but often one axle is enough to move the few feet needed.

SPOTTERS

Nobody rides for free. The person sitting in the passenger seat should assist the driver in keeping an eye out for hazards, particularly on that side of the vehicle. It doesn't take much skill to notice that the fender is in danger of being torn off, so virtually anyone can be of some use. Should the person riding "shotgun" be skilled and knowledgeable in the four-wheeling arts, so much the better. There comes a time when a view from outside the cockpit is needed and a clued-in person can provide walking disaster prevention.

Using a spotter comes with a price; the driver has to relinquish some control. The only way it works well is if the driver gives the spotter control of the situation and does no more and no less than ordered by the spotter. The driver, assuming he's the owner of the vehicle, retains overall veto power and the option to "fire" the spotter, but a spotter is worthless if the driver doesn't follow instructions. The spotter then takes responsibility for what happens, assuming the driver follows instructions. Friendships and closer relationships have gone awry in situations where mistakes were made and damage resulted. It pays to keep an adult perspective on these things, a little *que será, será* (whatever will be, will be) perhaps, and also to delegate spotting duties to people who are qualified. If you get help on the trail from relative strangers, it's a little more problematic. Another *que será, será* time, I suppose.

Basic Spotting Rules

There are some basic rules that both spotters and drivers should understand. Some clubs have adopted spotting rules similar to those used at events, but you can invent your own. The main thing is that both the spotter and driver are reading from the same page of rules. Even spectators can be helpful by understanding what's going on and letting the spotter and driver do their work without interference. That doesn't prevent you—thespectator—from helping, just do it in a way that doesn't disrupt the process.

General
1) At least 99 percent of spotting should be nonverbal. Use hand signals. This avoids words being misunderstood or drowned out by engine noises or spectators. Verbal conferences should be face-to-face with the vehicle stopped and secured.
2) There's only one official spotter: the person the driver has chosen. The spotter should ignore the more vocal armchair quarterbacks. If it gets to be a problem, make an appeal for silence. If you are not the spotter and you see a better or safer way, make a quiet comment to the spotter.
3) The spotter directs other helpers, such as in piling rocks, pushing, and so on.

Driver Tips
1) You have the right to refuse a spotter, or fire him, but you also take the responsibility for what happens.
2) You are giving over 50 percent of the control and 50 percent of the responsibility to your spotter.
3) Keep your eyes on the spotter. If you can't see the spotter, stop and get his attention. It's worse than uncool to run over your spotter.
4) Do no more and no less than your spotter directs. Continue with the last instruction until your spotter tells you to stop, or changes the instruction. If it becomes clear that your spotter isn't paying attention, stop and get his attention.
5) If you disagree with your spotter, don't just ignore him. Stop and have a conference. His perspective is a little different from yours, so it's good to know why he's made a particular decision.

With capable spotting, even stock rigs can be taken into extraordinary terrain. With 100-percent visibility, the spotter can direct the vehicle over the best lines and safely past the bad stuff. It's a team effort, with the spotter making clear, decisive hand signals and the driver following those instructions to the letter–responding no more or less than directed.

This spotter is standing far enough away to have a clear view of the terrain and be in clear view of the driver. The spotter should also be far enough ahead to be safe from an accidentally applied stab of the throttle or a foot slipping off the clutch or brake pedal. Moving around for vantage points is a dangerous time for spotters. It's easy to get caught up in the job and not pay as much attention to footing as you should. As the vehicle pulls closer, the spotter should stop the vehicle and then move carefully to another safe and strategic spotting location.

SPOTTER'S HAND SIGNALS

Stop immediately! Fists can be shaken for emphasis.

Come ahead at a slow pace. Can be performed one-handed in conjunction with other hand signals, such as come ahead, steer right.

Steer left. Driver to hold this steering input until directed to make a change.

Steer right. Driver to hold this steering input until directed to make a change.

Slow down!

Go back.

A little bit. The "little bit" signal can be added to any other, such as steer left a little bit.

Spotter Tips

1) Take the time you need to get a clear picture of the problem and a good solution before giving directions. The odds are good that you are dealing with someone's pride and joy. Take as much care as if it were your own.
2) Stay in view of the driver.
3) Make clear, bold hand signals that can't be misunderstood.
4) Don't stand too close to the line of travel. A foot slipping off a clutch pedal or an accidentally applied throttle could take you out. In some cases, standing 10 or 15 feet away gives you the advantage of being able to see the whole picture.
5) You are responsible for keeping any extra help clear of the vehicle when it moves. Rock pilers have a bad habit of getting run over if the spotter isn't paying attention.
6) Watch your step. Spotters spend a fair bit of time walking backward or moving around on instinct while watching their vehicle. While not always possible, it's better to stop your vehicle and find a spot to stand than to split your focus between walking uncertain ground and providing guidance. Seek the best way to protect yourself and the driver throughout the run.

MOMENTUM: THE TWO-EDGED SWORD

One dictionary describes momentum as "the impetus of movement" and a complex mixture of mass and velocity. Inertia is another word that fits. For our purposes, the definition of inertia, "a body in motion tends to stay in motion," is the most useful. The weight of your vehicle carries it along until friction, air resistance, and other factors slow it down. That inertia/momentum is a useful tool for

Momentum just right! The correct amount of momentum isn't always discernable in a still photo; this Defender 90 is using it correctly. Though on highly tractive slickrock, this climb is steep enough to overcome the available traction of a vehicle without lockers. A steady speed, faster than a creep, at a slow walking pace is enough.

Not enough momentum. This is what happens when there isn't enough momentum or traction. In the case of this unlocked Land Rover, this left front tire and the opposite rear tire have broken loose and are spinning on the rocks. Beyond approaching at too low a speed, this driver was making a couple of other mistakes. The first obvious mistake is the application of too much throttle for the available traction. The second is that he didn't air down significantly. Correction of either of these two errors might have resulted in a successful "one-shot" climb, even with a paucity of momentum.

Right: Too much momentum. Faced with a steep climb on a rock slab made slick by rain and mud, this driver chose to hit it hard. The results were spectacular! He did make the climb, but was risking severe damage in the process. He was betting on the strength of the upgrades made to the Jeep. Other drivers proved that a less radical approach could also make the climb.

Far right: Snow is a lot like mud. It can be deep and it's usually slippery. It's fun when only 4 inches deep like this, but you can come around the bend and be faced with a 4-foot-deep drift. Traction can also be marginal and variable from one stretch to the next. Maintaining a steady momentum is the key. This Discovery is actually going uphill and is maintaining about five miles per hour without wheelspin. Should he stop, it's very likely that he could not get going again.

the dirt

On Momentum: With practice, you can gauge the amount of momentum for assorted obstacles pretty accurately. Momentum can be used in nearly any off-highway situation, from crossing mud to climbing hills.

No Banzai:
In general, if crossing a soft area will require a high-speed banzai charge, look for another way across, or a way around.

Keeping up momentum on soft surfaces like mud, sand, and snow, will keep you on the surface rather in it. Making a turn in the sand is one such example. The tires will begin to dig in and slow the vehicle down. There won't be enough traction to overcome the extra drag, so it's momentum that will carry you through.

four-wheeling, but it must always be used wisely.

It takes a certain amount of traction to put your vehicle in motion. When circumstances don't make that traction available, a *little* momentum can carry you through. Sometimes that just means a steady speed over a problem area and other times it means gaining a little speed on good ground before you encounter the obstacle. Emphasis is on the "little," at least at first. Always try going easy the first time and increase the level of intensity gradually until you reach the no-go point and abort the attempts.

Momentum in Mud, Sand, and Snow

All three of these ground conditions are similar in that they combine low surface strength and low shear strength. Not only do you sink—you have no traction. Momentum can launch you completely across some soft areas or provide you with just enough help to claw your way across with the minimal traction available. With enough speed you can actually hydroplane across a soft surface, but control is just about impossible. Using momentum across soft ground requires that you evaluate the surroundings along with the obstacle. Are you going to end up sideways or lose it completely and slam into a tree or a rock?

Momentum on Hillclimbs

There are many hills on which you could not start from a dead stop, but if you have a little motion, you can keep going. Than means a steady speed on a hill. You may encounter spots of lesser traction, or a steeper slope, and momentum may be enough to carry you past it. If not, you must be ready to respond instantly before you come to a stop. Sometimes that means a little more throttle, other times it means backing off for torque control.

Momentum can also be used at the start of a low-traction climb to help you up. The momentum is built up on flat ground. On a short hill without enough traction to climb slowly, this may take you up without spinning a tire. On a long hill, safe and sane levels of momentum may just carry you halfway and leave you perched with spinning tires and a failed climb maneuver to perform. The approach to a hill also may limit your momentum options with a sharp transition from horizontal to vertical. In other cases, you may be able to build up quite a head of steam, but just as with soft ground, you can have control problems with too much speed.

Momentum for Rockcrawling

Momentum is as useful in rocks as anywhere else, but since rocks are unyielding by nature, contact usually results in the vehicle getting the short straw. As often as not, momentum for rocky terrain comes into play when weight transfer unloads one axle and overloads the other. This can happen on a straight climb, usually a very steep one if a highly tractive rock face is involved, or on ledges. On a straight climb on rock faces, such as slickrock, play the game much as you would elsewhere: maintain a steady speed and react appropriately if needed. On a boulder-strewn landscape, your speed potential will be severely limited, but even the momentum imparted from speeds as low as 1/4 mile per hour can be useful. Again, try to maintain whatever movement you can rather than starting and stopping. Climbing in loose rocks may require momentum, just as with soft ground, but too much speed can result in

Above right: Momentum is necessary even on rough surface climbs such as this. It requires thoughtful line picking and commitment. You pick the line, select a reasonable amount of momentum, and go for it. The mistake many novice drivers make in this situation is backing off too soon. Stay with it until it's clear that you are stopped. The second most common mistake is inducing wheelspin from too much throttle. The biggest danger on terrain such as this comes from wheelhop and tire spinning, and the end result can be broken-drivetrain parts. In fact, one of the next vehicles on this Moab, Utah, trail destroyed a driveshaft U-joint and a front axle universal simultaneously.

This is about as deep as it's practical to go. This Classic Range Rover is in snow about a foot deep, and though the axles are plowing some, the soft powder and solid bottom are allowing the vehicle to continue. Were the trail headed uphill or a bit deeper, he might miss his ski appointment. *Courtesy Land Rover*

Momentum in rockcrawling. This lightly modified Wrangler is negotiating a particularly difficult climb consisting of large boulders and ledges, all covered by a dusting of sand. Few vehicles can crawl this section, so a careful application of momentum is in order after selecting a line and committing to it. Despite how it looks (low shutter speed accentuating visual wheel speed), this driver had the right amount of "mo." This situation was a bit on the hairy side, requiring good judgment and calm application of basic principles.

bouncing, slamming, cut tires, or a loss of control.

The ledge scenario involves the use of a "Bump." Usually the front axle is up, though unloaded by weight transfer, and it's the rear axle that can't make the climb. The Bump combines momentum with a judicious stab of throttle at just the right time. If the driver applies a stab of throttle just as the rear tires hit the ledge, the momentum has the effect of momentarily "gluing" the tires to the rock by increasing ground pressure. This can make the rig hop up that ledge like a jackrabbit. As you can imagine, the forces acting on the tire, suspension, and drivetrain are great, so the amount of momentum used, the amount of throttle, and the duration of the throttle application must be carefully chosen. On a typical ledge, a "roll" of just a couple of feet is enough momentum for the bump.

EASY DIRT ROADS: MORE DANGEROUS THAN YOU THINK!

One of my jobs here is to warn you—or remind you—about situations where complacency leads to trouble. One of those areas is the dirt or gravel road. They can come at the beginning or the end of the more difficult four-wheeling. Many people regard the end as the most dangerous part for many reasons. You're tired by then and not paying as much attention. Perhaps you are in a hurry to get home, so you are combining fatigue with fast travel, and that's the devil's brew. Perhaps your vehicle has suffered some unseen damage and, just like on the highway, the more speed that's combined with a failure of some kind, the greater the chances are for a very bad result. As it often happens, the dirt road is a transition area from the more difficult parts of a trail to the highway. Because they are not highway-smooth, many drivers delay airing up their tires until they reach the edge of the pavement to maintain better ride quality. That's fine as long as the driver understands how handling is adversely affected.

LOCK IT DOWN

"Locking it down" is a trail term for parking, but unlike the street, there are many angles on the trail that make your vehicle prone to rolling

It's steep, but there's a good bit of traction on the rocky surface, degraded only by a powdering of sand. This Range Rover is not low-geared enough to no-brake this slope, so the driver will control wheel lockup with careful application of the brakes.

traction is needed going down as well as going up. The difference is that if you lose traction going down, you will continue going down, but in a less controlled manner.

A descent starts with a look at the hill. Many times you can see your path from the driver's seat, but if you can't, step out and have a look. Evaluate the surface for traction and contours. Evaluate the steepness and where it ends up at the bottom. Just like going up, you can handle some very steep angles if there is enough traction. A very steep descent on a loose surface, however, could be the "yeeha" toboggan ride of your life.

The general rule is to select the lowest possible gearing combination. That means the lowest transmission gear and low range in the transfer case. That rule is variable, of course, according to the conditions and your vehicle's gearing. On a mild descent with good traction, second gear might be OK. Try to let the engine and drivetrain be the primary means of slowing

away if it's not properly secured. You read about the park pawl and the parking brake in chapter 4. Always take care to lock your rig down on the trail by applying the parking brake (bearing in mind the caveats discussed in chapter 4) and using Park with an automatic or putting the manual trans in gear. On steeper terrain many prudent drivers will also throw a rock behind a tire or park in such a spot that the ground provides natural wheel chocks. Someday, you will have to park in steep terrain and the precarious nature of the spot will no doubt encourage you to lock 'er down good!

DESCENDING A SLOPE

Gravity can be a friend or an enemy. Gravity will "help" you down the hill, but like some of your most "helpful" friends, it may be more help than you want at the moment. People often forget that

Mud and a steep descent is a difficult combination. In this case, the mud has partially dried to a more tractive consistency, well out of the greasy consistency but not quite back to regular dirt. There is enough traction for a controlled descent, but there could be patches of more slippery stuff to catch you unawares. In this situation, you would be ready for steering correction and perhaps a stab of throttle to keep you going straight downhill.

A descent may be combined with irregular terrain. In the case of this stock Nissan, it resulted in moderate rear tire lift. No worries at this level, but the factors to keep in mind are the reduced traction and the weight transfer. Remember that you need traction as much for a controlled descent as for a climb. Traction is reduced by one tire in this case. Weight transfer would be a concern if the terrain increased the angle. In this case, the driver used his brakes for a very slow, controlled descent.

the dirt

Braking on Descents:
Engine braking alone may not provide the safe, slow descent you need. This is especially true with automatics. In that case, you'll need to gently apply the brakes. The key is to keep the wheels rolling.

your vehicle. In compound low, especially with a manual trans, it's amazing how much holdback you can get from the engine alone. The nice part about engine-compression braking is that it's evenly applied to all four wheels, though weight transfer may influence traction.

The less speed you have at the top of a descent, the less you'll have at the bottom. In cases where you can see well enough to drive over the edge without getting out to survey, you may be tempted to not even stop before doing so. On a mild hill this can be OK, but on a steeper hill, it can induce extra speed that you will have to deal with. In these cases, creeping over with the least possible momentum is the better choice.

On very loose surfaces, too low a gear may cause the tires to slide, especially the unloaded rear tires. If you choose a higher gear to maintain traction, you may go down the hill a bit faster than is comfortable or safe. Gauge the potential problems of that situation against the limited traction and decide if this is a hill you really need to go down. If there is a clear rollout at the bottom with no major undulations, a little speed shouldn't be much of a problem.

If you are caught on the hill in too low a gear, it's usually best not to shift up—especially with a manual trans. The moment you push that clutch pedal in, the vehicle will take off as if a JATO (Jet Assisted Take Off) rocket were strapped to the roof. The correct response is to increase speed with the throttle until the tires reacquire grip. You may be going faster, but at least you'll be in control and you can always back off on the throttle when traction is reacquired.

Because a good deal of weight will transfer from the rear to the front tires on a steep descent, be prepared for the rear end to try to swing around on you. This is an extremely dangerous situation because a rollover is usually imminent. If you are on the brakes at the time, as is most often the case, you have either locked the tires or are exceeding the available traction. Either get off the brakes entirely or ease up as needed and steer slightly in the direction the rear end is going (just like a skid). That alone may or may not get you straight, but the next step is to get on the throttle. It may not take a lot of throttle. The adrenaline rush may cause you to mash on the accelerator a little more than is prudent, so beware of the JATO effect. In reality, most situations as outlined above are pretty easy to control. The first time will offer the highest fear factor.

One: Complications to a descent could include a situation similar to "The Slide" on Red Cone Pass. It's a long, steep descent on a face covered with scree and rock powder. It's doable by most stock vehicles. The run is complicated by relatively deep holes that must be crossed at a low speed to avoid going airborne. Even at a low speed, they cause articulation and weight transfer. The steepness and loose surface guarantees locked-up tires with more than a tiny bit of brake application, so step one is to go over the edge at a very slow speed to reduce momentum at the start. In this case, there was a hole immediately after the top, and as the front tires went into it, it was possible to increase brake pressure momentarily and slow the vehicle significantly.

Two: The front wheels come out of the hole, and it's time to reduce brake pressure to avoid lockup. The Range Rover is beginning to build up some speed at this point, but the driver is resisting the urge to mash hard on the brakes.

Three: Dipping into another hole provides an opportunity to slow down a bit more by increasing brake pressure.

Four: More holes provide opportunities to slow down.

Five: The holes that severely articulate the suspension can be tricky. In this shot, the front and rear are articulated opposite each other, thus unloading one front and one rear wheel. These wheels tended to lock up with more than a tiny amount of brake pressure, but the ABS braking system aided the driver at that point and there was no adverse effect. With a non-ABS rig, momentary lockup at a very low speed would not be significant. From this hole on, it was a flat-surface run-out to the bottom and engine braking was enough to maintain control.

Climbs are straightforward stuff from a technical standpoint. Find the smoothest path to the top, choose the correct gear, and apply the required amount of momentum. At this steep angle (near 50 degrees), a short-wheelbase rig such as this CJ-7 has transferred a good deal of weight from the front to the rear. A rig with less rubber on the ground might lose traction in the back due to overloading. Bear in mind that only on a very tractive surface—in this case Utah slickrock—can grades this steep be successfully climbed.

Failed Climbs:
Above all, don't hit the brakes hard in a backward descent. The front wheels will probably lock up and cause the tires to slide, or slide more, leaving no traction for steering. Very cautious use of the brakes with a light front end is a vital necessity.

ASCENDING A SLOPE

Going up is easier than going down in many ways, because gravity or lack of traction may stop you before things get hairy. It becomes a go/no-go situation at the outset. As mentioned before, traction is the limiting factor. Evaluate the trail surface for traction potential and gauge the climb against your approach, departure, and ramp breakover angles. Don't forget the transition to horizontal at the top.

The goal is to use the *highest possible* gear to avoid wheelspin. This is variable according to the vehicle, with gearing and transmission type being the controlling factors. An SUV with 3.23:1 axle ratios and a manual trans with a 3:1 first gear will obviously need first gear, but a pickup with 3.73:1 axle ratios and a 6.4:1 first gear may be able to use second. With auto-

matics, the trans is allowed to make the selection, though there may be times when you should manually select the correct gear to prevent an inopportune upshift or a downshift because of having to use a little throttle on the climb.

The application of momentum is a useful tool. There are times when you need a little speed going up, but you don't want to fly over the top like those jeeps in the old *Rat Patrol* TV show. This is controllable by backing off the throttle by the right amount at the right time. Back out too much and you may not clear the slope, because momentum will disappear quickly.

Failed Climbs

The sad truth is that you won't make every climb. Learning the failed climb technique makes the sting much easier to bear. Imagine that you get to some point on a climb and you stop... not by choice. The first decision becomes whether you are safe enough to spend a few moments deciding what to do next.

If the vehicle is sliding downhill with locked brakes, get into reverse ASAP, get off the brakes, and steer it straight down the hill. If you have a manual trans, make sure you have let out the clutch. It's highly likely with a manual trans that the engine has stalled. For engine braking purposes, it doesn't matter if the engine is running or not, but it's nice to have power steering and brakes from a running engine. Most likely, the engine will restart on its own with the clutch out. If you have fuel injection, watch for a surge as it restarts. The idle speed controller may overcompensate for a moment when the engine restarts in this situation.

If you are safely held on the hillside by your brakes, you might evaluate whether you can make a try at continuing. Perhaps you started in too high a gear and what you need to do is downshift. If your basic technique was good, but there was insufficient traction to get you past the spot where you stopped, it's unlikely you can start from a hillside. It doesn't hurt to try, depending on the overall circumstances, but it's usually better to back down and try again. The next try should introduce a new element into the equation, perhaps in the form of a little more momentum or a better line.

There are some potentially hairy situations to be prepared for with a failed climb. First, the steering can be unpredictable and hypersensitive backing down, so it's easy to overcorrect. Weight transfer unloads the front tires, so your ability to steer on low-traction surfaces may be somewhat reduced. How responsive the steering is depends on the ground surface. The front end may try to swing downhill and put you sideways. As with a regular skid, you can steer into it, but with steering effectiveness reduced by weight transfer, you may find it has little effect. You may have to apply a little throttle to make the rear axle pull the vehicle straight.

SIDEHILLS

Sidehills are a part of the four-wheeling game that many people like to avoid. In extreme situations, they are very hazardous, but in the "normal" realm they are nothing to generate adrenaline over. What's normal? Anything under 10 degrees is a cakewalk on a tractive surface. Many four-wheelers will do 20 degrees without batting an eyelid, but almost everyone gets sweaty armpits over 20 degrees. Most vehicles are safe to somewhat safe over 30 degrees (not counting the dynamics of the vehicle in motion) and many have advertised being stable past 40 degrees. I've been at 40-plus degrees and freely admit to a dry mouth and a tightly clenched sphincter muscle. At 30 degrees it feels like the door handles are scraping the ground. At 40, you're waiting for the crunch of metal and the crash of breaking glass.

The first rule on sidehills is to avoid the really steep ones if you can find a safe, treading-lightly way around. On slippery surfaces, even a mild sidehill becomes potentially

dangerous, depending on what's at the bottom of that slippery slope. Don't forget that a vehicle in motion has some dynamics that may work against you. If one downhill tire lurches into a hole, the sudden weight transfer and suspension movement may momentarily lean you over farther than you expect, and perhaps far enough to be trouble.

The second rule is to stay straight and square in the seat. The natural human inclination is to lean into the slope, as if the minor weight transfer of your body shifted a few degrees will prevent your behemoth from rolling over! If you stay square in the seat, you will stay in touch with the vehicle's true angle. By most accounts, the driver's POV is also improved by seeming less "wacky"—you are only looking at one tilted angle: your vehicle vs. the terrain instead of two, you vs. your vehicle vs. the terrain.

The sidehill escape maneuver, to be used when rollover is imminent, is to steer downhill. Sometimes a quick application of throttle is also needed. Many an imminent rollover has been forestalled by quick application of this trick. In my years as an instructor, it seems this is 180 degrees from some

Even sidehills as mild as this one become "driver conditioning" the first few times out. The human body seems to quickly accept up-and-down angles, but side angles take longer. This easy sideslope would only be a danger if it were muddy instead of rocky. No worries here!

When the bottom of the upslope tire is even with the top of the downslope tire, you are at the upper limit (or beyond) of sideslope ability for most rigs. The Land Rover Defender is more capable than most in this area, but one might wonder why the driver chose this anxiety-fraught route over the easier one below. For practice, I suppose. Anyway, he made it without a hitch.

Sidehills:

If you think you're about to roll, turn downhill quickly, with a quick application of throttle if that feels necessary. This move both reduces the side angle and applies some centrifugal force to keep those uphill wheels on the ground. Steering uphill uses the same physics in reverse, and to your detriment.

Gullies that are along the line of travel can be straddled if they can't be avoided. This Steyer-Puch Pinzgauer barely has the width to straddle this particular rocky crag, but it was preferable to riding on an angle with two tires in the gully and two tires up on the side. Careful pilotage is important to ensure that one set of tires doesn't suddenly slip into the hole.

Stock vehicles with limited clearance will almost always use a diagonal approach in crossing gullies. That means one tire at a time will dip into the gully. The angle at which you cross should be chosen carefully. Ideally, that angle is as close to right angles from the gully as clearance will allow. This driver chose a fairly obtuse angle and you can see the result; his suspension is articulated to the maximum level. The danger of that in an unlocked rig is that traction may be lost on each of the low tires—in this case left front and right rear—due to unloading.

natural human instinct to steer uphill. That maneuver is likely to put you on the roof.

CROSSING GULLIES

This is one of the more common four-wheeling scenarios. Assuming the gully is not too deep to be crossed, you have two choices: the right-angle, or straight-through approach, or the diagonal approach. Which you choose depends on the gully and your vehicle's basic dimensions and clearances.

The straight-through method offers the best traction but requires more clearance and better approach, departure, and ramp breakover angles. The technique is to ease both front wheels into the ditch simultaneously and across the ditch to climb out the other side. Depending on the size of the gully, your rear wheels may be in the ditch at this point also. The key elements are to take it slow and to make sure you have all the angles and clearance you need.

When clearance or approach and departure angles are a problem, the diagonal approach reduces the need for clearance. Rather than dropping one end of the vehicle in at a time, you will dip one corner at a time. This has the effect of reducing the angle, though it will require more traction because both of your axles will be articulated. As discussed earlier, the downhill tire is unloaded and may lose traction. The diagonal approach works best for long-wheelbase rigs because one axle will be farther out of the bad angle, less articulated, and more able to apply some good traction.

SOFT GROUND: MUD

Mud, sand, and snow all fit into a similar category and the driving techniques are roughly similar. They share the trait of having low shear strength and low surface strength. That means little traction and a tendency to sink into terra firma.

Traction supplies movement across the mud and floatation keeps you on top of it. Mud can create a great deal of drag, even if only the tires are in it, and the deeper your

Above: Shown here is your ordinary mud hole with a few inches of water on top. Step one is always to evaluate. There are tracks in and out, so the odds are good that it's navigable. Local knowledge also indicates that bottomless slime pits are unknown in this area. If in doubt, probe for depth with a stick or shovel. Pick a line that takes you straight across, or as straight across as possible. Enter the mud hole with a bit of momentum—just enough to make a little splash with the tires—and maintain that momentum using light throttle and avoiding wheelspin. Emerge safely on the other side and test your brakes when clear. Note the many bypasses around this small obstacle. This driver is taking what appears to be the main route, thus avoiding further damage.

Some drivers think that they are better off keeping two tires up on solid ground when crossing a mud hole. Not if you have open diffs. Creating a situation where one tire is on solid ground and the other is in goo creates the classic open differential stuck scenario outlined in the earlier Traction 101 chapter. Better to have even traction on all wheels. You can get away with this if you have a locker or a very tight limited slip, but who wants to be tilted at 25 degrees in a mud hole? The weight transfer is putting more weight on the low tires, which could cause them to sink enough to hang the axles up on the edge of the hole.

Too fast for the situation. This is a mild mud hole, so making a big splash will just increase your time at the carwash, or, in the case of this rather wet mud hole, could drown the ignition. There are times when an aggressive approach is needed. This isn't one.

tires or undercarriage go into the mud, the more drag is created. If the drag exceeds traction, you stop moving. The idea in most types of mud is to keep the undercarriage out of the goo, and that's where the floatation of a big tire footprint comes in.

As for traction, tread design will either get you across or leave you stranded. Aggressive mud tires act more or less like a paddle. The danger is that some mud will stick to the tires, fill the treads, and turn it into a "mud donut." When this happens, it prevents the cleats from applying trac-

tion. In some cases, spinning the tires will allow centrifugal force to sling the mud off and allow the cleats to grab.

Types of Mud

There are many types of mud and each needs a slightly different technique to get through. Here are the basic types and subtypes, with some explanations, and the methods for dealing with them. The names and descriptions are mine, so don't go looking in the index of any other texts for information on Chocolate Ice Cream Mud.

Greasy Mud is usually not very deep, but because it contains lots of clay, it's as slick as oiled spaghetti. Greasy mud can be found almost anywhere, but is often seen in the southeast and the northwest. It often has good floatation but poor traction. Because it will really gum up your tires, you need a good self-cleaning tire tread. You are more likely to need the spinning tire technique in Greasy Mud to clean your tires and get traction. Tire chains are a useful tool here. You are also more likely to need momentum to get across, but not too much. It's easy to lose control and prang a tree or rock when your ability to steer is reduced.

Gumbo Mud is much like Greasy Mud but a lot deeper. It can be found almost anywhere, but is often seen in the southeast. It still contains very slick stuff but it's more watery. Well-traveled Greasy Mud holes often turn into Gumbo. Gumbo is tough because it offers neither floatation nor traction. Apply the same techniques as with Greasy, but have your winches and tow straps ready.

Chocolate Ice Cream Mud has the consistency of freshly scooped ice cream with grit in it. It's usually found in mountainous areas. Traction is often better than floatation.

Malodorous Mud is usually found in or around swamps and bogs. It's usually a form of Chocolate Ice Cream Mud but often more watery and with

Greasy Mud, and rather badly rutted at that. You have no choice but to ride the ruts in this kind of mud. The clay is just too slippery to climb out of. This is where extra clearance from a lift and larger tires would come in handy. This Range Rover pilot is spinning up the tires and using the Wiggle method. In this case, the wiggling is allowing the cleated edges of the tires to bite on the edges of the ruts and add to traction.

Gumbo Mud in its milder form. The only thing keeping this Pinzgauer from sinking deeper is that it's resting on its belly. Yep, he's stuck, as most rigs would be without huge, aggressive tires and lots of tire-spinning power. You might use lots of momentum to cross a patch of Gumbo in a mild rig, but it'd be risky. With no other route choice, you could try to get as far across as possible and then winch out. In this case, not only did this driver have a steep descent into the mud, but a steep climb out. Momentum was in short supply.

Chocolate Ice Cream Mud, but a bit on the greasy side. With all-season–type tires that are badly loaded up, this Discovery driver must spin the tires a bit to maintain forward motion. It's also deep enough to allow the diffs to ride in the goo, thus increasing drag and the need for traction.

a stench. It can have, well, *stuff* in it ... usually decaying vegetable matter. Sometimes it also has leeches and other critters you don't want to know about. Treat it like Chocolate Ice Cream Mud but adjust for the more watery consistency.

Nitty-Gritty Mud usually contains heavy grit and small pebbles and is most often found in mountainous areas. Floatation is usually good. This stuff isn't much of a worry most times, but it can chew up pretty wheels.

Rocky Road Mud is any basic type of mud with larger rocks in it, from fist-sized on up. The danger here is undercarriage damage or cut tires. If this type of mud is combined with a slope, as is common at the popular four-wheeling spots around Arkansas and Oklahoma, you can have some of the most difficult situations around. While there is not often much danger of sinking, the slicked-down rocks prevent your tires from getting traction. Airing down too much gets you cut tires. Too much air and the tires won't conform to the irregular surface and give you traction. Traction may be on and off, so if you are spinning, you may suddenly acquire massive amounts of traction and, snap, there goes a drivetrain part.

U-Boat Mud can be of any basic type but it hides under the water. It can be found in steams, rivers, or ponds, as well as puddles. Sometimes it's silt, sediment, or even sand. In standing water, the bottom is often Rocky Road, Greasy, or Gumbo. Rocks and clay hold water best.

Chop Suey Mud can be mud of nearly any type, but it contains sticks, wood, logs, pieces of 4x4s that went before, and whatever. Chop Suey Mud can often get you cut tires, torn-off exhaust systems, and broken brake lines.

Gear Choices

Choosing the right gear for a mud crossing is important. Because gearing multiplies torque to the wheels, too low a gear can cause a loss of traction. In the case of needing to deliberately spin the tires (read below), a higher gear will make your tires spin faster. In general, you will be crossing mud at a moderate pace, in a higher gear, and at a comfortable "lugging" speed for your engine. With manuals, you will generally use second-gear low range.

Rocky Road Mud. Slipping from one greasy, diff-denting rock to the next can be lots of fun. The key is to keep the speed low and pick a good line through. Try to pick rocks to drive over that provide a surface you won't slip off of. Slipping off a rock and high-centering on another is the biggest danger. You can also get high-centered on one large rock with four tires in goo.

Chop Suey Mud. This is an old Colorado mining road that was once paved with logs (they called them Corduroy Roads) that have deteriorated. This creates a mix of goo and sticks that can puncture tires, tear off brake lines, and cause body damage. If you need to get through, about all you can do is to pull out the chunks you can see and go for it.

With automatics, use "D" for three-speeds or "3" for overdrive types and let the automatic choose the gear it likes.

Tire Spinning and Throttle Control

This is a two-edged sword if ever there was one. There are two ways to spin tires: the major, mud-slinging, tractor-pull way, and the more conservative style. Each has its time and place.

You've seen competitive mud rigs wound up to 5,500 rpm, throwing 20-foot rooster tails and crossing bogs that could swallow a Kenworth. Pro mudrunners do it, so it stands to reason everyone should, right? Not necessarily. Try this technique in the average 4x4 and you'll usually sink even deeper.

The Wiggle! When traction is fading fast and your tires are turning into mud donuts, try rotating the steering wheel a quarter- to a half-turn to either side rapidly. This will sometimes give the cleated edges of the otherwise overloaded front tires the bite to keep you going. It seems to work best in Greasy Mud and is a very useful tool for rigs with nonaggressive tires. I've seen rigs perched, tires spinning, in Greasy Mud, and the Wiggle would get them moving again.

Or break something. It works for dedicated rigs built for mud because they use the "hydroplaning" effect of huge, spinning tires to keep them from sinking to China, while the aggressive paddle treads pull them across. The drivetrains are extra stout, the tires extra wide, and the engines built for high rpm.

Whether you should try the "wild and crazy" method depends on your equipment and the opposing mud stretch. If your rig has the qualities

mentioned above, you might get by. But this technique is necessary only a fraction of the time. Charging across a mud hole that's only a foot deep and 20 feet across, with your tires spinning up rooster tails, will make you look a little dumb … especially when the next guy idles across!

The more conservative approach is best when traction is marginal but flotation is good. In these cases use a higher gear and get the tires spinning a little. You will find that by adjusting the throttle up or down, you may be able to maintain forward motion. As the vehicle speeds up, you can usually back off a little on the throttle.

Wiggle, Wiggle

Here's a scenario. You're crossing Greasy Mud that requires some wheel spinning. You're moving nicely for a while but you begin to slow down. Increasing or decreasing throttle has no effect. Here's another tool we'll call the "Wiggle" method. Try turning the steering wheel rapidly from side to side a quarter or half a turn as your tires spin. You may find that, suddenly, you start to move again. What's happening is that the cleated edges of the tires are given a better chance to grab.

SOFT GROUND: SNOW

Winter can take your favorite two-wheel-drive, one-finger-on-the-steering-wheel trail and turn it into a Grade-A challenge. How well you do depends on two basic factors: snow depth and consistency. In general, there are two types of snow: powder or frozen, crusty snow. Many more exist if you want to count mixtures or gradations of the two. Often you can find powder under crust or vice versa.

Snow depth is the major controlling factor in whether you can mogate or not. Once your rig has sunk down to the point where the diffs are plowing snow, you are generally stopped. At some point, there simply won't be enough traction to push all that snow. Some types of dry, light powder will

Trail running in snow can introduce some complexities not seen on street snow—angles, for example. This Wrangler encounters an off-camber section that would pose no problem on dry dirt. With the icy snow and a drive-straight-through approach, the rig is sucked sideways to the bank and into some deep snow. Forward progress is stopped, but he can back out. The driver then chooses a different line and he first swings hard to his left and then steers right uphill. The Jeep's rear will not quite follow the front and slides downhill so the vehicle is actually moving through the slot in a diagonal "crab-walk." Eventually, the driver steers into it and the vehicle begins to go straight as the ground levels out. A similar scenario could occur on Greasy Mud.

Starting on sand can be a chore. Note how the F-250 has sunk into the sand, despite the wide tires. It isn't stuck, but to get moving again the National Park Ranger will have to use throttle finesse—no wheelspin but enough throttle to overcome the resistance of the partly buried tires. Bringing the front wheel straight ahead will also help by reducing rolling resistance. Low-powered vehicles may find it more of a struggle in a case like this. No worries here; the Rangers on the Cape Cod beaches have always been pretty good at sand driving, even 15 years ago when this shot was taken.

let you plow more easily than a heavier, wetter snow.

Snow will either support the weight of your vehicle or it will compress or compact enough to keep your undercarriage mostly clear of the snow. Many times, there is only a fragile crust between you and being stuck. It might support your rig only when you are exceedingly smooth on the throttle and avoid tire spinning.

Whatever types or depth of snow you encounter, you will experience a loss in traction. This can make even mild grades tricky. Snow generally offers the traction of Greasy Mud and equipment upgrades can be a great aid to winter wheeling. Most of the time, you will do better with a light foot on the throttle, but you will encounter times when the pedal must see the metal. Be ready for anything, because the winter landscape can change radically from one 20-foot stretch to another. Instant good judgment as the situations change is the key.

Avoid tire spinning where possible. It often just digs you deeper into the snow. Conversely, once you've broken through and found bottom, judicious tire spinning may provide traction, just as in mud. Sometimes you will go right down to dirt and find traction there. Sometimes all you find at the bottom of the snow is ice or frozen dirt.

Momentum plays a big part. Once you are running well on top of snow, back off on the throttle, get into a higher gear, and keep the revs low to avoid the torque multiplication that will break traction. You may find

slippery areas that cause you to slip and slide. If you are going too fast, you may slip and slide into an obstacle, or slide off the trail. For this reason, speeds over a few miles per hour, or any speed beyond which you can maintain total control, should be avoided.

The vehicle up front has the hardest time, because it's breaking a trail through the snow. It's best to rotate the trail-breaking machine to avoid punishing one vehicle too much. It also shares the fun! The vehicles behind are often best off running in the ruts. Many times you have no choice.

SOFT GROUND: SAND

Sand is a good deal like snow, except that there's often no bottom to it. Sand comes in many consistencies, from a gravel-like material to something so fine it's like talcum powder. Sand is generally found on beaches and in deserts, but pockets of it can be found just about anywhere. Driving sand successfully is all about floatation, momentum, throttle control, and gentle turns.

How you drive on sand is first determined by the sand itself. Floatation is the main concern so you need enough rubber for a big footprint. Everybody will air down in sand, some more than others, but if you have smallish tires and the sand is the fine stuff, you're probably better off aborting. That doesn't mean that you can't traverse short stretches of

the talcum-like stuff, but if miles of it lie ahead, you're asking for agony if you proceed.

Many experts will advise using an all-terrain tire on sand, and that's not bad advice. In fact, some beach areas run by government agencies will not allow aggressive tires onto the sand at all. Still, if you are running a radial mudder, you don't necessarily need to fear sand. My own recent experience with modern radial mudders on sand (BFG Mud Terrains, Dunlop Mud Rovers, ProComp Mud Terrains) shows that they do quite well. Of course, my opinion will not get you past the Park Ranger's shack on Cape Cod!

Beach sand is often pretty stable stuff, especially near the water, generally at the high-tide mark. It's usually coarse, and when damp, it's pretty solid. Many times it's good near the water, too, but you can run into quicksandlike stuff there and if the tide happens to be coming in, your rig is in for a destructive salt-water bath unless you can do a very quick recovery. Beaches near lowlands, salt marches, and tidal pools are often treacherous because of water flow under the surface. It doesn't hurt to know the beach's layout before you go too far. Playing in the surf, as all of us have been tempted to do, can be great fun but it's risky and not so hot for the vehicle. It's easy to get stuck and the salt spray is very corrosive.

"Blow sand," the type you see on coastal or desert dunes, is much finer and more treacherous. Beyond established routes, playing on blow sand needs a lot of rubber for floatation or a lot of speed and skill. For the average four-wheeler, blow sand will be encountered in short stretches in the deserts and momentum can usually carry you from one patch of solid ground to another. The coarser sand usually found in desert washes and streambeds is firmer stuff and relatively easy to traverse, even at relatively high tire pressures.

Silt is another form of ground sometimes present near water and in desert dry lakebeds. Since it's most like

sand, we'll include it here. Silt was once ocean or lake bottom and it's a fine talcum-like substance that can be found in a concreted form, or as a dry powder. Given a little water, the seemingly solid stuff turns absolutely bottomless. The silty stuff makes blow sand seem like child's play. These silty areas are sometimes called alkali flats, or when wet, alkali mudflats. The wet stuff is corrosive.

You will find that sand tends to make your rig grunt a little. That's because the tires are pushing a small wave of sand. It's as if they are continually trying to climb a slope. As a result, most rigs will need low range and first gear to get started (unless they are low geared or high powered), but once the vehicle has some momentum, you will want to run in the highest comfortable gear. That means not grunting along, but moving in an rpm range where the engine has enough torque to respond to throttle input. The vehicle may momentarily bog down, and the engine has to have enough oomph left to respond without your having to do an aggressive downshift and possibly start the tires spinning.

Turning hard can also result in an unscheduled appointment with the shovel. Too sharp a turn will cause the

Dune-type blow sand is treacherous for the stocker, but the use of copious amounts of momentum can get just about any rig through. Notice how the Jeep Liberty's tires have sunk deep into the sand and are plowing up four little waves. The 3.7L engine feels as if it's making a perpetual climb. Note also how much sand the driver's side tires are tossing up. That's a sign of sinking even deeper. As long as he doesn't run out of momentum before the turn is completed, this rig should stay on top of the sand. *Courtesy Ken Brubaker*

the dirt

Sons of Beaches:
Overall, you can consider beaches–at least the few that still allow vehicles–as pretty safe places for a stock or near-stock 4x4, assuming you have a safe and sane attitude about it.

the dirt

Driving on Sand:
On sand, starts and stops need to be gentle–starting too aggressively results in tire spin and a vehicle that goes down instead of forward. The same thing happens when you stop. The tires can lock on the low-traction surface and as you come to a stop, you will do so in four nicely dug holes.

tires to dig into the sand. Going deeper into the sand increases the rolling resistance (you're plowing up even more sand with the tires), which will probably leave you short of traction, as well as slow you down. If you run out of momentum before you stop turning, you may come to a stop. Don't forget that aired-down tires also limit your handling abilities. It's just as possible to roll a tire off the rim in sand as it is anywhere else.

WATER CROSSINGS

Water is not a natural environment for 4x4s, but it's an obstacle four-wheelers have to deal with relatively often. This can get complicated for some of us. Most modern 4x4s are ill-equipped to deal with water of any serious depth, but older units are much less vulnerable. In the end, the vehicle will determine whether you cross that creek or not.

Whatever rig you drive, your first job is to determine its fording limits. This specification can be found in the owner's manual, if the manufacturer has established one. Fording depth limits used to always be included in four-wheel-drive vehicle specifications, but these days it's harder to find. In some cases, all you get is a vague "below the level of the hubs," which works out to be a meager 8 inches or less.

You wouldn't dive into murky water of unknown depth, so why should you drive into the same situation? In most cases, the crossing will be part of a well-established trail, but don't take it for granted that the bottom conditions or depth haven't changed since the last rig went through. Also, just because a truck with 38-inch tires and an 8-inch lift got safely across, doesn't mean your unlifted rig with 31x10.50s will do the same.

Sometimes you can probe a bit from the banks with a stick to determine the water depth and bottom condition. You may have also observed a vehicle not too different in capability from yours cross safely, and this is as

good as a green light most of the time. If it's a large ford, you may have to resort to a bit of wading to determine if you can safely cross with your vehicle. By wading across, you can determine depth and bottom conditions firsthand. Obviously, common sense must prevail in this. You won't want to wade into any potentially dangerous situation, such as fast-running water.

Bottom conditions are as important as depth. In general, moving water is the safest, because deep silt is not usually present. Many streams have a rocky bottom, which is good in the sense that you won't sink, but bad in offering more danger of cut tires or large, diff-denting rocks. Larger rocks can hide under the water and cause damage or get you hung up. Stagnant or slow-moving water often hides deep silt, or the U-Boat Mud mentioned earlier. Make your evaluations carefully. Water recoveries are just about the worst in terms of cold, nasty work.

Use low range and a lower gear. Even though your pace will be slow and steady, it's best to keep the engine revved up a little, perhaps as high as 1,500 rpm. This gives you a little leeway to keep the engine running if water splashes on the ignition system and causes misfiring. In fast-moving water, it's best to cross diagonal to the current. Being broadside to a torrent of water may be enough to sweep your vehicle downstream. Remember that fast-moving water can wash the sand or gravel out from under your tires, so it's best to keep moving.

Enter the water slowly. As you nose in at an angle, the vehicle is most vulnerable to scooping water into the engine compartment and creating problems. Once fully in the water, proceed at a steady pace. Go too fast and you are pushing water into places it shouldn't go. Ultimately, your speed through the water is somewhat variable according to bottom conditions. A soft bottom might require more momentum to avoid getting stuck. A rocky bottom needs a slower speed to avoid tire or undercarriage damage.

Be ready to react quickly to changing conditions. These could include

On Water Crossings:
Before taking the plunge, evaluate the water depth, bottom condition, and the exit on the far side. It's quite common to forget about the exit and then find that the vehicle cannot climb out.

Don't drive where you won't dive! If you have to get out and check water depth the old-fashioned way, so be it. Just make sure it's safe for you to do so. Take note of water depth, bottom conditions, the entrance and exits from the water, and the current.

When you enter the water, do it sedately. Dipping in at an angle will momentarily place the engine compartment in a low position and a slow entrance will reduce the "tidal wave" effect in the engine compartment if the water is deep.

Once in the water, maintain reasonable momentum, just enough to generate a modest bow wave. The bow wave is mostly an indicator of correct speed. Too fast, and you are pushing water into areas where you don't want it. In some vehicles, the bumper pushing water creates a depression under the engine compartment, keeping the water level lower than it might otherwise be.

When current is present, a diagonal approach is best. In areas of very fast water, a vehicle broadside presents a greater surface area for water to push against. This force can overcome what little grip your tires have on the bottom and push you downstream. This Range Rover is in to the tops of the tires and somewhat over its maximum-rated fording depth.

If, for whatever reason, your engine stops in the water, the exhaust may fill up with water. In and of itself, this is of little consequence as long as it isn't deep enough to work itself up into the engine through the back door. When the engine starts, it will quickly and spectacularly push that water out. The more worrisome aspect is why the engine quit; you can read more about that in chapter 9.

In many parts of the country, water crossings will be accompanied by rocks. If you are lucky, the rocks are visible. If not, you may slam and bam your way across, rolling over the hidden rocks, assuming you don't get stuck on one. For that reason, a rocky ford is best taken slowly to avoid damage. In extreme cases, it's advisable to have a spotter to point out the offensive rocks.

holes, soft bottoms, or rocks. In mud or silt some extra throttle might be needed quickly, or even the Wiggle mentioned in the mud section above. If you fall into a hole—and hopefully it's a small one—momentum may carry you through. If it's a big one, you may have time to stop and back out. If you hit a rock, get off the throttle quickly, back clear, and steer around or over it. If it looks as though you'll go deep enough for your engine to ingest water via the intake, shutting the engine off before that happens may prevent serious damage.

Once clear of the water, take the time to put your rig back into dry land form. If you hit a rock, make a quick damage inspection. When you get under way, make a few stops to test and dry the brakes. Wet brakes are considerably less efficient, and a couple of hard stops will generate the heat needed to accelerate the drying process. Drum brakes dry more slowly than discs because they're enclosed and do not have a constant-contact self-cleaning design.

In deep water or extended soakings, it's very possible that the axles, axle universals, CV joints, or driveshaft U-joints have inhaled some water. If you were deep enough, even the trans and transfer case can take on water (though this is less likely unless you drown the rig completely). Remember, oil seals are designed to keep what's inside, inside, not what's outside from getting in. Better drivetrain designs use double-lip seals that prevent outside contamination. Even then, worn seals can allow small amounts of water in but will not let oil leak out.

Unless you have good reason to suspect there's serious water contamination, you can wait till you are home for a thorough underside inspection. At that time, I always recommend a couple of squirts of grease into all the lube fittings (suspension and driveline) to drive water out, and to check the diff oils for water contamination. Serious water contamination will result in gear oil that turns white and this goo must be

flushed ASAP. Small amounts of water will usually evaporate via the heat generated by driving. Units with closed-knuckle front axles (most early rigs and some later rigs such as Land Rovers and Toyotas) will need further inspection to ensure that water has not entered these housings.

CROSSING LOGS

In wooded areas, deadfall across your path is common. Sometimes these logs are small enough to cross, other times you have to get them out of the way by whatever means are practical. Crossing a log is done diagonally, similar to crossing a gully. The main requirements are that your rig have the ground clearance under the diffs, room under the belly, and enough approach and departure angle. If you have the clearance, simply put one tire at a time up and over the log until you are clear. The climb up the face of the log, and stepping off, are both done very slowly. If the log is only slightly beyond your clearance, you can build up the approaches and step-offs for both sets of tires to gain the required clearance.

The important complications to crossing logs include the fact that the log may roll, move, or shift as you go over. Smaller timber may actually flip up and strike the vehicle or spectators. There also may be soft or slippery ground on either side of the log that will reduce the traction available to climb over, or cause you to sink into the ground enough to reduce ground clearance to the point of hanging up.

BASIC ROCKCRAWLING

There are many types of rockcrawling, from boulder-strewn trails to vast expanses of sandstone commonly called slickrock. The key skills for successful rockcrawling of all types are a smooth driving style, good throttle and brake control, and the ability to pick lines.

After a Water Crossing:
Don't get lazy with the post-fun cleanup. Undiscovered damage, grit, and lubricant contamination will shorten your fun by shortening your vehicle's life span; depending on their nature and extent, these conditions can sometimes present a serious safety hazard.

Crossing a log is simply a tire-by-tire operation. One at a time, you carefully put one tire over the log. Stick-shift vehicles will require clutch, brake, and throttle finesse for this. Automatics will need left-foot braking. How big a log you can cross this way is determined by your overall clearance.

If the log is slightly taller than your clearance, use local building materials to build a ramp for both sets of tires. Often you need only a few inches' extra clearance.

One of the most common mistakes is to come off rocks too quickly. That's often because people do not use left-foot braking. Even if a rock is only a foot high, your rig will pick up speed on the downslope of the rock, and it may come down before you can get the right foot from the throttle to the brake. Coming down hard off the rock will compress the suspension, perhaps enough to use up that little bit of clearance and allow the undercarriage to hit somewhere.

One of the key insights in rockcrawling is learning that you are maneuvering both ends of the vehicle. If you need to put a front tire up on a rock so the diff will clear, you may have to maneuver the rear tire over the same rock or over a completely different one. Only some of the time will you be lucky enough to have a straight-through traverse. Many times, you'll be maneuvering around several rocks at the same time. Overall, many of the techniques you have learned in other terrain types apply here, but a few words on each type of rockcrawling scenario are in order.

Loose Rocks

These can range in size from gravel to basketball-sized rocks and from smooth to jagged. The smaller-sized rocks, especially weathered and rounded riverbed types, tend to slip and slide a good deal, so traction may be a problem. Climbing or descending a track covered in small rocks can be like driving on marbles. Throttle control is vital, as is the use of momentum. Keep moving and avoid large applications of throttle. On regularly driven tracks, you may find a "sweet spot" where the rocks have been compacted into a fairly stable surface. Outside of this area, you might find really loose stuff.

The larger rocks will move around as well. Many are anchored, but the loose ones have a bad habit of looking stable but moving at inopportune times. At best, it's a small jolt as the tire falls off the rock. At worst, you are thrown off onto another rock that's looking for a 4x4 part to nail. Loose rocks also tend to roll under the tire and get spit backward. These rocks can move with some force, so bystanders should take care. Pick lines that will put your tires on the rocks you can't clear and you will be driving from one high spot to the next. This may involve a good deal of maneuvering, both to find the high points and avoid the things you can't go over.

Beware of the tire-killing jagged rocks of all sizes. Always drive slowly through them, avoiding scuffing the sidewalls against sharp edges, and don't let the tires spin. In a sea of jagged edges, you'll have your eyes full watching out for potential hazards. Jagged rocks are particularly dangerous when wet, partly because the tendency to slip and spin is increased. Also, the edges that aren't sharp enough to gouge tires when dry tend to cut when lubricated by water.

Large Boulders

Creative line picking becomes vital when you get into the big stuff. You'll literally be driving from one boulder face to the next, finding a path for all four wheels and fighting to keep the body and undercarriage clear of harm. How far you can go into this realm depends on the vehicle. Lots of clearance

is important, as are low gearing, the added traction of a locker, and sticky tires. In all but the mildest "Boulder Bashing" environments, lifted tires are common, so a locker becomes a necessary part of the equipment package. This puts most boulder scenarios into the more advanced category covered in chapter 7.

Slickrock

Slickrock: The term gives many people an image of ice-covered boulders or perhaps soapstone. It's just the opposite, actually. Driving on slickrock has been compared to driving on 100-grit sandpaper and the analogy is a good one. Massive amounts of traction allow you to make climbs and descents that would otherwise be impossible. The question is, why do they call it slickrock? The answer goes back more than a century, when pioneers were using horses shod with iron shoes and wagons with wooden wheels covered with iron hoops. Where a rubber tire grips slickrock with authority,

Smaller logs can spring up as you drive over. In this case, no damage was done, but it's not uncommon for the flipped logs to strike the vehicle, or another vehicle, and cause damage. A spectator could also be in harm's way.

85

Picking your way uphill through a sea of rocks is slow, bouncy work. The key tip is to pick the line that keeps you clear of the taller rocks and your tire sidewalls away from any sharp edges. On a very steep uphill, the increased need for traction can cause the tires to spit the rocks out behind the tires.

an iron shoe slips as if it were on ice. The popularity of Moab, Utah, has made "slickrock" a common term for four-wheelers, mountain bikers, ATVers, and motorcyclists.

Not all slickrock is created equal, but all the usual techniques apply. Some slickrock has a crumbly surface that shears away and reduces traction somewhat. In addition, slickrock with sand on it can be spooky. Much of what you will face is ledges and the Bump technique will serve you well. The key to working a stock or near-stock vehicle over slickrock is keeping the tires on the ground and as evenly loaded as possible. Loss of traction due to articulation or weight transfer can stop an unlocked rig quickly.

Techniques for Preserving the Drivetrain

One of the problems of driving on many types of rock is that you can almost have too much traction. Many four-wheelers will respond to that by saying, "There's no such thing as too much traction!" True, of course, when you think just of getting over the obstacle. But if the excess traction is combined with angles and maneuvers that can put all the engine torque on one wheel or put the drivetrain into a bind, things go snap, crackle, or pop, and we're not talking about Rice Krispies.

If you've ever driven on pavement with your rig in four-wheel drive and the hubs locked in, you have an idea of what it feels like to put the drivetrain in a bind. As soon as you turn, tires start barking and the steering wheel starts bucking in your hand. Your front and rear tires are turning at different speeds and something has to slip or give. You hope it's the tire exceeding its traction and slipping and not a drivetrain part breaking. In conditions with less traction, such as in dirt, this slippage is less apparent.

Part of the rockcrawling scene is angles and lifted tires. That means weight transfer may put most or all of the weight on one tire. If you combine that with a locker, that means all the torque is going to that one tire. If it happens to have more grip than some part of your drivetrain has strength, then, *snap*, something lets loose! This is controllable by driving techniques that include knowing when to back off, having a feel for these severe-angle situations, and going easy, or picking other lines.

Some drivers of vehicles with weak links in the drivetrain will use tire pressure to prevent breakage. Reducing the tire footprint by maintaining a relatively high tire pressure will decrease traction.

THE END OF THE TRAIL

Wise 4x4 skippers stop at the end of the trail to look the rig over for any damage. This check starts with the tires, since they are the most vulnerable part of your 4x4, and one of the most potentially dangerous failures. Look for cuts, blisters, and gouges, especially on the vulnerable sidewalls. Minor cuts and gouges are part and parcel of four-wheeling, but the important question is how you can tell if a slightly damaged tire is safe. The general rule of thumb is as follows: if you can see cord material in the damaged area, the tire is probably not safe. Below that visible point, the tire may still be fatally damaged; predicting exactly whether an apparently slightly damaged tire is safe is sometimes a mix of gambling and black magic. I have seen tires with little obvious damage fail in a short period and tires with a nasty-looking gouge that lasted for years. "If in doubt, swap it out," is always good advice, especially if you have a full-sized spare. You can then have it checked by a more knowledgeable party, such as a tire shop, when you get home. Bear in mind that tire shops and other outside sources will always err on the side of extreme caution in their judgments.

Beyond tires, have a quick look at wheel rims for obvious hits and at the

A spotter/rock mover can be invaluable when you encounter boulder fields such as this. Note the jagged, tire-killing edges of these rocks. This is a place to take care.

suspension components for obvious damage. You will have noted any serious hits as they happened on the trail and probably had a look right then and there. It wouldn't hurt to take another look before you hit the pavement just to make sure there was no damage and that no problem has developed since you last checked.

The Road Home:
Once you're off the trail and headed for home, be extra sensitive for the first few miles, listening for any unusual noises, vibrations, or odd characteristics in the way your vehicle drives. Keeping the radio(s) off will help you determine whether anything sounds suspect.

CHAPTER 6

THE TOOLBOX

Basic Vehicle Tuning and Buildup

Well-chosen modifications can turn the ordinary 4x4 into a trail hero. It took little more than a set of sticky tires and a rear locker for this otherwise stock Toyota pickup to climb this steep slab of rock.

HERE WE'LL COVER:

Tire fitment, tricks, and treads
•
Lifts and suspension alterations for increased clearance
•
Component upgrades to keep you on the trail longer and with fewer worries
•
Making your engine more water-resistant

Star Trek's Mr. Spock once constructed a computer from crude materials he described as "stone knives and bearskins." That was science fiction and in this real world any tradesman will tell you that without the right tools and equipment, the job stops at some very basic level. While driving skill alone can carry you many miles into the outback, having the right equipment will take you farther and make it a better and safer experience. That equipment includes modifications to the vehicle itself and items carried within it.

MODIFICATION 101

The first lesson in modifying any vehicle is that you have to think beyond just one part. The whole vehicle must be balanced in strength and ability according to the uses you plan. When you get right down to the core of it, there are only two things you need in a four-wheel drive: traction and clearance. Make improvements in those two areas and you're set.

Most of us don't have unlimited funds, so modifications must be chosen carefully to bring a good result for the money spent. The two most common mistakes are buying something on the basis of popularity instead of need, and buying based on bottom-line price. Popularity sometimes represents a commonality of need, but sometimes it represents merely what's "cool." What's cool may also serve a use or need, but maybe not for you.

As to price, remember the old apples and oranges adage. Unless you are looking at nearly identical products, don't shop on the basis of price alone. Look first at *what* you get, *then* check the price and compare it to the other items that fit into the same general category. Remember—you get what you pay for! Some products are designed and built simply to be the lowest-priced item on the market and the prime candidate for those who shop by price alone. They are often far from being the best in terms of performance. Moderation of goals is a far better form of thrift than selecting the lowest-priced products in any category.

What's first? That depends a great deal on the vehicle, but generally safety and recovery come first. After that, it's traction and clearance (or clearance and traction). The buildup usually starts with tires, which may or may not include a lift and gearing changes. A locker or limited slip often comes next.

To wrench or not to wrench? You can save a lot of moola doing the repair and buildup work yourself, and you don't necessarily have to be a certified technician. An old-timer such as this Willys MB is about as easy as it gets in terms of low-tech. Some of the money saved from outside labor will be taken up by new tools, but generally you can come out ahead. If you are new at wrenching, the learning curve can be steep—but with patience, common sense, and a good manual, you can get to the top.

What's First?

Some of this depends on the vehicle and its particular pluses and minuses. Recovery and safety items should obviously come first. Beyond that, some of your choices will be dictated by the type of terrain you generally traverse. Typically, tires and wheels follow recovery and safety items. A tire upgrade may necessitate some suspension modifications or a body lift, or both, in order to fit them. After that, lockers and drivetrain durability mods are of paramount importance. Depending on your rig, body and chassis armor fits in there at about the same point. These basic items can be supplemented, or complicated, by your personal needs and wants.

Do It Yourself?

One of the big questions we all face is whether to do the work ourselves. Labor prices being what they are today, you can save a lot of cash doing the work yourself—but only if you and your toolbox are up to it. In my opinion, a reasonably intelligent person armed with the necessary tools, including a manual, and a large dose of *patience* can accomplish a great deal. Note the emphasis on patience. Lack of experience is largely mitigated by patience and the ability to follow instructions. Roping in a knowledgeable friend for tricky parts doesn't hurt, either.

A novice wrencher who wants to expand his mechanical horizons should start by buying the service manual and tackling some of the maintenance chores. Most towns have basic automotive repair courses and there are books available on the subject as well. You should be able to track down a factory repair manual for your vehicle, either through a dealer or on the Internet. At some point, you can even do some of the easier modifications. The biggest mistake I see is people setting their sights too high. That could be anything from choosing to overhaul and upgrade an automatic transmission as their second project to starting a locker installation Sunday noon on a daily driver that needs to be used Monday

a.m. Both of these extremes are setups for angst and failure.

Bear in mind that there is an initial investment in tools that will reduce the bang-for-buck aspect. Still, most tools are forever. Aside from a few specialty tools with a narrow range of uses, whatever basic hand tools you buy can be amortized by the labor savings in the first few jobs and can be used until you pass them along to your kids. As always, you get what you pay for. Bargain-rate tools are no bargain when they fail at home or in the field.

FREE PERFORMANCE: TRAIL TIRE TUNING

Correctly adjusting tire pressures for the trail is an important part of successful four-wheeling. The benefits of lower trail pressures can be dramatic. Your tires have three main tasks in the dirt. First, they provide a tractive grip on terra firma to move the vehicle, stop it, or turn it. Second, they are a part of your 4x4's suspension system and absorb a lot of the bumps. Third, they supply floatation to keep your rig *above* the ground and not *in* it.

From the traction standpoint, to recap what we talked about in chapter 2, lower tire pressures allow the tire to spread out and put a larger footprint on the ground. More footprint equals more tire surface to grip the ground. Also, since the trail consists mostly of irregular surfaces, the tire conforms to it better at lower pressures, wrapping itself around rocks and other obstacles. A relatively small irregularity, such as a fist-sized rock, can lift a "pumped up" tire off the ground and reduce grip to nothing, perhaps at a moment when you really need it.

Finally, the aired-down tire provides floatation due to the increased footprint. Your rig's total weight is supported by those four small patches of rubber on the ground.

Low Pressure Caveats

Whether you should air down a significant amount for the trail, or at all, depends first of all on whether you have an onboard compressor. All trails eventually lead back to the pavement, and driving home on low tires is dangerous and hard on the wallet. If you can't air back up at the end of the trail, it's better not to drop your pressures much, if at all.

If you do choose to air down, there are some important factors to keep in mind while out there on the trail. The first is that handling will be adversely affected at any speed above a crawl. A low tire can be suddenly deflated in hard or overly quick turns by literally rolling the tire bead off the rim. An aired-down tire is more vulnerable to sidewall damage in terrain with lots of sharp-edged rocks. Also keep in mind that an aired-down tire reduces the rolling diameter, which decreases ground clearance by a small amount.

An aired-down tire is vulnerable to all sorts of contortions. This wadded-up sidewall did not tear, but such extreme flexing can result in damage to the carcass that might not immediately show. Airing down is a great boon to outback travel, but your tires carry the burden of it. You can minimize the impact by airing down according to conditions. Reserve those major air-downs for when they are needed, namely, more extreme terrain.

TIRE PRESSURE AND FOOTPRINT

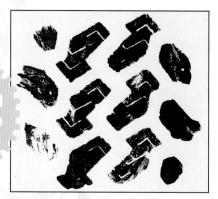

A ProComp 12.50x35-15 Mud Terrain mounted on the front of the author's 4x4 at 30 psi. There are approximately 1,500 pounds of weight on the tire. The actual size of the footprint is 8.25x 9 inches, for a total of 74.25 square inches. That combination of pressure and weight yields a ground pressure of 20.2 pounds per square inch. Notice that the outer edges of the tread are indistinct. My normal front pressure is 28 psi.

Our ProComp at 10 psi. The actual size of the footprint is 14.25x 10 inches, a total of 142.5 square inches. Ground pressure would be 10.5 pounds per square inch. Note that you can see the sharp edge of the outer tread block, indicating that the tire is flat on the ground. The footprint has grown 5.25 inches in length and 1.75 inches in width.

The same ProComp tire at 23 psi. The footprint measures 8.50x 10, for a total of 85 square inches. With 1,500 pounds, that footprint yields 17.6 pounds per square inch. Notice that the edges of the tread are a little more distinct and that the footprint has grown longer.

Suggested Trail Tire Pressures
Courtesy Oasis Off Road Manufacturing

John Williams at Oasis created the chart below, which outlines some heavy-duty four wheeling pressures based on GVW and tire size. These suggestions are subject to three general rules that John has also supplied.

1) Increase pressure approximately 3psi for each 10mph over 20mph, until normal highway pressures are reached. For example: A 3000 lb. vehicle with 31x10.50R15 tires travelling at up to 40mph should be set at about 15psi (9+3+3=15).
2) Decrease pressure by approximately 1/2 for extremely soft snow. The exception to this is a 33x9.50R15 tire, which usually benefits form an increase in pressure.
3) Decrease pressure approximately 1 psi for every additional two inches in tire diameter beyond this chart, assuming a corresponding increase in the width of the tire.

Tire pressure for GVW

Tire Size	2000	3000	4000	5000	6000	7000	8000
215/75R15	11	13	15	N/R	N/R	N/R	N/R
235/75R15	10	12	14	16	N/R	N/R	N/R
29x8.50R15	10.5	12.5	14.5	15.5	N/R	N/R	N/R
30x9.50R15	9	10	12	14	16	N/R	N/R
31x10.50R15	8	9	10	12	14	15	N/R
32x11.50R15	7.5	8.5	9.5	11	13	15	18
33x9.50R15	9	10	12	14	16	N/R	N/R
33x12.50R15	7	8	9	10	12	14	16
35x12.50R15	6	7	8	9	10	12	14
36x14.50R15	5	6	7	8	9	10	12
38x15.50R15	4	5	6	7	8	9	10
225/75R16	11	13	15	N/R	N/R	N/R	N/R
245/75R16	10	12	14	16	N/R	N/R	N/R
265/75R16	9	10	12	14	16	N/R	N/R
285/75R16	8	9	10	12	14	16	N/R

LESS PRESSURE, LESS CLEARANCE

Shown here is the right front tire at 30 psi, approximately 1,500 pounds on the tire. From the ground to the rim measures 8-3/8 inches.

The same tire at 15 psi has dropped to 7-1/2 inches from ground to rim. This action has decreased ground clearance under the diffs by 7/8 inch.

At 15 psi, the sidewall bulge is very pronounced.

OE Airing Down:
Use more caution in airing down stock rigs with OE-sized tires. In these cases, 15 psi is usually as low as you dare go—sometimes not even that far.

the dirt

Airing Down:
The old rule of thumb for airing down was to lower the pressure until the tire profile is reduced by 25 percent. That's still a useful tool for all but the largest tire.

The Science of Low-Trail Pressures

Assuming you have the ability to air back up, the question becomes how low you should go at any given moment. It depends in part on the terrain. An easy day of 'wheeling might only require a small drop in pressure just to smooth out the ride a little. A more radical day might require a more radical drop in pressure. A drop of 10 psi (say from 35 down to 25) isn't going to be a huge problem for most rigs, but finding that low-as-you-can-go number may be a little trickier.

Just how low you can go on a non-beadlocked rim depends on two main factors: tire size and vehicle weight. Beadlocked rims are in a class by themselves and we'll talk about them further along. A third factor is the tire and rim combination. The volume of air in the tire is what keeps the bead seated, and a larger tire has more of that and can be aired down more. Look at the charts from Oasis on page 92 for some guidelines on trail pressures.

One item I would add to the Oasis chart is to equalize front and rear tire profiles. Using those charts, set the pressures, and then measure the profile of the tires at the lightest end of the vehicle. The heavy end will be lower at the same pressure, so increase tire pressure at that end to equalize tire profiles front and rear.

The Mechanics of Lowering Trail Pressures

Airing down can be as simple as crouching down with a tire gauge and letting out the appropriate amount of air. This is the cheap and simple, but time-consuming, approach. My tests show it takes two minutes and 15 seconds to go from 30 to 15 psi on a

TIRE CONFORMATION AT LOW PRESSURE

At 30 psi, there is little conformation of the tire to this small rock. Were this a small knob on a bigger rock, little traction would be offered here.

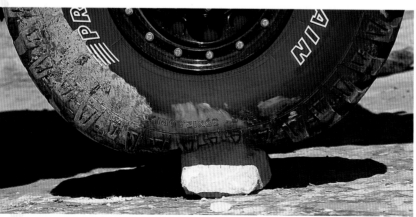

At 20 psi, the tire is doing a pretty good job of absorbing the rock. At this pressure, the tire could grip this knob like that hand in the old Uniroyal "Tiger Paw" commercial.

35x12.50-15 tire using an ordinary "pencil"-type gauge. Some owners with large tires will temporarily remove the valve core and this is fast and cheap, but a little risky if the core blows out of your fingers. My test shows this reduces air-down time by about 30 seconds per tire, including fussing with the valve core, but there is still a finite amount of time needed. In some informal tests where tires were timed on how long it took them to fully deflate from 30 to 0 psi with the valve core removed, it took a 30x9.50-15 tire about three minutes, a 33x12.50-15 about five minutes, and a 35x12.50 about seven minutes.

Methods of Re-Inflation: Compressors

Compressors come at assorted prices, with the price reflecting robustness and performance. The three most important performance specifications are airflow capacity in cubic feet per minute (cfm), duty cycle, and tire fill time for the particular size tire. The cfm rating is expressed two ways: at zero pressure or at "X" psi. The better performance spec is cfm at pressure, as it indicates the compressor's ability to pump against pressure. This could be at 30 psi or 100 psi (or whatever). A compressor making 3 cfm at 100 psi is significantly more powerful than one that puts out 3 cfm at 30 psi.

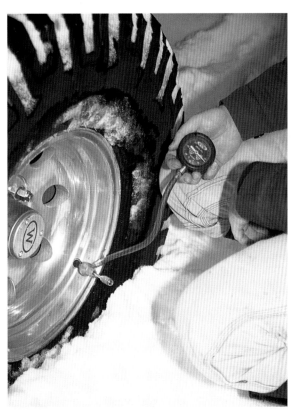

Airing down can be accomplished simply by working at it with a cheap pencil-type gauge or with a whiz-bang tool such as this. This gauge screws onto the stem and removes the core for a more speedy pressure drop.

Duty cycle is another important consideration. Some compressors can run continuously, but most cannot. They need time to cool, with that time increasing according to load and ambient temperature. The most useful way to read a duty cycle specification is when it's in time-on vs. time-off: 10 minutes running vs. 20 minutes off for cooling, for example. This time is

These adjustable devices from Oasis Manufacturing can be preset to the pressure you desire. When you get to the trailhead, you screw them on and continue on your way. The tires air down to the preset pressure as you drive.

Some owners build hose setups whereby they can air down or air up two or more tires at a time. In some cases, an adjustable regulator is built onto the inlet/outlet to control pressure.

calculated based on the maximum rated operating temperature of the unit reached while it's pumping against 100 psi pressure at 72 degrees Fahrenheit ambient temperature. When expressed as a percentage, duty cycle become a little more variable. A 100-percent duty cycle, of course, means the unit can run continuously. A typical unit with a 25-percent duty cycle can run 10 minutes with 30 minutes' rest. Depending on how the manufacturer rates their unit in time-on vs. time-off, the run/rest times could vary somewhat but stay at a 25-percent duty cycle.

How duty cycle relates to your choice is connected to fill time. If, for example, your compressor takes 5 minutes per tire to air them up to

Most compressors are electric. This ARB unit does double duty by supplying air pressure for the Air Lockers as well as for tire filling. It's a quality unit, but a bit low on cfm, so it's best suited for airing tires no bigger than 31x10.50, or, preferably, smaller. These small units can be mounted in a variety of locations.

This Oasis compressor is currently the king of the electric units, with performance that matches some garage compressors. If you have big tires or air tools, here's the "Big Kahuna" huffer for you. The downsides are weight, amp draw, and cost.

Four-Wheeler's Math

1) Effective Gear Ratio
The "effective" gear ratio illustrates the changes that occur when larger tires are installed. For example, by replacing 29-inch tires with 33-inch tires, your 3.54:1 axle ratio will perform like a 3.11:1.

To obtain the effective gear ratio:

$$\frac{\text{old tire diameter}}{\text{new tire diameter}} \times \text{original ratio} = \text{effective ratio of new combination}$$

2) Engine RPM at Speed
This formula is useful for determining the changes in cruising rpm that might occur from axle ratio changes or larger tires.

$$\frac{\text{mph} \times \text{total gear ratio} \times 336}{\text{tire diameter (inches)}} = \text{engine rpm}$$

3) Equivalent Ratio
This formula is used to find the axle ratio needed to bring the overall tire/axle ratio gearing back to an approximation of stock after you have installed larger tires. This will put your cruising rpms back to near-stock levels and improve acceleration. Bear in mind that the larger rotating mass of the bigger tires will slow acceleration regardless of ratio changes. For that reason, some owners go about 10 percent lower on the gear ratio than they actually need based on the formula. This helps compensate for the increased diameter of the tires.

To obtain equivalent ratios:

$$\frac{\text{new tire diameter}}{\text{old tire diameter}} \times \text{old ratio} = \text{new ratio}$$

4) Speedometer Correction
Use these formulae to determine your correct speed after swapping tires or tires and gear ratios. Going to larger tires will make the vehicle go faster than the speedometer indicates. Don't forget to add in your overdrive ratio, expressed as a fraction (usually .7–8:1 on most rigs).

Speedometer correction (tire swap only):

$$\frac{\text{new tire diameter}}{\text{old tire diameter}} \times \text{indicated mph} = \text{actual mph}$$

Speedometer correction (tire and gear swap):

$$\text{indicated speed in mph or KM} \times \frac{\text{new tire dia.}}{\text{old tire dia.}} \times \frac{\text{old gear ratio}}{\text{new gear ratio}} = \text{actual speed}$$

To find final drive ratio (in OD):

$$\text{OD gear ratio} \times \text{axle ratio} = \text{final drive ratio}$$

---

street pressure (that's 20 minutes for four), and if the duty cycle is 20 percent (8 minutes continuous), then you will have exceeded the unit's duty cycle midway into the second tire. By regularly exceeding the duty cycle, you will shorten the compressor's life, if not smoke the unit at an early stage.

Ultimately, the best way to select a compressor is based on tire size. A compressor that offers reasonable fill time for your tire size and the duty cycle necessary to complete the job without undue strain is the "just right" choice. The accompanying sidebar lists many current compressors and their performance, including tire fill times for many.

Airing-Up Tools
Beyond the compressor, the most important addition to any system is an air tank. A charged tank can reduce tire fill time significantly. The name of the game is volume, and a charged tank may contain enough air to

Compressor Performance

Model	Type	CFM at 0 psi	CFM at Pressure	Tire Time	Max Pressure (psi)	Current Draw (amps)	Cost Index	Max Tire	Duty Cycle
ARB	E12, H, P	1.68	1.41 at 20 psi	160	105	20 max	1.2	31x10.50	20
Big Red	E12, H, P	1.38	0.95 at 35 psi	(1)	120	20 max	1.2	31x10.50	20
Chuffer (home)	(2)	5.50	-	48	-	NA	-	NR	NA
Chuffer (production)	(2)	0.75	-	480	-	NA	-	225/75	NA
"El Cheapo" (2)	E12, P	0.70	0.27 at 35 psi	1344	210	10 max	-	225/75	10
Extreme Aire	E12, H	4.00	-	(3)	150	35 max	3.0	35x12.50	100
EZ-Air	E12, H, P	-	1.36 at 30 psi	(4)	150	20 max	1.9	33x12.50	20
Oasis Trailhead	E12, P, L	14.0	7.00 at 50 psi	(5)	125	180 max	2.8	UNL	100
QuickAir1	E12, P, H	1.31	0.73 at 40 psi	(6)	115	11 max	4.2	31x10.50	65
QuickAir2	E12, P, H	2.18	1.45 at 40 psi	(7)	105	26 max	3.2	33x12.50	65
QuickAir3	E12, H	3.65	2.05 at 40 psi	80	70	46 max	2.1	UNL	65
Ready Air 12100, 12200	E12, H, P, L	-	1.05 at 75 psi	-	120	30 max	2.7	35x12.50	100
Ready Air 12500	E12, H, L	-	1.10 at 175 psi	-	175	42 max	1.3	UNL	100
Shop Compressor (8)	E220, H	14.0	10.2 at 90 psi	28	140	-	-	UNL	80
ViAir 100	E12, H, P	1.38	-	290	-	17 max	2.7	31x10.50	15
ViAir 200	E12, H, P	1.94	-	135	-	23 max	1.8	33x12.50	20
ViAir 500	E12, H, P	2.93	-	(12)	-	-	-	-	-
York Conversion	B, H, L	-	4.00 at 90 psi (9)	45	(10)	NA	1.4 3.5 (11)	UNL	100

Notes on categories:

Model: Make or model of compressor.

Type: Key to codes: E12—12-volt electric; P—portable; H—hardmount; L—large and heavy over 30 pounds; B—engine, belt-driven; E220—electric 220-volt.

CFM at 0 psi: Airflow (in cubic feet per minute) and zero psi. This is the startup rate. As the compressor gets hot and has to pump against increasing pressure, the flow rate drops. These are manufacturer's specifications.

CFM at Pressure: The most important specification. This rate is much less than the zero PSI rate because the unit is pumping against pressure. Compressors with high flow rates at higher pressures are the better choice. These are manufacturer's specifications.

Tire Time: One of the more common standards is the time it takes to pump a 31x10.50-15 tire up from 10 to 30 psi. This is the default figure. If the available test information differs, it will be shown in the numbered notes below. This test info was compiled from my own tests as well as tests by manufacturers, or from published sources.

Max Pressure: This is the maximum pressure of the unit as given by the manufacturer.

Current Draw: In the case of an electric unit, this is the maximum number of amps needed by the unit. The amp draw increases the harder the unit works.

Cost Index: A measure of value, with 0 being the lowest value and 5 being the highest. At-pressure, cfm (or a reasoned estimate), and duty cycle are added and that value is divided by the current retail price for a hardmount unit. Values are averaged.

Max Tire: Since the volume of air needed to fill a tire is based on size, you need a larger compressor with a larger tire. This shows the largest tire suitable for a particular compressor, given reasonable wait times. These are my evaluations based on cfm flow rates. Use of an air tank could add enough capacity to bump this rating by one to two tire sizes. Key to abbreviations: UNL—unlimited; NR—not recommended.

Duty Cycle: The manufacturer's recommended duty cycle indicating the percentage of an hour the unit should be run continuously. This does not necessarily mean, for example, that a 20-percent-rated compressor can only be run 12 minutes before having to cool for 48; it merely means it must have some cooling-off time between 12-minute runs.

1: 33x12.50 from 8 to 28 psi in 180 seconds.

2: The homemade chuffer uses one cylinder of the engine as a compressor, so performance will vary according to the bore and stroke of the engine and engine speed. The tire-filling data was taken from a Land Rover four-cylinder of 3.56x3.5-inch stroke with the engine running at about 550 rpm and filling a 30x9.50 tire. The downside was that a certain amount of the air–fuel mixture was pumped into the cylinder, which puts a potentially explosive mixture into the tire. The manufactured chuffers use the compression of the cylinder to drive a small piston, and their performance was considerably slower, but safer. The production chuffer cfm is shown at 550 rpm. I have not seen a chuffer for sale in a number of years.

3: 35x12.50 from 10 to 35 psi in 185 seconds.

4: 35x12.50 from 15 to 35 psi in 408 seconds.

5: Manufacturer's rating is 50 seconds to fill a 35x12.50 tire from 15 to 30 psi

6: Manufacturer's rating is 180 seconds to fill a 31x10.50 tire from 15 to 30 psi.

7: Manufacturer's rating is 150 seconds to fill a 33x12.50 tire from 15 to 30 psi.

8: A typical medium-duty shop compressor of the type many dedicated home tinkerers may purchase. Shown here for comparison purposes.

9: These specifications are from York, who evidently tested their unit as a compressor at some point. The large-displacement York, 10.3 ci, is shown. They also offer 6.10-, 8.69-, and 12-ci units. This number is variable according to compressor speed and simulates an "average" engine at idle. Since pulley sizes vary, the compressor can run faster or slower and airflow will change. The GM R-4 and R-6 rotary compressors have a similar capacity.

10: These units can generate upward of 200 psi but are usually regulated to 120–150 psi.

11: Although the installation kits (not available for every application) are not overly expensive, the cost depends on whether you buy a new compressor or a used one. This is also a labor-intensive installation, though the performance is as close to a shop compressor as you can get. A dedicated junkyard scrounger and tinkerer could do this relatively inexpensively.

12: Manufacturer's rating is 125 seconds for a 35x12.50 tire from 15 to 30 psi.

essentially inflate one tire without much help from the compressor. Tests have shown that a charged 2-1/2-gallon tank added to an air system with a moderate-performance compressor can reduce the fill time of a 35-inch-tall tire by a minute and a half when going from 12 to 30 psi.

Another important element to any compressed air system is the size of the air lines. The use of 3/8-inch-inside diameter (I.D.) tubing or hose assures adequate airflow with all but the most powerful compressors. Overall airflow capacity is limited by the smallest inside diameter in the system, wherever that might be (usually at the valve stem of the tire). The largest and most important line should be from the compressor to the tank. Air tools will need 3/8-inch hose direct from the tank to operate efficiently, but the restrictions at the valve stem make only a 1/4-inch I.D. line from the tank necessary for tire filling. Speaking of air tools, a sufficiently powerful compressor and air tank make air tools a very feasible option. Once you've used a good air wrench, turning nuts and bolts by hand feels like slow motion.

A final tidbit on the airing-up subject would include the anecdotal observations of industry people and four-wheelers that rubber valve stems seem to flow more air than do metal ones. Metal valve stems seem to slow both airing up and airing down.

Methods of Re-Inflation: Filling With CO2

One of the new trends in four-wheeling is the use of CO_2 tanks for tire filling. These are high-pressure tanks that contain liquid carbon dioxide. A certain amount of the CO_2 evaporates to fill the volume of the cylinder and maintains pressure at about 1,800 psi until the last of the liquid evaporates and pressure gradually decreases. An adjustable regulator, with a high limit of 150 psi, controls output pressure, and you can fill approximately 27 31x10.50 tires from 10 to 30 psi (in a quick 42 seconds each) from one 10-gallon tank. The 5-gallon units cut that tire number in half but retain the same fill time. A 15-gallon tank is also available from some manufacturers. The capacity refers to the amount of liquid CO_2 the tank will hold.

The bottles are made of aircraft-grade aluminum and can be filled at welding or fire extinguisher shops for $10–$20. When full, they weigh in at 40–70 pounds with the carrying handle and all the regulator pieces. A 5-gallon tank with mount, regulator, and hose is around $350, with the 15-gallon tanks passing $425 with a mounting bracket. This puts them in the same realm as a midpriced compressor alone, or a lower-end compressor and

A CO2 tank such as this is a very viable option. The smaller ones hold enough liquid CO2 to fill a couple of dozen tires from 10 to 30 psi and come in a variety of capacities. They can also run air tools. The cost is about the same as a middle-level compressor without a tank, but the performance exceeds all electric or engine-driven compressors on the market. The downsides are the continued cost to refill ($10–$20) and the chance of running out when you need it most.

Recovery Points:
DO NOT use a receiver ball as a recovery point. Shock loads can break them off and turn them into cannonballs. If you must use a ball hitch for recovery, remove the ball and use the hole where it mounted to attach a shackle or ring.

the dirt

Tire Footprints:
A taller tire will offer more clearance with only a slight increase in footprint. The wider tire offers a bigger footprint increase with no extra clearance.

tank, but their performance is exceeded only by the most powerful and expensive compressors. You can also run air tools off these tanks.

RECOVERY POINTS

Recovery points are a basic necessity. Every 4x4 should have at least one up front and one in the rear. Recovery points can take many forms, including hooks, rings, shackle brackets, and others. The important part is that the individual pieces be rated for at least 1.5 times the curb weight of your vehicle and be solidly mounted to the chassis. The individual pieces of hardware can be purchased at four-wheel-drive shops, at a marine chandlery, and even the better-equipped hardware stores. The better pieces will have a safe working load (SWL) listed on them indicating their continuous rated load capacity (see chapter 8 for more details).

Here's a tire upgrade from a 225/75R-15 (28 inches tall) to a 32x11.50-15. The increase in rubber is apparent, as is the increase in diameter, but it takes a 3-inch lift to fit this upgrade on the Grand Cherokee.

The front points may be the most difficult to fit. The more utilitarian rigs usually have bare chassis horns up front for attaching hooks, but later-model SUVs and trucks often have bumpers and plastic in the way. You or your favorite 4x4 shop will have to get creative in that case. A few late-model 4x4s still have recovery hooks. The new Chevy Trailblazer is one that comes to mind.

In back, hooks can also be attached, but welded or bolted-on receiver hitches can count as a rear recovery point in most cases. These are often generically called "Class III" hitches and have a 2x2-inch receiver. There are class IV hitches that share the same 2x2 receiver but differ in weight ratings. Bolted-on ball hitches, called Class I hitches, are usually not stout enough, though some are. Some pickup step bumpers are stout enough for recovery; many are not.

TIRES AND WHEELS

A tire upgrade is one of the biggest bangs for your upgrade bucks. Bigger tires provide more of both of the primary four-wheeling elements: traction and clearance. A sticky tire can decrease the need for a limited slip or locker. A rig with open diffs is essentially limited in traction to the amount of grip one tire on each axle can supply. As soon as one tire slips, the ball game is over. If the tire is sufficiently grippy, and stays planted on the ground, that slipping point may never come, or will come less often.

Tire-size increases come in two dimensions: height and width. Most times, a bigger tire comes with more of both. In some cases, you can buy a wider tire of the same mounted diameter or a taller tire of the same width.

Unless a gear ratio change is planned, an increase in tire size would be limited by what your vehicle's existing gearing will accept. With a rig that has "high" gears (numerically low, such as 3.07, 3.31, 3.54), the effect on acceleration from a tire swap can be like starting in second gear. The effect

Tire Fitment Guide

Derived from a variety of aftermarket suspension supplier sources. Use as a rough guide only, because individual manufacturer's tire specs vary. Also take into account wheel size and offset. Your rig may be completely different. If you don't see a particular combo, there's probably a good reason why.

Key-
Setup 1 = Stock vehicle, maximum tire size that can be fitted.
Setup 2 = With a lift. Approximate suspension lift required is shown in parentheses.
Setup 3 = Suspension lift required is shown in parentheses; some fender trimming or metalwork may be required.
Setup 4 = Combination of suspension lift, in parentheses, and body lift, in brackets. May also require fender trimming.

Vehicle	Setup 1	Setup 2	Setup 3	Setup 4
Chevrolet/GMC				
S and T Series mid-sized	30x9.50	31x10.50 (2)	32x11.50 (2)	-
			33x11.50 (2.5)	-
'73–'87 pickups; '73–'91 Blazer and Suburban	31x10.50	33x9.50 (1.5)	38.5x15 (6)	35x12.50 (2.5)[1]
		33x12.50 (2.5)	39x15 (6)	36x15 (4)[1]
		35x12.50 (4)	40x17 (8)	38.5x15 (4)[3]
		36x15 (6)		44x18 (8)[3]
		38.5x15 (8)		
'88–up pickups; '92–up Blazer, Yukon, Tahoe, Suburban	31x10.50	33x9.50 (4)	35x12.50 (6)	36x15 (6)[1]
		33x12.50 (4)		38.5x15 (6)[3]
Dodge				
'74–'93 Ramcharger, Trail Duster	31x10.50	32x11.50 (1.5)	32x11.50 (0)	32x11.50[1]
	33x9.50	33x12.50 (2.5–3)	35x12.50 (4)	36x15 (4)[3]
				38.5x15 (6)[3]
'72–'93 W-250/350	31x10.50	32x11.50 (1.5)	32x11.50 (0)	32x11.50[1]
	33x9.50	33x12.50 (2.5–3)	35x12.50 (4)	36x15 (4)[3]
				38.5x15 (6)[3]
				40x17 (6)[3]
'93–'99 Dakota	31x10.50	32x11.50 (3)	-	-
		33x12.50 (3)		
'94–'99 Ram pickup	32x11.50	33x12.50 (3)	35x12.50 (4)	-
'98–up Durango	31x10.50	33x12.50 (3)	-	-
Ford				
'66–'77 Bronco	30x9.50	33x9.50 (2.5)	32x11.50 (0)	-
			33x12.50 (3–4)	
			35x12.50 (4–6)	
'78–'79 Bronco	32x11.50	33x12.50 (2.5)	33x12.50 (0)	38.5x15 (6)[3]
		35x12.50 (4)	36x15 (4)	
'80–'96 F-150, Bronco	32x11.50	33x12.50 (4)	35x12.50 (4)	35x12.50 (4)[1]
		35x12.50 (6)		35x12.50 (2)[3]
'80–'88 F-250/350 (TTB)	33x12.50	36x15 (6)	35x12.50 (2)	35x12.50 (0)[2]
		38.5x15 (6)	40x17 (4)	40x17 (4)[2]
'83–'92 Ranger/Bronco II	225/75-15	235/75 (1.5)	30x9.50 (1.5)	-
		31x10.50 (4)	32x11.50 (3)	
		32x11.50 (4)	33x12.50 (4)	
			35x12.50 (6)	
'93–'97 Ranger	31x10.50	32x11.50 (4)	33x12.50 (4)	-
			35x12.50 (6)	
'73–'79 F-250	33x12.50	35x12.50 (4)	35x12.50 (2)	35x12.50 (0)[3]
		36x15 (4)	36x15 (6)	40x17 (4)[2]
'90–94 Explorer	235/75	30x9.50 (4)	33x12.50 (4)	-
		32x11.50 (4)		
'95–98 Explorer	235/75		31x10.50 (0)	-
'97–01 Expedition, Navigator	31x10.50		33x12.50 (3)	-
I-H Scout II				
All	31x10.50	33x12.50 (4)	33x12.50 (2.5)	35x12.50 (4)[2]

Tire Fitment Guide (continued)

Isuzu

Vehicle				
'87–'98 Pickup	215/75-15	-	-	30x9.50 [3]
'85–'91 Trooper	31x10.50			
'92–up Amigo, Trooper	265/75	32x11.50 (2)	285/75 (3)	-
	31x10.50	-	33x12.50 (3)	-

Jeep

Vehicle				
'42–'68 MB, CJ2A, CJ3A, CJ3B	30x9.50	7.50x16 (1)	-	-
		31x10.50 (1)		
		32x11.50 (2.5)		
'54–'86 CJ5, 6, 7, 8	7.50-16	32x11.50 (2.5)	33x12.50 (2.5)	33x9.50[1]
	31x10.50	33x12.50 (3)		33x12.50 (2.5)[1]
				35x12.50 (4)[3]
'87–'95 Wrangler YJ	31x10.50	32x11.50 (2.5)	-	33x12.50 (3)[1]
		33x9.50 (3)		35x12.50 (4)[1]
'96–up Wrangler TJ	31x10.50	32x11.50 (2)	-	33x12.50 (3)[1]
'84–up Cherokee XJ	30x9.50	31x10.50 (2.5)	32x11.50 (2.5)	33x12.50 (3)[1]
'63–'91 Wagoneer SJ	30x9.50	32x11.50 (3)	31x10.50	-
		33x12.50 (4)	32x12.50 (3)	-
'74–'86 J-Series PU, Cherokee Chief (wide track only)	32x11.50	33x9.50 (1.5)	33x9.50	35x12.50 (4)[1]
		33x12.50 (3)		38.5x15 (4)[3]
'93–up Grand Cherokee	30x9.50	32x11.50 (2–3)	33x12.50 (4)	-

Kia

Vehicle				
Sportage	235/85	30x9.50 (2.5)	31x10.50 (2.5)	31x10.50 (2.5)[1.5]

Land Rover

Vehicle				
'58–'86 Series II, IIA, III	245/75	33x9.50 (2.5)	33x12.50 (3)	-
	30x9.50	33x10.50 (3)		
	31x10.50			
'87–'94 Range Rover Classic	245/75	265/75 (2)	33x10.50 (3)	-
	30x9.50	31x10.50 (2)	33x12.50 (4)	-
		33x9.50 (3)		
'86–'97 Defender 90/110	286/75	33x12.50 (2.5)	36x15.50 (4)	-
	32x11.50	35x12.50 (4)		

Nissan

Vehicle				
'86–'95 Pickup	30x9.50	32x11.50 (2)	33x12.50 (4)	33x12.50 (4)[3]
	31x10.50	33x10.50 (4)		

Suzuki

Vehicle				
Samurai	235/85	30x9.50 (2)	32x11.50 (3)	-
		31x10.50 (3)		
Sidekick/ GeoTracker	205/75	235/85 (1.5)	-	31x10.50 (2.5)[3]

Toyota

Vehicle				
'60–'83 FJ-40	31x10.50	32x11.50 (1.5)	-	-
		33x12.50 (3)		
'79–'85 pickup	32x11.50	33x12.50 (3)	33x12.50 (3)	35x12.50 (3)[1]
		35x12.50 (6)	35x12.50 (4)	
'86–up pickup, Tacoma	31x10.50	32x11.50 (2)	32x11.50 (0)	-
			35x12.50 (4)	-
T-100	31x10.50	32x11.50 (1.5)	-	-
		33x12.50 (3)		
'90–'97 4Runner	31x10.50	32x11.50 (2)	32x11.50 (0)	-
		33x12.50 (3)		

Here's a very cost-effective tire upgrade that offers performance in between the stock tires and the monster meats. BF Goodrich makes a 33x9.50-15 tire (in both an All Terrain—shown here—and a Mud Terrain) and it will fit on a standard rim. It offers about an inch of increased tread width over the factory tire (a 215/75R-15). When aired down it will offer a sizable increase in footprint over the stock tire and is over 5 inches taller. The best part about this tire is that it will fit with a moderate lift. It appears that this Wrangler has been lifted via longer shackles alone, not the best choice in lift options, which indicates a lift of only about an inch. It appears to have plenty of clearance for the tires. A potential advantage of a moderate setup such as this is that these tires are somewhat self-limiting in the traction area due to their moderate footprint. If the vehicle has some weak links in the drivetrain, this could help prevent breakage.

of going from a 28-inch-tall tire to a 30-inch-tall tire is like trading 3.54 gears in for 3.31s. If you have a low-powered rig for its weight, or a rig with exceptionally tall axle gearing, you may find that a 10-percent increase in diameter causes an unacceptable loss of performance. Powerful vehicles with a low torque/weight ratio may be able to accept more than a 10-percent change, if they have the room to fit the tires.

Changes in diameter of more than 15 percent should come with an evaluation of the drivetrain. Stress on the drivetrain, the axle shafts especially, increases with larger tires. In many cases, these pieces may prove to be adequate for a mild increase, but not always. Much depends on intended use. Mild four-wheeling will increase the chances that a marginal combination of tire size and axle strength will survive.

When it comes to actually fitting the tires to the vehicle, the main thing to remember is that it's an inexact science. The first impediment is that tire manufacturers all build to a slightly different standard, and even among tires with the same rated size, one tire's mounted dimensions will not be the exact same size as another's. This means you to have to get the actual mounted dimensions of the tires from each manufacturer for comparison.

Don't ask me to explain why, but one manufacturer's 31x10.50-15 tire may be 30.8 inches tall when mounted and another might be 30.3 inches. It's a simple fact that can mean one tire rubs and another doesn't. Ultimately, lifts are required to fit most significant tire upgrades.

The tire-fitting guide on pages 101 and 102 is a compilation of information gleaned from suspension manufacturers and four-wheel-drive shops. Remember that it's a *guide,* and not engraved in stone. It offers you a starting place, but the final test will be a trial fit. If you can make an arrangement with a tire shop to test fit the tires you want, so much the better.

Tire Tread Designs

As far as tread designs go, you have to pick your poison and stick with it or buy more than one set of tires! There are four basic tread types available, with a few subclasses. They are generally biased toward stellar performance in one area, but a careful choice will give you a tire that will be great for your particular environment and generally OK when you stray from it.

Highway Tread- This your ordinary passenger-car tire and is designed with pavement in mind. A subclass would be *All-Season* tires, which are tires

The perennial favorite for the trail crowd is the so-called "mudder." There was a time when an aggressive tire such as this Goodyear was only for the hard-core enthusiast. Tread design has progressed to the point where they are good all-rounders for the trail. They are still less than ideal for certain street environments, namely ice and snow, but they are not terrible in day-to-day use.

TRAIL ENDERS

Mudders and Ice:
Some MTs can be positively dangerous in ice, so if this is a regular part of your scene, think long and hard before running an MT tire on your rig.

Like the mudder, the so-called all-terrain tire has advanced. Where it was once a distant second in the trail environment, across the board, all-terrain tires have closed the gap. They remain a good choice for people who spend a lot of time on the street but still want a tire with some trail performance. This one is a BFG that wears its category as a name.

specially designed to perform better in inclement weather. These are potentially more useful to the 4x4 owner who doesn't hit the trail much. Another subclass would be *performance tires,* dedicated to cornering and braking performance. Highway tires often lack the robust construction qualities needed for the trail.

All-Terrain Tread- Even though BF Goodrich makes a tire of this name,

the term has come to represent a tire that is designed to perform well in a variety of off-highway conditions, as well as on the highway. The closed-tread design is usually quiet on the highway, though noisier than a street tire, but it performs well in rocks, sand, and on the highway. They are generally decent rain, snow, and ice tires also. As you would guess, they tend to load up in mud, but some of the AT designs are surprisingly good in the goo. An AT tire would be outstanding for a driver who mostly drives on the highway but wants acceptable trail performance.

Mud Tread- Mud tires come in a variety of styles, from the old bias-ply mudders that give new meaning to the term road noise, to modern radial mud designs that are surprisingly quiet and docile in other elements. As a rule, the radial MT designs are the weapon of choice for most four-wheelers. Their aggressive good looks play a part, but beyond their obvious attributes in soft stuff, they are generally outstanding in rocks of all types and good in deep snow. The MT is not good in rain and is worst on ice.

Snow Tires- Contrary to old myths, a good snow tire is not an open-lugged design similar to a mud tire. It is moderately open so that it can clean itself, but the tread design is close enough to compress the snow inside the tread and use its cohesion to supply traction. Snow tires also use sipes to aid in ice and wet traction situations. Often, the rubber compound is changed in a snow tire to offer better ice traction. Some snow tires are studded, though studs are not legal in every state. The metals studs actually dig into the ice for traction. There are mud- and snow (M&S)-rated tires of many types that are essentially standard tires reengineered enough to pass the DOT's requirements, and then there are all-out, full-gonzo winter tires, like the Bridgestone Blizzak.

Forgotten Tire: The Spare

A major aspect of tire upgrades—and one that is often overlooked—is the spare. You can mount the new meats easily onto the vehicle, only to find the spot designed for the spare won't carry the new-sized tire. The cure for this could entail relocating the spare to another location, such as an aftermarket swing-away tire carrier or a bed-mounted location. With some rigs, this can really be a can-o-worms because of the lack of availability for such items or the physical impossibility of using them.

Some owners in the "where-the-spare" pickle will go the roof rack route, and mount a spare up there. That's a reasonable solution, but I don't like the idea of the raised center of gravity. Other folks just ignore the problem and run with the OE spare. That can be a terrible solution if your rig has one of those tiny short-term spares, and only a bad one for the OE full-sized spare. It depends on the difference in diameter between the spare and the rest of the tires. Having a radically shorter tire is as hard on the drivetrain as having a different ratio on one side than the other. It will really fritz lockers, full-time four-wheel-drive systems, and traction control systems, because one wheel will be turning at a different speed than the others.

A spare to match the tires on the ground is important from the getting-home standpoint as well. A marginal tire reduces your traction by a significant amount. If you are stuck in a situation such as this, make sure your primary traction axle, most likely the rear, has the best tires, even if you have to do a front-to-back tire rotation.

Speedometer Correction

Speedo correction will likely be necessary with a tire swap. One correction method for mechanical speedometers is to determine overall ratio with the setup you built, compare the overall ratio to those offered by the factory, and look for a new speedo drive gear that was used on those rigs. Speedometer shops also have a correction device available with assorted ratios than can be calibrated to your particular rig. If you have an electronic speedo, there are electronic corrections available via reprogramming the ECU. There are also corrective electronic devices for popular applications that can be added, such as SuperLift's TruSpeed device. It can be calibrated to correct the speedo for nearly any tire-and-axle ratio combination. Ultimately, you can simply determine your error, post it on the dash somewhere, and hope you don't forget (particularly if you are discussing the situation with an understanding police officer). In some cases, correcting the speedometer is vital to late-model engine management systems, and not doing so can cause no end of drivability problems.

Wheels

Choosing a wheel seems like a no-brainer and subject more to looks and taste than anything else. No tso! While looks are a part of the choice, function must be the first consideration. There are thousands of cosmetic choices, but only a few functional ones. They boil down to size (dictated mostly by the tire size), offset, and material.

Original-equipment applications often involve a steel wheel with a stamped-steel center welded to a rolled-steel outer rim. The advantage of steel wheels is that they are strong, easily repaired, and cheap. There's nothing wrong with using a stock wheel if it will fit your new tires. The

The back side of an alloy wheel will usually list its rated load capacity and maximum pressure. Obviously, you wouldn't want a set of wheels not rated for your rig's GVW.

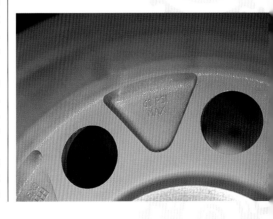

A steel wheel combines strength, low cost, and reparability. The single downside is weight. With big tires that are also heavy, the combined weight of the rotating mass tends to slow acceleration and decrease braking efficiency. The heavy wheel can also be a factor in drivetrain durability. None of these become huge factors until the tires themselves become huge. This is not a beadlocked wheel, by the way. It's a wheel from ProComp called the "Street-Lock," which has the gnarly appearance of a beadlock without the harsh realities. The extra material on the outer rim actually seems to be good protection against rock damage.

ROCK TALK

Negative Offset:

Negative offset means that the wheel's centerline is farther away from the center of the vehicle than the mounting flange. Deep-dish wheels have negative offset.

Backspacing is a very important consideration. Stay as close as you can to the OE backspace. If you increase rim width, add the width to both sides of the wheel to keep the centerline of the wheel on the original spot. If you do not, turning radius is affected, as well as wheel bearing life and steering effort. Measuring backspacing is a simple as this.

disadvantages to steel wheels are mostly in the performance area. A vehicle equipped with light alloy wheels will accelerate noticeably faster and stop shorter than a vehicle with ordinary steel wheels, since there is less rotating mass to start in motion or stop.

One-piece alloy wheels are the most commonly seen alloy type on 4x4s. The two-piece, or modular, wheels are too delicate and shouldn't be used. Forged alloys are the brutes of the alloy wheel realm. A cast- or forged-aluminum alloy wheel can weigh 30 percent less than an OE-style steel wheel and 50 percent less than some heavy-duty steel wheels. Both the forged and cast wheels are tough and generally repairable, but they can be made unsightly by the rigors of the trail fairly quickly.

Choosing the Right Wheel

In general, the rim diameter will stay the same during a tire swap, but the rim width is dictated by the size of tire being installed. For each tire, the manufacturer will list a rim width range. It's best to stay within this recommendation.

Wheel offset, or backspacing, is a critical dimension. These are two common terms used when discussing the orientation of the wheel rim (where the tire mounts) to the mounting flange (where it bolts to the hub). The centerline is the dead center of the rim. The mounting flange may or may not be on the centerline. If the centerline is offset to the outside (away from the axle), the mounting flange moves to the inside and the wheel has negative offset. If the centerline is to the inside, it's called positive offset. Backspacing is the distance from the inside of the rim to the mounting flange.

The first step is to determine the backspace needed. The stock wheels can give you an indicator of where the factory had things set up. If you need to, lay the wheel face down with a straightedge across the rim and measure down to the mounting flange to determine the backspace.

The OEM designs the wheel so that the load is placed evenly over the wheel bearings. Altering these dimensions radically can cause premature bearing wear, unwelcome changes in steering geometry that increase your turning radius, increased steering effort, and extra load on the ball joints or king pins. If you need a wider rim, the best option is to increase rim width by adding the extra equally on each side and keeping the centerline in more or less the stock location. If the OE rim were 7 inches, for example, with a 5-1/2-inch backspace, going to an 8-inch rim with a 6-inch backspace would keep the centerline exactly to stock specs. Interference between inner fenders, springs, and so on may make this impossible, so you just have to do the best you can. You may even have to limit your tire size to what will fit without a major compromise.

The next item is to find a wheel that is rated for the load you will carry. DOT requires the max load to be shown on aftermarket wheels. That rating, times four, is your maximum permissible gross vehicle weight.

Beadlocks

These devices physically lock the outer tire bead to the rim so it can be run at extremely low pressures. Are they necessary? To the die-hard gear grinder who runs the hard-core trails in a specially prepped rig aired down to practically nothing, perhaps. The average 'wheeler in a dual-purpose machine would probably find them an unnecessary expense. He may also find them a pain in the butt. Beadlocked wheels are often very difficult to balance. I don't know of any that are DOT approved for street use. I recommend against them for all but the most extreme four-wheelers who do not regularly drive their rigs on the street.

SUSPENSION MODS, LIFTS, AND BODY LIFTS

A "mild" suspension lift would be no more than 2-1/2 inches on SWB rigs and up to 4 inches on larger pickups and SUVs. Adverse effects would be few, but many rigs achieve a startling transformation. They can carry larger tires, get better articulation, and suffer only a minimal loss of street drivability. There are also modifications you can make to non-lifted rigs that can enhance trail performance.

Choosing Shocks

If you are buying a suspension kit, the shocks are usually included. Does this mean they are the best ones for your situation? Not always. Sometimes it pays to look at the upgrades available, or seek your own. If you are upgrading the shocks from a lift kit, be sure to match the required extended and compressed lengths needed for the lifted rig.

As to the type of shock, the need can be divided by slow movers, fast movers, and rigs that are mostly stock and run on the street. Slow movers are the rockcrawler types. They stay away from high-pressure gas shocks because they can cost some suspension flexibility. A good compromise can be had with shocks that use cellular gas or foam. Another good compromise is adjustable shocks. They offer the flexibility to dial-in the dampening for street or trail use.

Fast movers could include those owners who primarily run desert tracks or milder trails where you can get up some speed for more than just a short stretch. For these folks, low-pressure gas shocks are a better choice to deal with the heat and foaming that comes from taking a bumpy road at speed. If you are a very fast mover, high-pressure gas or even remote-reservoir shocks may be your ticket. If your truck is to remain fairly stock, or will spend most of its time on the highway, then some of the trick, self-adjusting units are a good choice. Low-pressure gas is always a good choice for stock or mildly built rigs.

As to quality, there are some hallmarks to watch for. Among the commonly touted shock specs are piston and piston rod size. In this case, bigger is better with the larger piston running cooler and dampening better. A variety of seal materials are used, from simple neoprene to Teflon to more exotic materials such as Nitrile. The durability of the seal is vital to shock life.

A larger shaft is stronger, though the material it is made from will play a part. They range from cast or sintered iron, to induction-hardened steel, to silicon bronze. The best shafts are made from forged steel and machined to a microfinish. The shaft is usually chrome plated, and the quality of this work will help determine how long the shock will last. Once the shock loses pressure and oil, it's history.

Some shocks have eyes on both ends or on just one end. Either way, the quality of the welding will dictate how long that eye stays attached in tough situations. Cheap shocks are attached by a couple of spot welds. Better shocks are continuous- or double-welded for more strength.

Sway bar disconnects allow for the best possible handling on the street when connected, but the most articulation on the trail when disconnected. When used with a lift kit, the disconnects must be longer by the amount of the lift. This would hold true for the normal sway bar links as well. Disconnects sometimes come with lift kits.

Shown here is too much body lift. This is at least 3 inches and look how the mount is tilted and tweaked. A very rigid chassis is needed to make a 3-inch body lift practical for rigs used on the trail. It's best to keep body lifts no taller than 2 inches and to use them mainly for final correction of tire fit problems.

Sway Bar Disconnects

When weight transfer in cornering causes the vehicle to lean, the sway bar tries to keep the body level. You could look at it two ways—it either jacks the low side up or pulls the high side down. While the sway bar is great for pavement handling, it does restrict suspension articulation on the trail.

Over the past few years, several companies have developed sway bar disconnects. With the pull of a pin, you can unhook the sway bar from the axle and gain an instant increase in articulation. That keeps the tires on the ground better for improved traction. When you get back to the pavement, a few minutes will have you hooked back up for good handling. They are very effective and useful for some rigs and less so with others. Solid-axle rigs benefit the most. How much articulation you can gain is partially limited by your vehicle's suspension travel.

Choosing a Lift Kit

Lifts are accomplished various ways, depending on suspension type. We will deal with the mild forms of lift in this chapter, but if you are interested in more radical methods, flip to chapter 8. In recent years, some states have imposed lift laws that limit or regulate the amount of lift you are allowed to use. Research before you buy.

Leaf Spring Lifts

For leaf spring rigs, the front lift is always done with new springs that are longer and have more arch than the originals. With heavily arched leaf springs, uptravel must be restricted to prevent reverse-arching the spring, which could damage it, so a bump stop extension may be included. That's the downside to highly arched springs: they lose flexibility. A more mildly arched spring (less lift), however, may be able to use much of its newly gained uptravel, assuming the larger tires you also selected don't hit anywhere.

In the rear, leaf spring lifts are done with new springs

when the spring is mounted under the axle (a.k.a. spring under) but are often done via lift blocks on pickups and full-sized SUVs where the spring is mounted above the axle (a.k.a. spring over). The lift is equal to the thickness of the block. As the name implies, a lift block is a steel or aluminum block that's inserted between the spring and the axle perch. It requires longer u-bolts. Their main advantage is low cost and simplicity, but by retaining the OE spring, you are retaining stock ride and articulation. At low lifts, they work well, but at higher lifts spring wrap can be a problem.

Add-a-leaf products are offered by most aftermarket suspension manu-facturers. This is another very inex-pensive method to acquire lift, though the amount of lift available is less. With some small variations, they all involve adding a single, heavily arched leaf to your existing leaf pack. It can raise the suspension 1 to 1.5 inches with a corresponding increase in spring rate—which may not be at all desirable.

You will see some 4x4s lifted with longer spring shackles. This is a poor way of doing it. Shackle changes may be necessary with a lift, but they are best used for minor suspension geom-etry correction purposes than for true lift. If used only for lift, they can

adversely affect geometry. Shackles will add lift, but only to half of their actual length. If you put on a shackle that is 2 inches longer than stock, you only gain 1 inch of lift because you are lifting only one end of the spring.

Coil Spring Lifts

Coil spring rigs with solid axles are lifted by either longer springs or by spacers placed on top of the springs. A longer shock or a shock extension is also used. With a mild lift, a spacer is acceptable.

A leaf spring lift block can be used only on rigs that are in spring-over configuration, either factory or conversion, and only on the rear. The thickness of the block equals the thickness of the lift. The extra leverage of the block tends to increase spring wrap, especially on light-duty springs. Lift blocks seem to be the most trouble-free on trucks with stiff springs, but a 4-inch block is about the limit. A block can be combined with lifted springs as well, such as a 4-inch lift spring with a 2-inch block for a total 6-inch lift.

TRAIL ENDERS

Lift Blocks:
Some leaf-sprung pickups use spring-over front axles, but never, ever use blocks up front due to spring wrap and the dangerous possibility of the u-bolts working loose.

the dirt

Add-a-Leaf:
An add-a-leaf can be used to bolster sagging springs. Usually it's a pretty hefty leaf, but the versions with a longer, thinner leaf provide a better ride than the short, very thick ones.

the dirt

Coil Spring Lifts:
Suspension geometry is not always an issue with mild, solid-axle, coil spring lifts, but in some cases, new suspension links (a.k.a. radius arms, trailing arms) are necessary. This is what can make a coil spring lift complicated or expensive.

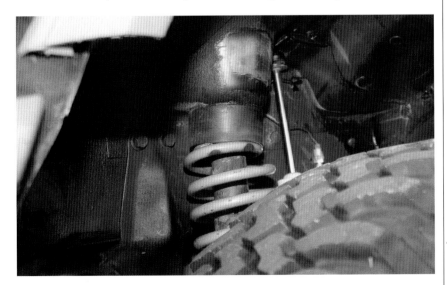

If used only for a moderate amount of lift, coil spring spacers are viable choices for those rigs that can use them. This includes the coil-spring Jeeps and Land Rovers. One to two inches of lift from this method is OK.

An IFS lift kit uses brackets to lower the entire suspension. This retains the original suspension geometry, for the most part. Front driveshaft angles become an issue because the differential is lowered. This is a kit designed for a 1990s Chevy IFS truck. *Courtesy Rancho*

Driveshaft angles are critical at every lift level, but especially so with short-wheelbase rigs. Even a mild lift can be a problem if your rear driveshaft is less than 24 inches long. Level one of the fix would be a CV joint, though in some cases the shaft may not be long enough to use a CV. In that case, the answer is either relocating the t-case forward or shortening up the transfer case with a short tailshaft conversion. In addition to a CV rear driveshaft, this rig uses a high-pinion Dana 60 differential—normally used up front—which raises the driveshaft several inches. It's an expensive answer. The upside is that you solve the driveshaft problem and end up with some beefy 35-spline rear axle shafts. On the downside are the cost, the extra weight, and loss of clearance. Running the differential at reverse its normal rotation costs some strength (20–30 percent), but a Jeep such as this is probably OK with an axle of Dana 44 strength; the reverse-cut Dana 60 is above that.

The suspension links are designed to offer specific steer and axle geometry. When a longer spring is installed, the angle is increased, effectively shortening the eye-to-eye distance of the arm, relocating the axle, and changing caster and pinion angle. To correct this, longer and reshaped control arms, or corrective brackets, must be used to bring the suspension geometry back to normal.

IFS Lifts

The only real gain with most IFS kits is lift for bigger tires, and there are usually no performance improvements, such as the increased articulation you might gain from a solid-axle lift. The IFS rigs are usually more limited in tire size, not so much by available lifts but by the strength of the front drivetrain components, which is considerably less than most solid axles used on vehicles in the same category. Some kits involve cutting original bracketry from the chassis, leaving them more difficult to convert back to stock specs.

IFS lift kits share some common characteristics. First, they usually lower the entire suspension assembly and differential to obtain the majority of the lift. This is a plus as it retains the original alignment of the suspension. When evaluating a kit, pay special attention to the way these brackets are built. Since they support the vehicle, they become the source of continued life for the occupants.

Some kits also use whatever extra lift they can gain from jacking up the torsion bars. This increases the angle on the front CV axle shafts. Just like with driveshaft U-joints, the "Rzeppa"-style CV joints have a maximum and an ideal operating angularity. Life and strength are reduced when they are operated out of their best ranges. Angularity is complicated on the outer CV by the need to steer, which imparts an even more complicated set of angles onto the joint. The rear of IFS trucks is usually leaf sprung, so all the tricks shown in the leaf spring sections apply.

Suspension Lift Complications

With almost any amount of lift, there are complications not directly

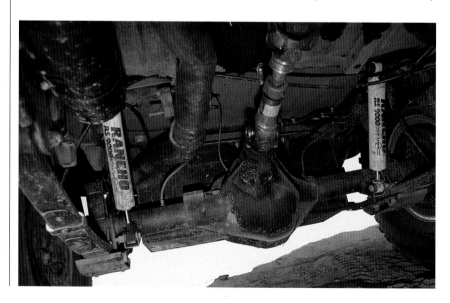

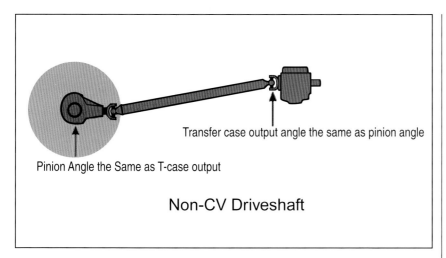

Pinion Angle the Same as T-case output

Transfer case output angle the same as pinion angle

Non-CV Driveshaft

Many 4x4s come with non-CV–type driveshafts. When lifts are performed, it's vital to keep the pinion angle and t-case output angle identical to avoid vibration. There are no bad effects until driveshaft angularity is increased to the point that U-joint life is affected. One hundred percent U-joint life is possible at angles of up to 3 degrees, but as that angle increases, service life declines. At 15 degrees, life is reduced to 25 percent of normal service. As driveshaft angles near or exceed 8 degrees, it's time to start thinking about a CV-type driveshaft.

related to the suspension. The first of these would be driveshafts. One major effect of lifting or lowering any vehicle is a change of driveshaft and pinion angles, as well as driveshaft length. Changing the operating angles of the driveshaft universal joints can have many negative effects, the mildest of which is vibration and a shorter life.

The two universal joints, or U-joints, on each driveshaft should both operate at the same angle and at the same speed. That means the pinion end of the differential and the transmission/transfer case output must be parallel on two planes. If not, then one universal is operating at a slightly higher or lower speed than the other and vibration is the result. The greater the difference, the greater the vibration. A difference of 3 degrees or less is usually regarded as "in the ballpark," though some rigs are very sensitive to any variation. The axle is the easiest place to make corrections. On leaf-sprung rigs, tapered shims are fitted between the spring perch and the spring. On coilers, the correction can sometimes be done via adjustable or offset control arm bushings, or adjustable control arms.

Driveshaft angle, or more specifically universal joint operating angle, becomes a problem, especially with short-wheelbase rigs. The driveshaft angle increases more per inch of lift the shorter the driveshaft. The maximum angularity for most U-joints is

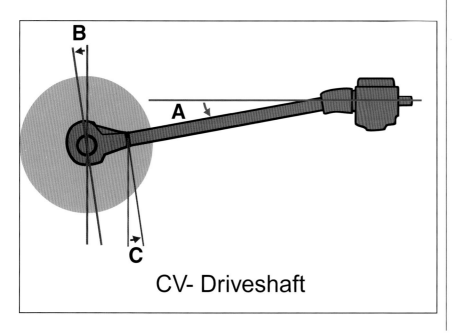

CV- Driveshaft

With a CV joint–type driveshaft, the driveshaft angle is split by the two universal joints contained in the CV joint. The difference between this setup and the standard driveshaft is that the pinion angle (B) must be altered until the rear U-joint angle (C) is within 1 or 2 degrees of the driveshaft angle.

about 30 degrees. This is a short-term maximum number. Continuous angularity is rated at 15 degrees for most universals, and service life will be cut by 75 percent at this angle. One cure for rear driveshaft angularity problems is a CV joint. More accurately called a Double-Cardan, the CV takes two standard U-joints and couples them together with a housing that has a centering device. If you have a 20-degree angle, the CV essentially splits this between the two joints, giving them 10 degrees each, well within their operating range. If you want long U-joint life, start thinking about installing one when your operating angle reaches 8 degrees. Many front driveshafts are already CV-joint equipped.

Up front, you run into more problems than just driveshaft angles. Any alterations made to the pinion angle to correct driveshaft angle or U-joint angles will change caster angles. Since caster affects straight-line tracking and braking performance, it's important to keep it within an acceptable range. Pinion angle and caster are inexorably tied together. If you change one then you will change the other, and the only way to alter this relationship is by rotating the axle tubes inside the diff case.

Bear in mind that your pinion angle changes with suspension movement or by the torque effect of the axle (solid axles only). The rear pinion will climb under a torque load and the front will drop. If this occurs at low driveshaft speeds, it isn't much of a problem because the U-joint can deal with the extra angularity while going slowly. If you happen to be spinning the wheels or are in a high gear with the drivetrain turning at a higher speed, it's a different deal and U-joint failure is possible.

Body Lifts

On vehicles that have a separate body and chassis, small pucks can be inserted between the chassis and the body to lift the body off the chassis. This allows for extra clearance in the fenderwells for larger tires. It's an

acceptable and cost-effective means of fitting larger tires if not used to extremes. What's extreme? That's somewhat variable according to the vehicle and who you speak with. If you talk to me, I'll tell you that 3 inches is max and less is better. The part that spooks me is the extra leverage on the longer bolts. When the chassis flexes, it can tear out body mounts or snap mounting bolts, a possibility that increases with the body lift height. My opinion is based on actually using the truck on the trail. Some guys get away with tall body lifts because they don't hit the trail much.

Body lift pucks come in various materials, from a high-strength plastic to Delrin (a derivative of polyurethane) to metal. Within limits, they are all OK. I have seen the plastic pucks break and I have seen dissimilar-metal corrosion problems with aluminum pucks on steel bolts. The former case is unusual and the latter situation can be remedied with a coating of antiseize compound between the bolt and the puck.

Body lifts are best used for corrective purposes, that is, to gain that last inch of clearance needed for the new tires in conjunction with other modifications. It's a good alternative for IFS vehicles needing a little extra room in the wheelwells.

DRIVETRAIN

At the basic level, with stock or near-stock gearing and only a moderate increase in tire size, most of your concerns are with traction. OE drivetrains are generally (but not always) safe to about a 15 percent increase in tire size, or more, and that puts most of the harder-core upgrades into the advanced buildups chapter further on. Still, there are some durability aspects to consider apart from major upgrades.

Upgrade As You Break?

As a precursor to all of the other drivetrain stuff you will read in this chapter and in later ones, let's discuss the "upgrade as you break" option. Let's say that you snap a rear axle in your largely stock rig. Let's also say that there is an alloy replacement available that's 20 percent stronger than stock. Why not replace what you break with better parts? Of course, you'd need to replace both axles in that case, but you've substantially increased that system's durability. In the case of an axle shaft, the alloy unit may only be a slight to moderate increase in cost over a bolt-in replacement. And if you're paying labor costs anyway, why not apply them to stronger parts?

Automatic Transmission Upgrades

Trail work can cause your 4x4's automatic transmission to generate massive amounts of heat. That tendency is increased with heavy loads, tall gears, and more difficult terrain. Overheated oil may go unnoticed in most OE rigs because they do not have trans fluid temp gauges. A few have a warning light. The risk of damage presented by overheating makes a tranny temp gauge one of your first trail upgrades if you have an automatic.

With the gauge installed, you can monitor trans temp during your heaviest-duty wheeling. Ideal temps are below 200 degrees at all times. Hot tranny oil can be cooled by stopping, putting the tranny into neutral, and fast-idling the engine at about 1,000 rpm for a while. If you find yourself in the red zone often, then an auxiliary cooler is in order.

Where to monitor temperature is the big question. Most gauge kits offer an inline sensor that mounts in one of the trans cooler oil lines. Mounting it in the return line (oil going back to the trans from the cooler) tells you how effectively your coolers are working, and this return oil is most often used to lubricate the "hard" parts of the transmission, so cool oil is vital. This is the second-best place to monitor trans oil temp. The ideal spot is the transmission oil pan, since this is the holding area for a major volume of oil used for all purposes. Installing a plug for a sensor in

the oil pan is more difficult and complicated than an inline sensor.

As for coolers, an oil-to-air cooler can knock off a good deal of heat. If you live in a warm climate, mount the new cooler so that the radiator (oil-to-water) cooler outlet feeds into the oil-to-air unit and then returns back to the transmission. If you live in a consistently cool or cold climate, reverse this so the outgoing oil from the trans enters the oil-to-air cooler first and then feeds back into the radiator cooler. This prevents overcooling, which is also detrimental over the long term.

I did some tests and found that the factory radiator oil cooler on my old Blazer could knock at least 40 degrees off trans oil temp. With a medium-sized oil-to-air cooler, another 50 degrees of capacity was added, though bear in mind that an oil-to-air cooler's efficiency is relative to ambient air temp and airflow. It is more efficient on cooler days and with more airflow.

Traction-Aiding Differentials

The most logical first step here is a rear limited slip or locker. A "loose" limited slip or an on-demand locker meets the demands of day-to-day driving. A limited slip with really smooth characteristics on the street, however, would be easily overcome in rough terrain. In mild terrain, especially where traction is relatively even for both tires (no lifted tires, radical side-to-side weight transfer, or one tire on solid ground and the other in goo), a limited slip would be an acceptable choice. Brake-pedal modulation to encourage lockup would be a useful technique in this case. In addition, a set of wider, stickier tires would be an asset, holding off tire slip as long as possible.

There is an option that fits below the on-demand locker in terms of cost and complexity but with better performance than a limited slip. TracTech's nearly seamless Gearless unit (as mentioned in chapter 2) is a viable option and gets very near to a true 100 percent lockup, especially with moderation in tire-size selection.

Tranny Oil Temps:
The 250-degree mark is the hottest your transmission should ever be allowed to attain. At that temp, the oil is beginning to seriously degrade and, if ignored, may result in shortened tranny life or immediate failure.

Cool Automatics:
Beyond an auxiliary transmission-oil cooler, an upgrade to synthetic transmission fluid can help your transmission survive longer at high temps because it does not break down as quickly and has a higher temperature rating.

The fuel tank is a vulnerable spot that either isn't protected on OE rigs, or is protected by just a thin piece of sheet metal. It doesn't help when it's hung way out the back. All Custom Fabrications builds this major fuel-tank guard, which encloses the tank completely.

the dirt

Front Axle Weak Links:
Up front, the axle universal joints and sometimes the locking hubs are weak points on solid-axle rigs. For IFS-equipped vehicles, the CV joints may be the first item to go. Other weak links would include the CAD axle disconnect devices on both solid and IFS front axles, not so much from breakage as engagement problems.

There are no serious downsides to this unit in the short term, but because it uses clutches, its performance will degrade with time and use as the clutch plates wear. This is also true of any clutch-type limited slip. Eaton's Command Traxx units are another viable option in the same vein, though they use more durable carbon fiber clutches.

Not much can beat an on-demand locker when it comes to performance.

They are totally transparent on the street but give you a 100 percent lock-up when you need it on the trail. This locker would be the more expensive option and its complexity leaves it a bit more vulnerable to glitches, but the idea offers lots of bang-for-buck. If it were an ARB Air Locker, which uses a small electric air compressor, your tire airing-up needs might be addressed as well.

The rocker panels are one of the universal areas of vulnerability that should be addressed by anyone traveling where rocks can bite. The "rock sliders" on this Cherokee have prevented major damage in this case.

If cost is the bottom line for you, there are a number of relatively inexpensive options, such as Power Trax's line of Lock-Right Lockers, and the TracTech EZ Locker. It all comes down to your wallet and your willingness to live with cranky manners.

Axle Upgrades

The main weak points for many axles are the axle shafts and the differential parts (carrier, side gears, spider gears). This applies to the front or rear, but since the rear is the most heavily loaded of the two, a weak axle shaft will be at great stress in the rear.

In the case of vacuum-actuated CAD devices (many older Jeeps, GM S-10), it's mostly a case of keeping the hoses connected, leak-free, and protected from damage. For the thermally or servo motor–activated units (IFS-equipped, full-sized GM products and others), the situation is more dire. They're unreliable and it's very common to experience problems getting the unit to engage, or to remain engaged. Not having the front axle engaged can ruin your four-wheeling day.

The aftermarket has responded with two devices. Vacuum-operated devices are available from Rancho and Warn. These are both adequate, but when the vacuum bleeds off, the units will disengage. The most beef in this area is the 4x4 Posi-Lok.. This is a cable-operated mechanical device that is fully-by-God-locked, and stays that way, when the driver actuates the control. These units are available for both the S-Series rigs and the big trucks.

ARMOR

With minimal ground clearance, some well-chosen armor is an investment in keeping your four-by looking good. What you actually need depends on the particular vehicle you drive. The most vulnerable areas typically are the rocker panels and the rear-mounted fuel tank, followed closely by the rear quarter panels, the transfer case, and the front diff housing. Remember that gnarly-looking brush bars, nerf bars, and the like are popular visual enhancements, but offer little real protection. They're good for one hit—perhaps not even that. My advice is to opt for more substantial items.

ENGINE

Unless you drive a heavy rig with a small engine, you are probably adequately powered for the trail. The engine is usually the last place to spend your four-wheeling dollars. More power is the American way, I know, but more than an adequate amount is of no real benefit on the trail in most cases. Most trail power problems are due to tall gearing, anyway. There's a lot to talk about with engine performance, but I'll leave that to other books.

For most late-model, fuel-injected engines, there is little to be done, other than a few waterproofing tips outlined in the next section. If your trip will take you to an elevation above 3,500 feet for any length of time, I would recommend that you adjust the ignition timing for that altitude. To keep the engine running at some semblance of normal power at higher altitudes, the timing is usually advanced 1 or 2 degrees for every 2,500 feet over 2,500 feet of elevation. The exact specs vary according to the manufacturer. It's important to reset the timing back immediately after returning to sea level to avoid detonation (a.k.a. "pinging"). This is a moot point for the latest rigs without a distributor. They either largely adjust themselves or must be recalibrated for altitude electronically at the dealership with computerized equipment. In any case, these newer engines seem to self-compensate for altitude more accurately than any in the past.

Carbureted engines are most in need of tuning for the trail. Angles of any significance and severe motion are the bane of carburetors. Because they have an internal float bowl, the fuel within that bowl is subject to sloshing, resulting in fuel starvation or flooding that can make the engine die, sputter,

For engines with distributors up front (Fords, many Chrysler V-8s, Land Rovers, and others), sprayback from the fan during water crossings can be a problem. This little cover is something I've seen on a number of late-model Ford engines that I think could be adapted to many distributors. Even a simple step such as this can help keep your engine running when water is splashing about.

or belch black smoke. Some carburetors are more resistant to these problems and some balk at the slightest climb, sidehill, or descent.

There are simple cures for these problems in some cases, but many times you must simply endure, or swap to an aftermarket fuel injection system. These are usually bolt-on throttle body injection systems that replace the carburetor with a throttle body device that holds two or four injectors. There is also a smaller selection of bolt-on multiport injection systems. In many cases they are emissions legal.

Engine Waterproofing

"Waterproofing" is really a misnomer. About the best you can do is make your engine water-resistant. The overall goal is to make the engine safe from a moderate amount of splash. After that, coordinate any changes with a look at other vehicle systems so that everything is safe to one level of immersion. We discussed fording requirements in some depth back in chapter 5.

The information that follows is by necessity somewhat vague. Because there are many different models and thousands of equipment variations, I can only offer general tips: I may not hit some of the more oddball situations at all. It falls upon you to capture the gist of the idea and translate it to your own rig.

Step one in the engine compartment is to address the air intake. Many newer rigs have the air intake ducted to the front, usually to one side of the radiator. In some cases this is in quite a low position. This is ideal for going down the road, but detrimental if you go diving. With most rigs, you can temporarily disconnect this duct and direct it to another location for the duration of the crossing. Definitely direct it away from the

Snorkels such as this ARB unit are useful in more ways than preventing water ingestion. They deliver cool, clean air to the engine. After some tests for a story, I determined that a TJ such as this essentially delivered warm radiator air to the engine, despite the intake duct being located to the front. Warm air lowers power output. Clean air is the other aspect. On the long, dusty, outback roads of Australia, plugged air filters are common. With a high-mounted snorkel, dust ingestion is reduced. Whether you like the looks or not is up to you. *Courtesy ARB*

fan. The ultimate cure may be a snorkel kit, but only a few applications are covered, most of them by ARB.

The next place to look is the ignition wires. Are they in good condition and do the boots at both the distributor and the spark plugs fit tightly? If additional sealing is needed, use only self-vulcanizing tape such as Pro Tape, available from Accel. RTV silicone is not useful because it does not seal to the boots or cap. The distributor cap can be sealed to the distributor with RTV. The RTV will stick to the distributor body to form a sort of gasket. Some 'wheelers have found large o-rings that work and, in fact, some caps and distributors have o-rings from the factory. Many distributors have small vent holes at the

bottom and most people advocate covering that hole. The distributor doesn't usually need venting to the atmosphere. Electronic ignition control modules are usually sealed, but the connections can be affected, so some protection from splash might be in order.

Most newer engines are completely sealed, but older engines can have filler caps, vent tubes, or dipstick tubes that may allow water to pass. Ancillary items should get a look, such as power-steering pump cap vents, vents on brake booster, EFI MAP sensors, vapor canister vents, and so on. Most of these are already splash-resistant, though if any item is mounted particularly low, a vent extension might be in order.

CHAPTER 7

GRIZZLED GEAR GRINDERS

Advanced Skills and Buildups

Extreme 'wheeling often involves steep angles and lifted tires. Sometimes, it all happens at the same time. One of the first skills is learning to be comfortable and calm in any position. Except upside down, of course!

Advanced four-wheeling is nothing more than an extension of the basics applied in more adrenaline-charged environments. For that reason, there's less to talk about and more to look at. The majority of the advanced techniques will be presented in photographic form.

Advanced terrain needs a vehicle up to the task: a built-up vehicle is absolutely necessary in the majority of cases. It's difficult to keep a stock or near-stock rig in one piece in tough environments, let alone get it through. It still comes down to traction and clearance, but getting more of those two elements requires more compromises and a greater level of commitment.

THE RISK FACTOR

At the higher levels of four-wheeling, the vehicle damage risk factors are greatly increased. That includes mechanical problems and damage. The potential for injury is also higher in some cases, but because advanced machines have better safety systems, that potential is kept relatively low. The worst consequences of even the most difficult 'wheeling is often no more than a rollover. Adequate protection in the form of a roll cage and a safety harness usually results in nothing more than a good war story and shelling out some cash for repairs.

There are extreme risk-takers in our group—those are the high-flying

four-wheelers who like to perform sidehill maneuvers at the edge of a 300-foot precipice. Some of this is done by highly skilled drivers in well-equipped rigs and sometimes by people with more raw courage than smarts. Obviously these folks are at a much greater risk, regardless of how well-built their roll cage may be. This is where free will comes in. If you are willing to face those risks for braggin' rights, so be it. Unless Osama is on my tail, you won't see this fella in those places.

More extreme terrain results in more chances for this. Truth be told, these incidents are uncommon and don't often result in human injuries worse than hurt pride. Still, one of the reasons most hard-core rigs are Spartan in style is that they are repairable. This Jeep was righted and driven the rest of the way. The sheet metal was repaired, probably with used bolt-on parts, and the rig is probably still four-wheeling somewhere. If this were a newer SUV, it would probably be a total. That's assuming you had coverage. Your insurance may not cover you in a situation such as this.

Side angles are one of the least comfortable positions that you can encounter. This driver seems supremely comfortable, with the flat ground below apparently disdained for the more drastic situation above.

Advanced driving is as much about outlook as anything—the ability to "see" the obstacle and the ways over it. It's an instinctive knowledge of the vehicle and its capabilities that comes from experience. I'm not sure it's possible to teach this in a book. That's why this chapter includes many photos with captions that explain the situation and the solution. These may be of some aid at the point of starting in advanced situations, but when it comes down to the nitty-gritty, it's confidence and practice that count. The learning will never stop until that day when you hang up your 'wheeling spurs for good.

THE ADVANCED MACHINE

The advanced 4x4 is to the OE rig what the Six Million Dollar Man is to OE humans... "better, stronger, faster," yada, yada! How a machine is built is somewhat variable according to the intended terrain. Most advanced rigs are built with all the basic performance enhancements and are designed to be useful in all types of terrain. There is also specialized equipment for specific terrain, such as a rockcrawler or a mud-bogger. Either of these machines might be useful outside of their own element, but perhaps less effective.

THE ADVANCED DRIVER

If the basic skills are the same, what puts the advanced driver ahead of the beginning or intermediate one? It's simply a matter of degree. With practice comes skill and eventually mastery. Four-wheeling is akin to mathematics. Basic addition and trigonometry are both mathematics, but at vastly different levels of difficulty. Without the basic addition down pat, you can't learn the more advanced stuff.

Never get comfortable here! Extreme rigs get into extreme pickles. This rig and driver were well equipped for calamities such as this and were on their way in a few minutes with nothing worse than a bit of scraped roll-bar paint.

Sometimes obstacles are combined with tight clearance. Wooded areas in some states combine steep climbs and big trees. The key is to have a pretty good idea of what's going to happen. This climb tended to suck the rigs toward the tree when the tires spun, so a light throttle was essential. Coming down steep wooded trails can be the yeeha ride of your life, especially if the ground is slippery.

This is almost as steep as it looks. Drivers of very short rigs, such as this CJ-3B, need to make sure that they won't nose over on the way down. The key here is to keep finely attuned and avoid any sudden brake application that would surely flip you "arse over tip" as the Brits would say. If the rear end does come up, a quick blip of the throttle should put it back down. One other cure is to have a strap attached to another rig, and it can lower you down.

Tight quarters and steep angles. This full-sized Bronco is only inches away from some custom body work. The key here is to plan the maneuvers and avoid slipping the tires. As soon as traction is lost, this rig's headed for the rock. Also, too much right rudder will run his tail into the big rock.

The only way to cross this famous Moab, Utah, crack without major tail dragging is to enter it diagonally and drop one wheel at a time. It's tough to do without a locker because many rigs pull a wheel or two, and the ones that don't unload the low wheel enough put that axle out of action. Even with a diagonal approach, rigs without really big tires or with lots of rear overhang will scrape tail, if not hang up.

The drive out may be different from the drive in. A heavy rainstorm created a flash-flood situation in an area that had been dry a few hours before. In some parts of the country, flash floods are a serious worry and can go from a trickle to a torrent in a matter of minutes. Fortunately, this one didn't get much bigger than this and everyone made it out OK.

The harsh environments are much harder on equipment. Prepare for more damage and breakage, but don't give in to the defeatist, "Ain't had fun unless sumthin' broke" philosophy, spoken by people unwilling or unable to improve their skills or equipment. Give up every dent or broken part as if it were your last dollar. Be willing to analyze every broken part and take steps to correct the situation. Was it pilot error or does something mechanical need improvement?

It often comes down to money. Are you driving in terrain beyond your budget? If you can't afford the buildup beforehand, it stands to reason that you won't be able to afford the repairs afterward on a rig that's not prepared. There are two cures to this dilemma: add more money for the buildup items, or ratchet back your four-wheeling a few notches to limit breakage.

An advanced machine doesn't have to be a trailer queen. You can build in a lot of capability and retain a safe amount of street prowess (with a sane driver, at least). If you drive to and from the trail, however, you may be frustrated by breakage or damage that strands you in a town waiting for parts, or having to rent a truck and trailer to haul the carcass home. An advanced machine driving to and

Driving across deep snow requires the utmost care. This snow was several feet deep and although the Range Rover was aired-down for floatation, it broke through the crust in a spot where recovery was difficult. This vehicle was part of the 1994 Mount Washington expedition, where several vehicles from Rovers North were the first wheeled vehicles to reach the top of Mount Washington, New Hampshire, in winter. The entire trip was a balancing act atop snow as deep as 6 feet.

Wedgie! This driver is using the sidewall of his left front tire to help pull him up and over these boulders. He couldn't quite get the tires up the far side of the boulder on the right. His rear tire has just contacted the boulder and will walk him up and around. There was a bit of contact with the body sill, but it was armored with some plate. Serious rockcrawlers often think beyond the conventional approach. Taken slowly on smooth surfaces, sidewalls are fair game.

the dirt

Tires:
The tires are your main connection to terra firma and that connection is the key to getting though any sort of advanced terrain.

from the trail needs to be better built, better driven, and better prepared than one that only has to make it back to a trailer at the trailhead.

The advanced machine is usually an adaptation of one of a few commonly available rigs. It comes down to available buildup goodies and the general suitability of the platform. Sometimes the fickle nature of popularity comes into it as well. With unlimited funds and lots of time and skill, you can build a trail monster out of most anything.

Tires

Most of what you need to know about tires was in chapter 6. There are only some conceptual things to add here. "Big" is the key word. Tall for clearance, wide for traction. You'll do what it takes to put on the maximum practical amount of rubber, and that usually

This 38.5x 14.50-15 Super Swamper is a lot of tire for a CJ-7. Though this owner tried to keep the center of gravity low by minimizing lift and maximizing fender trimming, this will be a relatively tippy Jeep. He did gain lots of clearance, however. In the terrain where this Jeep is used, mainly Arkansas and Oklahoma, these tires make sense.

An argument for beadlocks on the trail. An aired-down tire is more likely to pop off the rim at low pressures, so in hard-core situations a beadlock-type rim would have prevented this mess. The main criterion is how much street time your rig will see. In time, someone will come up with a DOT-approved beadlocked rim.

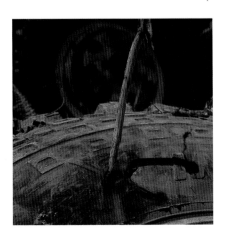

Another downside to airing down in a big way is the ease with which the sidewalls are damaged. There are times when the risk must be taken, but judge how much to air down by the terrain. An easier trip needs only a little airing down. Remember, you can always air down later if you need to.

Breaking trail in deep virgin snow is one of the most enjoyable parts of winter 'wheeling. It's also tough on vehicles. Rotate the lead rigs so that all can share the work and the fun. This Samurai poses on a fine winter morning in Utah's La Sal Mountains.

the dirt

As Gordon Lightfoot sang, "When you're caught by the gale, and full under sail, beware of the dangers below." Getting caught in a snowstorm on off-camber slickrock became a slippery experience one year at the Easter Jeep Safari. There was some slipping and sliding that earned more than a few excited comments. For some it came at a tricky moment. The big question here was to stop or to go ahead. With a better section ahead, and more snow coming, it was thought best to continue before things got worse.

There's nothing quite like a steep rock ledge with scree at the top and bottom. There isn't enough traction for a slow approach. You can see the trenches dug by the spinning tires of previous rigs. Momentum, but a light throttle, was what got this Jeeper up.

requires major upgrades in the drivetrain as well. The practicality aspect comes into play with drivability and a safe amount of lift to fit the tires. Short-wheelbase rigs require special care.

Drivetrain

A trail machine needs low gearing to compensate for the bigger tires and to improve performance. The combination of lots of torque multiplication and big, sticky tires will put major stress on drivetrain parts. Lockers are also a part of the game and one axle may have to handle *all* of the torque when weight transfer and lifted tires

STEPPING OFF

Stepping off a high, steep ledge requires careful execution if your rig is short of major clearance. Set up at a slight angle to the ledge.

Ease one tire down using the brakes and the traction from the three other tires. Manual trans rigs will be in gear with the clutch in unless they have really deep gearing.

One down, three to go.

Two down, but a pile of loose rocks ahead that may diminish braking capacity.

Three down but some holes ahead. A rig with less articulation and less articulation balance would have been very tippy at this point.

Ease that tail down as slowly as you can, even if you have armor in back, as this Toyota does.

It's a wheelbase kinda thing! Experience, sticky tires, lockers, momentum, and wheelbase enabled this full-sized Jimmy to walk to the top of Moab's notorious Pritchett Canyon's Rockpile in one shot. If you look closely, you can see the left front tire has bounded up a small ledge. This driver committed to a line and hit it, not backing off until the truck was at the top. The speed was not more than a fast walking pace and the engine barely above an idle.

This is another side effect of aired-down tires and using the sidewalls against rocks. It's unsightly, but not necessarily dangerous.

leave you with essentially one tire to push your rig up and over. You need enough beef in all components to handle these stresses.

The torque multiplication goes downhill toward the axles. If the tires slip before some drivetrain part breaks, you're safe. If not, well, there you are with some shiny scrap metal. People who 'wheel a lot in rocks will need the strongest drivetrain because there lies the best traction combined with the steepest climbs and the most weight transfer.

The transmission's job is comparatively easy. All you have to be sure of is that its torque capacity matches engine output. Depending on the gearing in the tranny, the transfer case will probably also have an easy time, though if a splitter is used between the trans and t-case, the input torque can get high. Changes in the internal gearing of a transfer case can result in transfer case output shaft failures due to torque multiplication. The load on the driveshaft and driveshaft universals is also increased by lower trans or transfer case gearing. The input load on the differential also increases in this case. In diffs that have weak pinion shafts, increased torque multiplication can result in a greater likelihood of pinion shaft breakage. For example, going from a 1.96:1 low-range ratio to a 4:1 ratio more than doubles the torque input to the diff.

Siping is a trick that offers improved traction on rocks as well as on the street in slippery conditions. Many tire shops can sipe your mud tires, but that may void the tire warranty. Some tires will "chunk," or throw off small bits of tread around the new sipes. Siping is generally a good thing. I found it measurably improved traction in rain and snow on the mudders I tested, but it was less effective on ice. It also made a big difference in rockcrawling.

Maximum Recommended Tire Sizes for Various Axles*

*For highway and moderate off-pavement use, stock engine. Equipment in good condition is presumed. If you don't see it here, it's probably not a popular unit. This was compiled via conversations with assorted industry experts, not from scientific study, so use it as a general guideline only.

AM General
AMC-20 IS	38 inches

Chrysler Corporate
AMC-20 (older Jeep), rear	33 inches
8.25-inch rear, 27 spline	31 inches
8.25-inch rear, 28 spline	33 inches
8.75-inch rear	35 inches
9.25-inch rear	35 inches

Dana
Dana 23 rear	31 inches
Dana 25 front	31 inches
Dana 27 rear	31 inches
Dana 28 IFS	31 inches
Dana 30 front, low pinion	31 inches
Dana 30 front, high pinion, small U-joint	31 inches
Dana 30 front, high-pinion, big U-joint	35 inches
Dana 30 rear	31 inches
Dana 35 IFS	33 inches
Dana 35 rear	31 inches
Dana 44 IFS	35 inches
Dana 44 front, small U-joint	31 inches
Dana 44 front, big U-joint	35 inches
Dana 44 rear	35 inches
Dana 50 IFS	38 inches
Dana 60 front	38 inches
Dana 60 rear, semi-float, 30 spline	35 inches
Dana 60 rear, full-float, 30 spline	36 inches
Dana 60 rear, semi-float, 35 spline	38 inches
Dana 60 rear, full-float, 35 spline	38 inches
Dana 70 rear	44 inches

Ford Corporate
7.5-inch rear, 28 spline	33 inches
9-inch, 28 spline	33 inches
9-inch, 31 spline	35 inches
8.8-inch, 28 spline	33 inches
8.8-inch, 35 spline	35 inches
10.25-inch, semi-float	38 inches
10.25-inch, full-float	44 inches

General Motors Corporate
7.25-inch IFS	30 inches
8.25-inch IFS	31 inches
9.25-inch IFS	33 inches
10-bolt front	35 inches
7.5-inch rear	31 inches
7.83-inch rear	33 inches
10-bolt rear, 28 spline	33 inches
10-bolt rear, 30 spline	35 inches
12-bolt rear	35 inches
14-bolt rear, semi-float	38 inches
14-bolt rear, full-float	44 inches

Isuzu
8-inch rear, 17 spline (early Trooper)	31 inches
8-inch rear, 26 spline (late Trooper, Amigo)	33 inches

Land Rover Corporate
8.5-inch, 10-spline, front or rear	31 inches
8.5-inch, 24-spline, front or rear	33 inches
9.25-inch, 24-spline (Salisbury)	33 inches

Mitsubishi
Front IFS	30 inches
Rear (small ring gear)	31 inches
Rear (large ring gear)	33 inches

Nissan
Front IFS (early)	30 inches
Front IFS (late)	31 inches
Rear, 27 spline	31 inches
Rear, 31 spline	33 inches

Suzuki
6.9-inch front and rear (Samurai)	31 inches

Toyota
7.5-inch IFS	31 inches
8-inch, front or rear	33 inches
8.25-inch rear	35 inches
9.5-inch rear (FJ-40)	35 inches
9.5-inch front (FJ-40)	33 inches

Picking lines through a sea of boulders the size of medium dogs is a tricky situation. This is why you get harped on about big tires and clearance. Without clearance, it's a bash-fest. The key is to go from one boulder to the next and put all four tires on lines that will keep the underside away from all the boulders. It's almost inevitable that a few boulders will have to be moved or positioned. This would also be a good place for a spotter.

From the pinion, torque goes to the ring gear and is multiplied by the ring and pinion ratio and transferred through the ring gear bolts to the carrier. This multiplied torque will find its way through the differential, whether it's open or locked, and into the axle shafts. The strength of the side gear and spiders, or lockers or limited slip, then comes into play. Even the carrier that holds all these pieces can be broken or distorted by too much torque. The differential housing itself is also subject to distortion from torque. Finally, the torque goes through the axle shafts and to the wheels and tires to the ground. These shafts are the final link in the mechanical chain and are taking the most abuse.

Your task is to determine just how much beef you need the whole way down from the engine and choose components that are strong enough for the job. This can be done, and I'll show you how further on, though it's a somewhat inexact science. It will give you an idea and, based on the information available in the sidebars, you can see if your current or proposed setup is close to being up to the task.

Transfer Case Beefing/Improvements

Older transfer cases were cast iron and, overall, are much stronger than the later aluminum units, but at twice the weight. The transition from iron to aluminum also marked the transition from gear to chain drive. Gear-drive, cast-iron t-cases are stronger overall, but aluminum t-cases have closed the strength gap, so don't automatically dismiss them. All the current transfer cases are aluminum, with the last all-iron units phased out by the late 1980s.

Talk about emptying the pool! This bone-stock Defender 110 driver is in a hurry and is making a bow wave the captain of the U.S.S. Missouri would be proud to see. The water is close to 3 feet deep, but this driver is getting away with an aggressive approach because the Defender, even stock, is particularly well-equipped for water.

Doors off water-wheeling can result in a bath, especially if you are in a hurry. Obviously an open rig such as this Jeep YJ will fill quickly, but drain just as quickly. In a closed rig with tight doors water may take quite a while to cover the floor, and you might get across before a significant amount comes inside. *Courtesy Ken Brubaker*

On the left is an NV-231 transfer case with a slip-yoke–type rear output. On the right is a similar NP-241 transfer case with a short tailshaft conversion. The conversion knocks quite a bit of length off the transfer case (variable according to the kit) so that longer driveshafts can be accommodated and driveshaft angles reduced with lifts. These conversions are available from several manufacturers for a small number of transfer cases built by New Process (NP), which later became New Venture (NV).

Gear-drive cases tend to be noisier than chain drive but have a longer life. A set of t-case gears will usually outlast the truck, but a hard-worked chain-drive unit may need a chain replacement at 80,000 miles.

Chain units use planetary gear sets instead of standard gears and because the dynamics of gear ratios can be built more compactly, it's easier to get lower ratios. While it's unusual to find a gear-drive transfer case with a ratio much under 2.0:1, chain-drive t-cases are at 2.61 or lower. With improved gear-cutting machinery, extralow gearsets are now available for some of the older gear-drive units, specifically in the popular Jeep Dana 18, 20, and 300 line.

In some cases, you can parts swap within certain families of transfer cases to produce a stronger unit—going to a wider "C" (Chevrolet type) chain in an NP-231J (Jeep) transfer case, for example, or swapping the early 10-spline NP-205 front output shaft with a 30-spline piece. The vast range of transfer cases that have appeared over the years make discovering swappable parts a rare event.

the dirt

Transfer Cases:
Chains usually last longer on part-time transfer cases because the chain doesn't come into play until the vehicle is shifted into four-wheel drive. The chain is operational all the time in full-time cases.

Textbook crossing: a perfect bow wave and crossing diagonal to the current. The bottom had been checked previously.

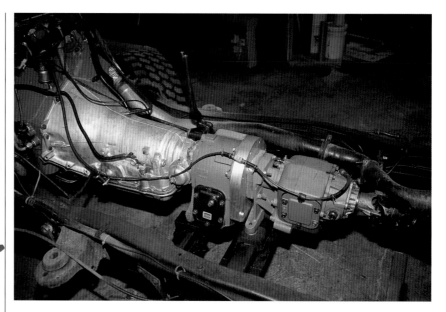

Splitters often fit between the transmission and transfer case. This is Off-Road Design's Doubler setup as installed in the author's rig. Up front is a GM 700R4 with the Double range box right behind. This cast-iron unit has a 2:1 reduction. Behind that mounts the legendary NP-205 transfer case. The NP-205 is one of the few transfer cases strong enough to handle the input of 2:1 reduction with a lot of torque to boot. The Doubler setup offers the standard 1:1 high range, 2:1 low range, or a 4:1 low-low range. In addition, the 2:1 reduction of the range box can be used in two-wheel drive. The Doubler is one of the heavy hitters in the splitter crowd, both in terms of its torque capacity and physical weight. Other splitters offer similar characteristics in lighter and more compact units.

In most cases, people who need a serious increase in strength make a swap—usually from one type of OE unit to another. Among trucks, for example, swapping out the chain-drive New Process or Borg Warner units for the beefy NP-205 cast-iron gear drive is common. This older gear-type unit, available for older GM, Ford, and Dodge trucks, is remarkably strong, though with a marginal low range of just under 2:1. Among Jeepers, the Dana 300 cast-iron unit is a popular swap. For the ultimate beef in combination with a deep low range, the Advance Adapters Atlas transfer case is a popular, though expensive, option. Adapters are made for many popular trans/transfer case swaps, either from Advance Adapters or others.

Some strength improvements can come from modifications done for other reasons. Later short-wheelbase rigs (Jeep YJs and TJs) are prone to rear driveshaft angle problems when lifted. This problem is alleviated by a short tailshaft conversion, which reduces the length of the t-case by replacing the slip yoke output with a flanged output and allows for a longer driveshaft at a less steep angle. In some of the kits, that conversion comes with a much stronger rear output shaft.

Transfer case gearing changes are a useful way to get deep gearing for the trail and reasonable gearing for the street. Some people also use extra-low

A more compact splitter is available in the form of the Klune-V. This one uses planetary gears for a more compact vehicle. These 6.5-inch-long units come with a 2.72 or a 4.0:1 ratio and fit in many transmission/transfer case combinations.

transfer case gears to give themselves extremely low gearing. Among factory t-cases for commonly seen light-duty rigs, the lowest I know of is the Land Rover, which is at 3.3:1. Most others in the "low" category are around 2.7:1.

Splitters and Underdrives

These are two names for the same type of device. In essence, they give you an additional gearing step-down, much like the transfer case. They are inserted somewhere in the powertrain before the transfer case. In most cases, they are added between the transmission and transfer—as with the Off-Road Design Doubler, the U.S. Gear or the Klune-V—but the Advance Adapter's Ranger II bolts between the bellhousing and the transmission. Any of these units adds considerably to the drivetrain length, so a shorter rear driveshaft and a longer front driveshaft are the result; these units are best for longer-wheelbase rigs.

The splitters have some advantages over the super-low low-range transfer case conversions, namely gearing flexibility. They retain the original gearing for mild situations but you can go lower when, or if, you need to. In some cases, the extra-low t-cases are too low for the situation and you have no middle ground between that extra-low gear and 1:1 high range.

Front Axles

With solid axles, the front is inherently weaker than the rear for several reasons. First, unless the unit has a reverse-cut (or high-pinion) ring gear (only a few solid-axle Fords and the Jeep Dana 30), the front ring gear is driving on the reverse side of the teeth. This weakens it by as much as 30 percent. A reverse-cut ring gear in front is effectively as strong as one in the rear, though if a reverse cut is used in the rear, it becomes weaker by the same 30 percent.

The other weak link is the axle U-joint. In truth, these are the major

The axle U-joint or CV joint is the usual weak link on the front axle. As offered on OE rigs, the differential is always at least 50 percent stronger than the axle universals. This is a Dana 60 unit, generally acknowledged as the strongest front axle commonly available. As often as not, the big Dana 60 is swapped just to get these tough universal joints.

the dirt

Splitters and Underdrives: The splitter bridges the gearing gap between the mudrunner and the rockcrawler. On the downside, a splitter adds drivetrain length, weight, and complexity.

The Dana 60 diff section is often overkill for smaller rigs and offers a weight and clearance liability. Some custom axle builders are installing the Dana 60 knuckles onto smaller front axles. The Toyota pickup solid axle is a perfect candidate for this conversion. It has a stout differential and housing, but the Birfield-type CV joints are notoriously weak when combined with big tires and lots of torque. The Dana 60–type 332 U-joint with custom axles eliminates the problems. Several of the big custom axle builders are performing this conversion on Toyotas, as well as on other types of axles.

One of the growing aftermarket trends is the conversion of IFS trucks to solid front axle. No rig needs it more than the older GM S-10 Series trucks and SUVs. The S-10s are an otherwise great package that's hampered on the trail by an inadequate front drive system. Stage West Four-wheel Drive Center in Glenwood Springs, Colorado, builds this conversion that fits supple, long-travel springs and an ordinary Jeep Wrangler front axle to the rig. The result is radically improved articulation and trail performance, good street manners, and the durability to handle 35-inch tires reliably.

the dirt

Front Axles:
Another front axle weak point is the outer axle shafts, which may actually snap before the U-joint. Some corporate axles and Dana axles have a necked-down section on the inner shaft that also reduces strength (see Axle Strength Chart sidebar).

weakness of most front axles. They are often weaker than the axle shafts and will break before anything else. Axle U-joints are generally what limit tire size. It boils down to this: the small Spicer 260-sized U-joints (older Dana 44 and recent Dana 30 axles) are conservatively limited to about a 31-inch

Converting a light-duty semi-float axle to a full-float has some advantages. If the axle does break, there is no danger at all of losing the wheel. Second, you will probably end up with a stronger alloy-type axle in the conversion. This is a kit from Warn (less the brake rotors) for the Ford 8.8 semi-floater. It has 31-spline shafts that are good to near 10,000 lbs-ft on paper.

tire; the Spicer 297 (very late Jeep Dana 30, Dana 44 axles, and many GM Corporate units) size can handle a 35-inch tire; the Spicer 178 (Ford Dana 50 TTB) and the Dana 332 (Dana 60 axles) can handle up to 38-inch tires. With the exception of a few late-model rigs that use CV joints, and the import rigs, which either use CV joints or U-joints of unusual sizes, all the solid front axles fit into these four U-joint sizes. In truth, my ratings are a bit conservative, especially with Dana 60s. Some of the axles can be made to handle more tire with careful driving. The CV joints are generally weaker than standard U-joints, merely because of the pieces selected by the OE manufacturer, but they are more difficult to upgrade.

An important fact to remember about front axle U-joints is that there is a torque multiplication effect that occurs with angularity (see nearby sidebar). At maximum angularity, torque is multiplied at the inner axle yoke and U-joint trunnions by approximately 30 percent. If your U-joints are on the ragged edge of being strong enough, this will snap them. As you can see by the chart on page 143, the effect is on a curve, so 15 degrees of angularity offers minimal multiplication.

There are a number of cures for weak front axles. The first is obvious:

swap the weaker part for a stronger unit—that is, a Dana 30 for a 44, or a Dana 44 or GM 10-bolt for a Dana 60. In some cases, the swap is a bolt-on; in others specially built or narrowed assemblies must be used. Bearing in mind that you are mostly swapping for U-joints, there are companies that will put Dana 60 U-joints on Dana 44 or 10-bolt axles. It's even done to the solid Toyota axles to replace the notorious Birfield CV joints. This is an expensive option, but a good one for lighter rigs that don't need the extra weight and loss of ground clearance that comes with a bigger axle housing. A heavy pickup or SUV really should go the whole nine yards to a Dana 60.

Internal upgrades to any front axle would include replacing the necked-down inner shafts (if equipped) with non-necked pieces. These shafts can come in the same carbon steel alloy as OE or in a stronger chrome-moly (4340) alloy. The outer shafts can also be replaced, though I don't know of any stouter pieces that are not made of 4340. These 4340 assemblies are very stout and are available from several sources, including Randy's Ring and Pinion. The only problem is that there are currently no U-joints available that match the axles for strength. A little birdie tells me that may not be the case by the time you read this.

Warn's hub fuses are becoming popular in harder-core circles to protect vulnerable drivetrains. If you have Warn hubs, one of the locking rings can be replaced by one that's designed to shear cleanly at a predetermined torque load. This piece is easier and cheaper to replace than an axle or U-joint.

Finally, we get to the IFS category. When it comes to hard-core stuff, IFS rigs are not all that common. While there are some successfully campaigned IFS rigs in the advanced realm, they are almost always less successful than solid axles. It's very difficult and expensive to make an IFS front end hold up with big tires and low gears. The performance issue is another matter. IFS rigs are more prone to lifting front tires, thus reducing the potential traction by one tire.

With the solid front axle fading fast with OE 4x4s, there is going to have to be a renaissance in IFS aftermarket products. FabTech is currently at the head of the suspension side of that process, but the drivetrain issue has not been seriously addressed. There are a growing number of swaps available that convert IFS to solid axles. Right now, that's the best option and 'wheelers are converting many IFS GM trucks and SUVs. For the most part, these conversions are pretty tough and are best done by a competent person with great welding skills. Even farming out the labor, the job can come out at about the same cost as high-end IFS lifts and the performance is better.

Rear Axles

In many situations, the rear axle has to handle 30 to 50 percent more torque than the front. This is most often due to weight transfer in climbs, or acceleration. Like the front, rear-axle buildups follow some pretty general guidelines. It starts with axle shaft size, which is commonly expressed by diameter and spline count. A larger-diameter axle will have more splines (some of the big full-floaters are exceptions, such as big 1.5-inch shafts with 30 splines) and this equates to less reduction in diameter and more driving surfaces.

In a general way, you can rate axles for tire size by their axle shaft size and spline counts. OE alloy 28 splines can handle 31-inch tires in heavy rigs and 33s in lighter ones. The 30- and 31-spline units are good for 33-inch tires in heavy rigs and 35s in lighter ones. The 32- and 33-spline units can handle 35s and sometimes bigger. The beefy 35-spline axles are easily good to 38-inch tires, more if they are full-floaters. There are some in-betweens also. Look at max tire recommendations on page 127.

When you get into the stronger alloy steels, the equation changes. These can easily jump

Drivetrain Defense:
A good defense strategy for drivers is to try to keep the tires as straight ahead as possible if a heavy torque load will be applied to the front axle. This reduces the chance of front axle failure, which often comes from a broken axle U-joint.

A small sample of axles. On the bottom is a 27-spline Dana 35 unit. In the middle is a 30-spline Dana 44 c-clip type, with c-clip. On top is a Dana 44 non-c-clip. The difference in strength between the 27 and 30 splines is approximately 30 percent.

DOUBLE LEDGE

Though the tires look big on this Samurai, they are only 31x10.50s and the tall ledge is a bit high for tires this short, so this enterprising driver takes the oblique approach. One front tire at a time goes up the ledge. The Suzuki was in constant movement throughout this sequence.

With both the front tires up, he maintains the diagonal approach with his right rear, but notice that he has turned right a little. When the left rear hits the ledge and gets a good bite from momentum, he will goose the throttle a bit to hop up.

He's up and still moving. Note the deformed front tire on the second ledge. That's the momentum of the first hop pressing the aired-down tire (about 4 psi) against the rock. In that instant, the front axle will have a really good bite of traction. The 79-inch-wheelbase Samurai is short enough to fit on the first ledge.

Still moving at a steady pace. The front tires are up the second ledge and the driver is watching the ledge. When his back tires hit, he will goose the throttle yet again.

And he's up, the shot capturing the moment the tires climb the ledge. This entire operation was done without slipping a tire and without slowing down. The Samurai was locked at both ends, fitted with low gears (about 120:1 crawl ratio) and a wide tire footprint considering vehicle weight (well under 2,500 pounds). Bear in mind that this obstacle, nicknamed the Double Whammy, is notorious for defeating short-wheelbase vehicles.

There's a time and place for mud-slingin', rooster tail–type mud driving and the mud-dragging sport is one of them. The idea is to see how fast you can get from one end of a muddy pit to the other. This is a fun event at many 4x4 Jamborees around the country.
Courtesy Ken Brubaker

the axle up to the next major tire size and sometimes two. Stronger alloys can also add an extra margin of beef within a tire size range. This latter tip is particularly useful for c-clip axles, where a snapped shaft strands you. Lockers can drastically increase the axle load, because they will allow all the torque to run to a single shaft.

With regards to full-floating axles, there are a few kits to convert popular half-ton semi-float axles to full float. This eliminates the danger of a lost wheel from a broken shaft. It also offers the availability of stronger 4340 shafts. The conversions do not offer a great increase in load-carrying capacity, just the separation of load-carrying and torque delivery duties. The axle then only has to drive the wheel, and not support the weight as well.

Size upgrades are available for some axles. These generally use the OE alloy, but are larger. An upgrade from a 1.28-inch, 28-spline shaft to a 1.31-inch, 30-spline shaft, for example, adds 20 percent more strength. Many of the OE light truck axles (Dana 44, GM-10 bolt, Ford 8.8, among others) had both 28- and 30- or 31-spline versions. A change of carrier (or a 30/31 spline locker) is necessary. There are some custom builders who do similar things, such as Superior Gear's 30-spline conversion for the 27-spline Dana 35, or the 33-spline conversion for Dana 44s.

Housing strength is a consideration in some cases, especially with

Three-wheeling! In some situations, it's necessary, and this happens to be one of them. Because of the steep approach, a diagonal attack was needed. The dip just before the wall complicated the situation. If this truck weren't locker equipped, he'd be stopped right here. The front doesn't have quite enough pull to get the rig up, and with one wheel in the air, an open diff in the rear would cancel out that axle.

Left: Driving uphill over 6 inches of sheet ice is not a common situation. Normally you use chains, but it was an interesting exercise in skill to air down and drop into the lowest gear and lug the engine down as low as it would go. That combo offered enough traction to "chug" this Land Rover across the slick ice. It was extremely cold at this point, and that also aided the endeavor.

No smoking! Steep angles will bring out weaknesses you may not have thought about. It's bad enough to waste costly fuel, but it's especially bad when it gets into runoff water.

half-ton trucks. Their light-duty housing is designed for their OE duties. Slap some big tires, low gears, and lots of torque to them, and they bend and twist like rubber. A hard-used half-ton truck can really use a heavier 3/4-ton axle. The fact that most 3/4 tons use eight lug hubs complicates the situation, though some 'wheelers will swap both front and rear axles (a Dana 60 front and 14-bolt rear in a GM truck or SUV, for example). There are five or six lug conversion hubs for front or rear Dana 60s available from DynaTrac, but depending on what axle you use, you may be forced to convert the front hubs to eight lugs and switch wheels all around.

Gearing

We've discussed compensating for tire size by appropriate changes in gearing. Doing this puts you in the same relative performance place as the stock vehicle with OE tire size and gearing. What about gearing from a strict off-highway performance standpoint? There are four major considerations: terrain type, transmission type (automatic or manual), drivetrain strength, and torque-to-weight ratio.

What we are really talking about here is overall gearing. This is commonly called the "crawl ratio" and is the cumulative ratios of the transmission first gear, low range in the transfer case, and the axle ratio. Crawl ratio has become a catchphrase and, like many trendy things, people can carry it too far in the quest to be "cool." With the gearing choices available today, owners of some rigs can easily get crawl ratios down into the 200:1 area and even lower.

Automatics are a bit tricky to calculate because their torque converter is what amounts to a variable-ratio first gear. On average, they have a 2:1 ratio, which you would multiply by the "hard" ratio for the first-gear planetary set. If you had a 2.41 mechanical ratio, you would multiply by 2 to get the approximate ratio. The problem is that this ratio changes with engine speed. Your converter may have a 2:1 ratio at 800 rpm, but by 1,200 rpm it's

only 1.3:1 and by 1,500 rpm, is very near to 1:1.

What's the ideal crawl ratio? This takes us back to the four considerations discussed above. Starting with terrain, rockcrawlers need the lowest ratio and mudrunners need the highest. Rockcrawlers need to be able to drive at a slow, comfortable speed and to have the multiplication to climb very steep stuff at an engine rpm that leaves flexibility to slow down and speed up. When Stephen Watson at Off-Road Design conducted an informal poll, he learned that a 100:1 ratio (torque converter included on automatics) is the weapon of choice for the rockcrawlers in his large customer circle. This poll covered V-8-powered rigs with good torque-to-weight ratios, essentially rigs that would otherwise be no lower than about 60:1. The dedicated mudrunners he polled were exactly the opposite at between 55 and 65:1, or higher. A dedicated mudrunner needs to get the tires spinning as fast as possible. Sand drivers are at the mudrunner side of the spectrum. The rest of us "all-rounders" fit somewhere in the middle, though biased toward the mudrunner ratios, with slight alterations to either side.

The torque multiplication of low gearing must be taken into consideration before going really deep, and I'll show you how. Compensating for a poor torque-to-weight ratio can be more difficult. These rigs will need much lower gears to compensate.

Combining all of the generalities together is difficult, but I've put some basic calculations together in the chart ob page 139. It shows the torque and gearing needed to climb a 45 degree (100 percent) slope. It shows how the ratio changes with tire sizes from 30 to 40 inches and with weights from 2,500 pounds to 6,500 pounds. You will see how light weight or lots of torque lessens the need for low gears and that heavy rigs or those with small engines need really deep gears to do the same job.

You can use this chart to estimate the overall gearing you need. Bear in mind that this chart is biased toward steep and difficult terrain. Flatland 4x4s may not need gears that deep and mudrunners probably will not. Rockcrawlers will probably go lower. You can obtain these overall gears from various combinations, from axle ratio changes to lower transfer case gears, or splitters, or transmissions with lower first gears. Most likely it will be a combination of these items when it comes to the deeper gears. With automatics, count your converter ratio. If you don't know what it is, use 2:1.

Torque Loads

To plan modifications, it's useful to have an idea of how strong the existing drivetrain is. For many rigs, the area of most stress is at the axle assemblies. We first need to calculate how much torque multiplication the drivetrain can generate. Next, we need to know how much torque it will take to break the tires loose. Then we need to know the breaking strength of the weakest part of the drivetrain.

The first two items are relatively easy calculations. The last one is more difficult. What is the weakest part? Certain information is readily available, but most of it is not commonly dispensed. Observation and logical deduction can point us to some of the more common failures for which there is some information. The yield strength of an axle shaft, for example, can be calculated based on its minimum diameter and composition. The axle strength chart in the nearby sidebar contains some common sizes and materials that you can plug into your own calculations. The calculation is fairly technical and you need a materials handbook with steel formulas to make it, so I've done the brain twisting for you on some of the more common sizes and alloys. There is information on U-joints as well.

Step one is to find your engine's maximum net torque (manufacturer's figures from 1973 on are net torque; prior to that, they are gross torque: reduce gross torque by 20 percent to get a close approximation of net) and multiply that times your first-gear

Axle Shaft Strength

These yield torque ratings were generated via an engineering formula and should be considered approximations. They are useful to show the differences that size and material have on yield torque.

Size	Material	Yield Torque	Note
1.00-inch	1040 carbon steel	2,657.3 lbs-ft	1
1.10-inch	1040 carbon steel	3,639.8 lbs-ft	2
1.125-inch	1040 carbon steel	3,787.5 lbs-ft	3
1.16-inch	1040 carbon steel	4,160.8 lbs-ft	4
1.25-inch	1040 carbon steel	5,184.5 lbs-ft	5
1.28-inch	1040 carbon steel	5,571.4 lbs-ft	6
1.28-inch	4340 chrome-moly	9,147.4 lbs-ft	7
1.31-inch	1040 carbon steel	6,044.1 lbs-ft	8
1.31-inch	1340 manganese steel	6,473.1 lbs-ft	9
1.31-inch	4340 chrome-moly	9,923.5 lbs-ft	10
1.32-inch	1040 carbon steel	6,121.6 lbs-ft	11
1.37-inch	1040 carbon steel	6,828.4 lbs-ft	12
1.37-inch	4340 chrome-moly	11,211.2 lbs-ft	13
1.50-inch	1040 carbon steel	8,966.2 lbs-ft	14
1.50-inch	4340 chrome-moly	14,721.2 lbs-ft	15

Notes
1) Old Jeeps, Dana 23 and 41, as well as old Land Rover Series rigs.
2) The necked-down section on GM 28- and 30-spline front axle shafts and 30-spline Dana axles. Also a close approximation of the old Jeep Dana 25 and Dana 27.
3) The OE stub axle of Dana 44 and GM 10-bolt front axles.
4) Dana 30 and Dana 35 front and rear 27-spline axles used on Jeeps and Ford Rangers and Bronco II. The 1.20-inch, 28-spline Ford 8.8 used on many small Fords is just slightly stronger. Mitsubishi trucks and SUVs are slightly stronger.
5) Jeep AMC-20 rear (29 spline) and AMG Hummer IFS/IRS (not CVs). Newer Nissan SUVs and trucks similar.
6) The GM 10-bolt front or rear 28-spline axle.
7) A 28-spline in 4340.
8) An OE-type 30-spline axle, to include Dana 44 in many rigs, most Toyota axles, GM 10- and 12-bolt axles, small-axle Dana 60 light-duty full-floaters.
9) A slight upgrade in material on a 30-spline axle.
10) A 30-spline axle in 4340.
11) The 31-spline Ford 8.8 OE axle. Old Nissan Patrol similar.
12) An OE 33-spline axle similar to those used in the GM semi-float 14-bolt.
13) A 33-spline axle in 4340.
14) An OE 35-spline axle as found in a front or rear Dana 60 or a 30-spline, 1.5-inch, 14-bolt full-float axle, a Ford 10.25 Sterling full-floater, or a Dana 70.
15) As in number 14 above, but in a 4340 alloy.

This is what happens when a driveshaft gets hit when under a torque load. Driveshaft diameter and wall thickness are controlled by the length and maximum rpm of the shaft. Diameters range from 2.5 to 4 inches, with the longer shafts tending toward larger diameters. Wall thickness runs from .065 to .083 inches. For low-speed, super HD applications, a 2-inch, .120 wall shaft is sometimes used.

Looks impossible! It is impossible for most rigs, but a determined driver with the right equipment who is not concerned about body damage can pick a way through this. The wet, sandy tires are not going to help. The biggest danger here is to drop down into that big hole in front of the CJ and get wedged. The line this driver chose took him out through the area in the foreground.

ratio, t-case low-range ratio, and axle ratio. Let's say you have a rig with the ubiquitous 350 Chevy engine with 290 lbs-ft of torque, an automatic TH-700R4 with a 3:1 first gear, a 2.61:1 low-range ratio and 4.10:1 axle ratios. That does not include the torque converter ratio, which can multiply the ratio somewhat according to engine speed (lower rpm provides greater multiplication). I don't usually factor that ratio in because most of the experts say that it's a "soft" ratio and isn't much of an issue in calculating strength. The torque converter's lowest ratios occur at just above idle (800—1,200 rpm) and the engine isn't producing much torque at that speed. With manual trans, of course, you don't have a converter and the above comments are moot.

By putting the numbers together we get 290 x 3.0 x 2.61 x 4.10 = 9,309.8 lbs-ft. That's 9,309.8 lbs-ft going to your carrier or locker, axle shafts, and tires! In truth, the engine will not be putting out max torque all the time and the transfer of torque is not 100 percent efficient, so the final answer is multiplied by a "real-world" efficiency factor of 0.85, which drops it to a "mere" 7,913.3 lbs-ft.

The old straddle works every time! This driver will have to be careful stepping off the boulder on the right. In fact, he needs a little left rudder (his left) in order to not step off too early and drop down into the hole.

Finding the Ideal Crawl Ratio

This chart shows the torque and gearing required to climb a 45 degree (100 percent) slope with perfect traction (yeah, right!). Any rig geared to do this would be adequately geared for hard-core trails. Find your approximate weight and tire size at the top. Follow that line down level with your engine torque. Go straight down to the bottom and read an approximate crawl ratio. If you want this to be accurate, weigh your rig in its loaded-for-bear mode, or use the GVW. Next, try to find a dynamometer graph for your engine and plot engine torque at a reasonable climbing speed, perhaps at the lower edge of the peak torque area. For V8s or older inline sixes, that will be around 2,500 rpm. For fours and smaller sixes, it might be higher, but you want a speed that allows the engine some reserve to slow down and be able to speed back up with a heavy load. For lack of anything else, find the maximum rated torque for your engine and note the rpm at which it occurs. Since you will probably not reach max torque on most climbs, reduce it by about 10 percent, more if your engine has an rpm peak above 3,500 rpm. The formula for working this out yourself is:

$$\frac{\text{engine torque} \times \text{crawl ratio} \times .85 \text{ (note 1)} \times 1,200}{\text{tire radius (note 2)} \times \text{loaded weight}} = \text{gradability in percent (note 3}$$

Note 1- This accounts for the friction loss in the drivetrain.
Note 2- Half-mounted tire height.

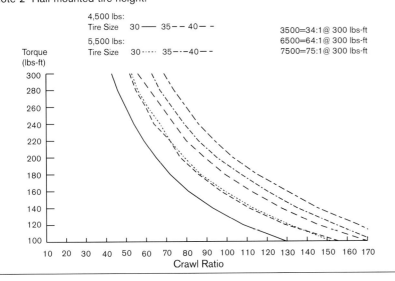

The previous calculations don't take into account one important factor—traction. Seldom, if ever, will your tires have the grip to handle that much torque. The tires usually break loose before the axle shaft (or something else) does. This is especially true with open diffs or loose limited slips. The chances of something breaking are based on how much traction you have versus the strength of the drivetrain parts. Logically, and in reality, that puts rockcrawlers at greatest risk.

There is a rough method of calculating traction, or more precisely, slip torque (the amount of torque required to break the tire loose from the ground). On level pavement, the cal-culation is fairly accurate. When you hit the trail, weight transfer, terrain angles, and such will be constantly variable, so we have to pick a high traction coefficient as the maximum possible number. Most times it will be less.

The first part of the slip torque formula involves knowing how much of the vehicle's weight will be on a particular axle, so you need to know front and rear weight. To get this, load your rig with a full tank of fuel, all your trail gear, and the extra bodies you commonly carry (or their equivalent weight) and go to the nearest scales. I go to the local landfill where they charge for dumping by weight, but truck scales or scrap metal yards are

Note 3- Subtract 10 percent if being able to stop and restart on grade is desired. Grade angle in percent is different from grade in degrees. Here is how they correlate.

Grade Percent	Degree Angle
10	6
20	11
30	17
40	22
50	27
60	31
70	35
80	39
90	42
100	45

Average Front Axle Universal Joint Yield Strength

Based on destructive testing of a small sampling of universal joints from various manufacturers. Interestingly, most brands, from high- to low-priced brand names, test within 15 percent of each other.

Spicer Number	Yield Strength
260	2,949 lbs-ft
297	4,401 lbs-ft
178	4,894 lbs-ft (estimated, only one test)
332	5,500 lbs-ft (estimated, only one test)

A sample of economy and choice use of funds. This Blazer has only a 2-1/2-inch lift but fits 35-inch tires. The center of gravity remains relatively low and the articulation is fantastic. Minor fender trimming was needed at the lower edges of the front fenders. The tires are also within the drivetrain's ability with only a few modifications. Following this general pattern with any other rig will lead to a very cost-effective unit. This rig was capable of performance into the lower end of extreme.

good places also. First, drive the front tires onto the scale and record the weight. Then drive forward to get total weight with all four wheels on the scale. Finally, drive the front wheels off to get the rear wheel weight. I weighed my own rig this way, so we will plug my numbers into the formula below.

My rig weighed 5,600 pounds with two people, 34 gallons of fuel, and my loaded-for-bear spares and tool kits. It has 35-inch tires with a rolling radius of 17 inches. Front and rear weight divided to 3,100 pounds front and 2,500 pounds rear. We'll calculate a simulated climb by increasing the weight on the rear axle with a 20-percent transfer from the front to the rear. That makes front weight 2,480 and rear 3,000 pounds. The basic formula is:

$$\frac{\text{weight on axle x coefficient of friction x tire radius}}{12} = \text{slip torque (lbs-ft)}$$

or, plugging in my numbers

$$\frac{3,100 \times .6 \times 17}{12} = 2,635 \text{ lbs-ft (for both tires)}$$

This formula only applies with equal traction on both tires and does not account for the type of differential. It really only applies if you have a true locker, which is capable of delivering 100 percent of the torque to one tire. With a limited slip, you could reduce that amount by the bias ratio. A 60-percent bias ratio (4:1 locking factor), or 0.60, times the number you got in the above calculation reduces the potential single axle load to 1,581 lbs-ft. An open diff will always share the load between both axles because as soon as one

tire slips, torque takes the path of least resistance and reduces the load.

Really good traction due to ground conditions could move the coefficient of friction up a bit. You can plug in any coefficient you want, up to perfect traction of 1.0, but it's unlikely you'll see it that high on the trail. Quizzing assorted engineers and experts helped to confirm this, though the sticky tires of today dictate working out worst-case scenarios if you are a dedicated rockcrawler with aired-down tires. Plug in a smaller-diameter tire and you'll see the effect tire diameter has on the torque load. A 30-inch tire (14.5-inch radius), for example, drops final slip torque to 2,247 lbs-ft. Bear in mind that slip torque is not the end-all. There are also shock loads to consider as well as metal fatigue that has weakened the components over time.

Let's put it all together. We have the maximum potential torque. We have the torque required to break the tires loose. All we need now is the component strength of the various parts. My rig uses 1.31-inch, 4340 chrome-moly shafts that have a breaking strength of approximately 9,923 lbs-ft. Put that number between the 7,913 lbs-ft from the gearing and the 2,635 lbs-ft needed to break the tires loose (1,317 per tire) and they come up with a lot of strength in reserve. The engine doesn't have enough torque to break the shafts and the tires don't have enough grip to exceed the breaking strength of the axle. The important part is that the axle strength exceeds the torque or the traction. The previous flanged, semi-float axle shafts I used were rated for about 6,200 pounds and I managed not to break them.

My own rig is geared a bit differently from the example. With the Off-Road Design Doubler, I have a choice of 2:1 or 4:1 low-range ratios. In my lowest gears, I can generate 14,268 lbs-ft, which is enough to break a shaft, but I still don't have the grip needed to break the axle. My modified diesel also generates considerably more torque than the example, even at 1,000 rpm.

Polyurethane is the bushing of choice for most suspension systems. It holds up better and usually offers more suspension movement. The greaseable type, as shown here, avoids the creaking for which unlubed poly bushing are notorious. Unlike rubber bushings, which consist of two metal sleeves with rubber bonding them together, the poly setup is made up of separate pieces. When the rubber bushing is flexed past its elasticity, the rubber tears away from the metal sleeves. The poly bushing is free to pivot as far as needed. On the downside, poly sometimes results in a harsher, noisier ride in the more cushy rigs where such things are important. Poly has not yet reached the same softness as rubber, though the time is near when it will. Most aftermarket suspensions come with poly bushings.

The Revolver shackle is an interesting design that can offer major articulation gains in leaf spring vehicles. It drops in a kneelike fashion to allow several more inches of downtravel. Not only that, it pivots to allow the spring to twist a bit as it drops. Spring twist, or the lack thereof, is a factor in articulation. The weight of the vehicle seems to keep the Revolver in place on the highway.

What's wrong with this picture? Radical body surgery is a part of the game in the quest for the ultimate clearance. In the case of this Toyota pickup, the prodigious rear overhang has been "bobbed" to a more reasonable amount. Along the way, some rear quarter panel protection was added. The body projects only slightly past the amount of frame needed to support the aft end of the spring. Some 10 inches of body were removed.

This is a custom-built front suspension made to convert a GM IFS truck to a solid front axle. It uses a coil-over–type shock. This type of unit combines a coil spring and a shock. You may remember a version of this idea that your dad put on the old Ford station wagon to keep it from tail dragging when the family went on vacation. Other notable features of this setup include a downtravel limit strap, Heim joints on the suspension arms and tie-rods and a very high level of workmanship. Custom work such as this is beyond many shops. Self-trained engineers and welders may be OK, but let them apprentice on somebody else's vehicle first! *Courtesy Ben Stewart*

A small item seen on many hard-core rigs is "Moab" rollers. Placed on areas that are guaranteed to touch in a tight clearance situation, they allow the offending part to glide rather than drag. In most cases, these are fabricated items. In this case, they are built by AOR (Advanced Off-Road Research) as a kit for Toyota trucks.

With your front-end weight, you can take the same formula to find the weak link there, which may be the axle U-joints. You could use the level ground figure, or the reduced figure from the climb. In that case, don't forget to also figure in the multiplication factor of a U-joint at its maximum angularity just so you know. The 297 joints are similar in strength to the 1310 series listed in the driveshaft U-joint sidebar. The Dana 60 332 joints are similar to the 1410 series listed in the same place. Incidentally, I cannot explain the disparity between the U-joint destructive tests done and shown in the sidebars and these Spicer ratings.

Another use for this information is to determine whether the driveline U-joints are adequate. By calculating slip torque in a different way, you can discover the amount of torque on the driveshaft at the point where the tire breaks loose. If you compare the figures from this calculation to the max short-term driveshaft torque ratings in the nearby sidebar, you will learn if you have any weaknesses there. Bear in mind that *usually* the driveshaft and yokes are rated for the same torque as the U-joints, but not always. Most smaller 4x4s have 1310 series joints, as do many half-ton full-sized rigs. The 1330 series are found in some half-tons and some 3/4 tons. Some 3/4 tons and many 1-tons use 1350 series joints. The formula is:

$$\text{driveshaft torque} = \frac{\begin{array}{c}\text{weight on axle}\\ \text{x coefficient}\\ \text{of friction}\\ \text{x rolling radius}\\ \text{of tire}\end{array}}{12 \text{ x axle ratio}}$$

Or, using our numbers from above:

$$\frac{3{,}000 \text{ x } 0.60 \text{ x } 17}{12 \text{ x } 4.10} = 621.9 \text{ lbs-ft}$$

That's inside the maximum short-term ratings given by Dana Spicer for all the U-joints listed in the sidebar.

SUSPENSION

We talked about basic lift conditions in chapter 6. More lift for bigger tires is just an extension of the same information. In an advanced rig, other factors come into play. Stability is

---

Average Front Axle Universal Joint Yield Strength

Driveshaft Universal Joint Dimensions and Torque Ratings
Note: This rating is for maximum continuous torque with no distortion or ill effects.

Series	Cap to Cap	Cap Diameter	Continuous Max	Short-Term Max	Deformation	Angularity
1310	3.22	1.08	130 lbs-ft	800 lbs-ft	1,600 lbs-ft	30 degrees
1330	3.63	1.08	150 lbs-ft	890 lbs-ft	1,850 lbs-ft	20 degrees
1350	3.63	1.19	210 lbs-ft	1,240 lbs-ft	2,260 lbs-ft	30 degrees
1410	4.19	1.19	250 lbs-ft	1,500 lbs-ft	2,700 lbs-ft	37 degrees

the dirt

Articulation Balance:
To avoid instability, your 4x4 ideally should have as much articulation in the front as the rear. In reality, a 40 percent front, 60 percent split rear is close enough.

An example of front-to-rear articulation disparity. The rear coil spring suspension of most Land Rovers is capable of prodigious flex with some relatively minor modifications. It's more difficult and expensive to coax flex out of the front, and this holds true for nearly all rigs. To maintain maximum stability, it's best to keep the front and rear at about the same amount of articulation. It's acceptable to go as much as 10 percent more on the rear.

Front Axle Universal Joint Torque Loads Due to Increased Angles

Torque at Tire	U-Joint Angle	Torque on Inner Axle Yoke/Trunnions
2,500 lbs-ft	0 degrees	2,500 lbs-ft
	5 degrees	2,510 lbs-ft
	10 degrees	2,542 lbs-ft
	15 degrees	2,594 lbs-ft
	20 degrees	2,661 lbs-ft
	25 degrees	2,763 lbs-ft
	30 degrees	2,897 lbs-ft
	35 degrees	3,097 lbs-ft
	40 degrees	3,269 lbs-ft

A sample of articulation with some other things to talk about. This completely home-built rig has had a spring-over conversion, where a Toyota axle was mounted under some standard Jeep springs (the old, narrow 1.75-inch type). Longer rear shackles were installed to tip the nose of the differential up for driveline angle purposes. This budget rig was rough to look at, but surprisingly competent and well thought out in many ways.

Longer leaf springs offer a combination of better flexibility and a better ride, though a conversion like this flatfender Jeep's is labor intensive and not for everyone. Note also that the springs have been attached outside the chassis via GM style-truck spring hangers. This also offers an extra measure of stability to an otherwise narrow and tippy short-wheelbase rig.

Coil spring suspension modifications are more technical than a leaf spring setup. The lifts must be accompanied by correction in the way the axle is mounted so that critical steering and driveshaft geometry is maintained. This usually comes in the form of longer arms with the corrective angles built in. On the Cherokee, note the drag link (the gold-colored bar running transverse), which is made almost z-shaped. This helps prevent bump steer. Note also that this rig has sway bar disconnects, currently disconnected.

important, so rigs with "nose bleed"-type tall lifts are at a decided disadvantage in uneven terrain. Articulation is another factor. The ideal is to have the suspension compliant enough to keep the tires on the ground as much as possible. Even a partially unloaded tire can deliver more traction than a lifted tire (assuming a locker is engaged). That said, articulation is another of those "cool" items in which people are immersed.

The main goal in a modified suspension is balance: balance in articulation front to rear; balance between the lift height and a reasonable center of gravity; and balance between street performance and trail performance for rigs that are not trailered. Ride quality is another important factor.

Lifts and Center of Gravity

The quest to fit big rubber often forces many compromises. Some rigs can easily swallow big rubber and others cannot without be being lifted to the moon. It often comes down to how much fenderwell and sheet-metal modification you are willing to make. In my opinion, it's better to compromise

Calculating Spring Rate

Formulas courtesy Skyjacker

These formulas work for leaf and coil springs. They can help you approximate ride height and your spring rate needs.

1) You will need to determine the weight on the front and rear axles. This can be done at a truck stop or any convenient truck scale.
   A) If your ultimate goal is to find a spring rate and ride height for a predetermined vehicle setup and load, weigh it in that configuration.
   B) If your goal is to determine a load capacity, you will need to weigh the vehicle once empty and once with the load.

   Sample Problem. Front weight: 2,400 lbs; rear weight: 1,800 lbs

2) Divide the front and rear axle weights by two to determine the weight per spring. Deduct the weight of the axles, wheels, and tires, since it is weight not supported by the springs. Here are some educated guesses. Dana 30/35 front/rear: 250/200 lbs; Dana 44: 300/250 lbs front/rear; Dana 60: 375/300 lbs front/rear.

   Sample Problem: Front 2,400 − 250 lbs = 2,150 ÷ 2 = 1,075 lbs per spring
   Rear 1,800 - 200 lbs = 1,600 ÷ 2= 800 lbs per spring

3) Find the rate of the spring in pounds per inch.

   Sample Problem: New spring rates front: 250 lbs/in, rear 200 lbs/in

4) Divide the load per spring by the rate per spring to get the deflection in inches.

   Sample Problem: Front: 1,075 ÷ 250 = 4.3 inches of deflection
   800 ÷ 200 = 4.0 inches of deflection

5) Now for some practical application. With coils, if you have the free length of the spring, you can calculate loaded ride height difference easily. By determining what the loaded height of the spring will be with the per spring load, you can figure mounted spring-seat-to-spring-seat height. With leaf springs, you need free arch measurements and then you can deduct the loss of arch according to the spring rate and per spring load.

   Sample Solution for Coil Spring:
   Front free length: 18 inches - 4.3 inches = 13.7 inches mounted height
   Rear free length: 18.5 inches - 4.0 inches = 14.5 inches mounted height

   If your original mounted heights were 11 and 12.1 inches, then you have gained 2.7 inches up front and 2.4 inches in back.

   Sample Solution for Leaf Spring:
   Front spring free arch: 7.6 in - 4.3 in = 3.3 free arch mounted at weight
   Rear spring free arch: 7.25 in - 4.0 in = 3.25 inch free arch at weight

   If your original free arch numbers were .9 inches front and .8 inch rear, then you have gained 2.4 inches of lift in front and 2.45 inches in back.

Extreme suspensions are available for many popular applications. They offer radical trail performance improvements with moderate to severe compromises in the street realm. In the recent past, the Black Diamond XCL kit converted the leaf spring Wrangler YJ into an all-coil trail monster with unbelievable articulation and wheel travel. It was a labor-intensive kit to install and more than a little hard on the wallet. Black Diamond was recently sold, and the ultimate fate of the XCL kit is uncertain at this writing.

To dual shock, or not to dual shock? For most rigs, dual shocks are unnecessary. Fast movers and particularly heavy rigs might consider a dual-shock setup. The better dual-shock kits use a bolted or welded hoop kit such as this one. Shocks are "soft" valved for dual applications, meaning they share the work. Two regular shocks would result in a harsh ride.

ROCK TALK

Spring Wrap:

Spring wrap, or axle wrap, or just plain "wrap," is an effect of torque. As torque is applied through the axle to the tires, the axle twists, pushing the snout of the differential up toward the floor when the vehicle is moving forward. The spring resists according to its stiffness but will actually go S-shaped. This happens to all springs, but in a spring-over situation, the extra leverage increases the effect.

An extreme leaf spring suspension for a Toyota. This is actually a converted IFS truck. Advanced Off-Road Research offers this setup for conversions on the solid-axle Toyotas. The springs are long and supple, with not much arch, and are mounted above the axle. The Bilstien dual shocks are high-end, remote-reservoir, gas-charged units. The nitrogen gas pressure in the shocks can be adjusted according to the terrain. The suspension is shown at normal ride height. Note how the shackle is tilted back slightly. All in all, this is near perfection in a leaf spring setup.

a bit with a smaller tire than to reduce stability to the point that it becomes a liability on and off the highway.

Articulation Balance

In most cases, it's easier to gain articulation in the rear, and many owners simply grab what they can get there and ignore the front end—this action results in articulation imbalance and leads to instability. Instability translates into more severe

roll angles in steep terrain. This means more tilt in certain situations and an increased propensity to roll.

Unfortunately, measuring articulation balance is not easy. You need an articulation ramp and lots of time for measurements. It's possible to do it in a shade-tree way if you have the ramp, but often you can observe it visually.

Articulation imbalance can be caused by more than a simple disparity in wheel travel front to rear. Mismatched spring rates may also be responsible. If the rear springs are too light compared to the front, they will do all the flexing as the front resists articulation. The cure in this situation is to either go lighter on the front springs or heavier on the rear to force the front to flex more. The section below and the nearby sidebar will fill you in more on spring rates.

Spring Rates

Correct spring rates for the weight and ride height of your vehicle result in good ride and articulation. Spring rate is expressed in pounds per inch of movement, or lbs/in. This is the amount of weight it takes to move the spring 1 inch. To move the spring 2 inches, it takes twice the weight, and 3 inches takes three times the weight, and so on. Obviously, the higher the

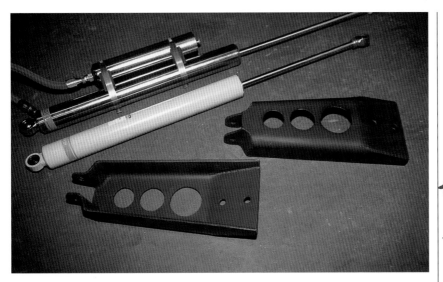

Mounting longer-travel shocks usually entails relocating the shock brackets. This is a kit to raise the upper mount for a Toyota truck and allows for 14-inch travel shocks.

rate, the more the load capacity and the harsher the unloaded ride. The rates are chosen to balance these two elements. This is the same whether the vehicle uses leaf springs, coil springs, or torsion bars. In leaf springs, however, the friction of the leaves sliding past each other results in a little extra "perceived" rate, especially if they have gotten rusty.

Since springs often come with lift kits, can you assume that they are correct for your vehicle? Not necessarily. Aftermarket springs are often a "one-size-fits-most" sort of deal. You can usually find a "standard duty" and "heavy duty" spring rate offered, the latter being stiffer. If you have the catalog, the spring rates are usually listed in product specifications. If the rates are close to stock rates, and you are satisfied with the ride and load capacity now, then you should be happy with the new springs. With leaf springs, a lift often requires more spring camber (arch), and this can require a higher spring rate to hold that arch. The procedure for selecting a spring rate is shown in a nearby sidebar.

Advanced Lifts

There's one type of lift that we didn't discuss in chapter 6: spring-over lifts. Some leaf spring rigs, such as Jeep CJs and YJs, as well as Toyota Land Cruisers and IHC Scouts, are spring-under vehicles. One way to get lift with these rigs is to move the axle to the underside of the springs. This results in a lift equal to the thickness of the axle tubes, plus the height of the new spring perch that must be welded to the top of the axle. The plus side is that you retain the supple OE springs and articulation. The downside is that you may experience problems with spring wrap and driveshaft angles.

The result of spring wrap is that the driveshaft and pinion angle changes—and if it changes enough, the U-joint binds and breaks. The other negative effect occurs if the tires lose traction. Suddenly released of torque, the springs snap back and

High-clearance steering is necessary in some applications. This does two things. First, it allows the drag link to run more or less level, thus reducing bump steer tendencies. Second, it puts the tie-rod and drag link higher out of harm's way. There are complications to this conversion, including interference with the spring. In some applications, the tie-rod mounts over the spring. Note that this Jeep has also had a spring-over conversion.

Big tires put more stress on the steering system. This can result in minor problems such as bent steering rods or more major situations including broken steering boxes or chassis cracks where the steering box mounts to the chassis. Steering box braces may save your rig from this malady. Not all 4x4s are particularly vulnerable to this, but many of the popular trail rigs that are have the option of a brace. This one is a Wrangler TJ kit from M.O.R.E.

again the driveshaft takes the brunt. Spring rate, the length of the spring, gear ratios, and engine torque all contribute to this tendency.

Several cures exist for spring wrap, whether it comes from a spring-over or not. These include stiffer springs and torque rods of all types (a.k.a. traction bars). Some spring manufacturers, most notably Rancho, include a half leaf on the leading end of some of their springs that goes from the eye to just past the u-bolts. Often this is just enough to prevent wrap. Several companies build torque rods but make sure they will not restrict articulation. Some do.

Dual and Long Travel Shocks

In nearly all stock suspensions, the shock length determines the limit of suspension travel. Ditto for many lift kits. One way to increase, or at least maximize, articulation is to install a longer shock.

The first step is to disconnect or remove your existing shocks and see how much more travel or articulation you can get. Simply disconnect one end of the shocks and jack the vehicle up by the chassis until the wheels are off the ground. If you determine that the lower shock mounts are significantly lower than the extended shock, then you have some long travel potential. From there you need to look at other factors to see if it's feasible to increase suspension travel.

Look first at your brake hose length. You may have to temporarily disconnect them even for the test. Solid-axle coil-spring rigs may drop to the point where the coil spring is released. With an independent front suspension rig, you may find that front axle CV joint angles get to be excessive if travel increases significantly. Steering geometry may be affected adversely. Axle vent lines may be too short. Driveshafts may be too short or operate at too steep an angle. Some of

The steering on a stock vehicle is designed so that the drag link (A) and the tie-rod (B) are parallel. This reduces or eliminates bump steer. While this is a common setup on solid-axle rigs, it's not the only type of steering system you may see. Even with the other types of steering systems, a similar effect occurs.

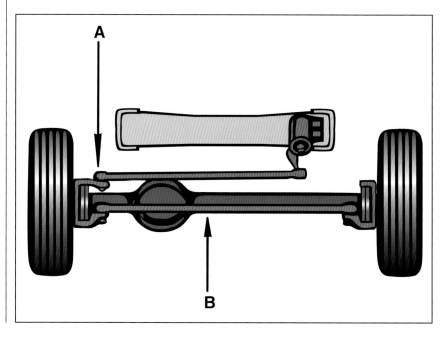

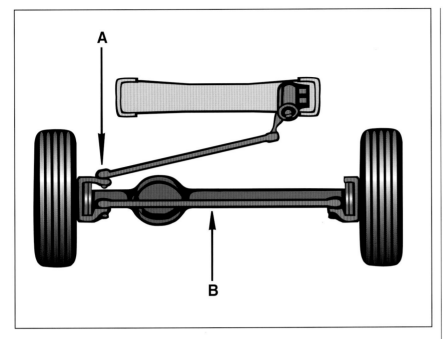

When a lift is applied, the angle of the drag link (A) increases. The distance between where it attaches to the steering box and the knuckle decreases, effectively making the drag link shorter.

these items can be corrected with effort and some cannot.

Next, uptravel needs to be considered. First, measure the distance between the shock mounts with the suspension extended all the way. Then compress the suspension all the way against the bump stop and measure again. You can simulate this measurement using the bump stop, or whatever else is your upward limiter, as a guide. Ideally you want a shock that has an extended length about a half-inch longer than your suspension's

extended dimension and a compressed length about 1/2 to 3/4-inch shorter than the compressed dimension. The extra downtravel adds a margin of shock and shock-mount safety. The collapsed distance is even more important, since the rubber bump stop has some give. If you accidentally bottom the suspension hard, you will still have some shock travel left. Bottoming the shock can damage it or break off the shock mounts. Taller bump stops or spacers can be used to fine-tune uptravel. Remember that tire/fenderwell clearance

ROCK TALK

Bump Steer:

Bump steer describes directional changes in the front wheels that result from suspension movement rather than steering-wheel input.

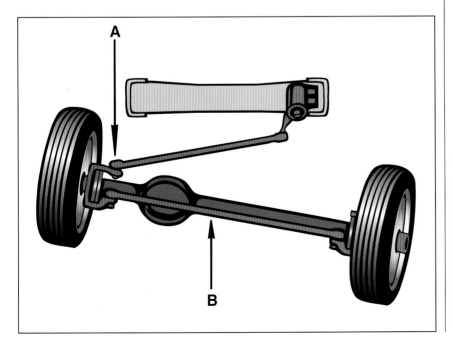

When the suspension moves, the drag link gets longer or shorter as the point-to-point distance increases or decreases. In this situation, the axle is compressed on the passenger side and the effect is to force the vehicle to steer left. This is called bump steer.

may be an issue with the suspension at the upper end.

The shock manufacturers will list the extended and collapsed length of their shocks. If you are lucky, you will find one that fits your dimensions. Most likely, you will have to relocate a shock mount to get the longer shock installed. There are various methods to relocating shock mounts, including kits, fabrication, or even a few bolt-on tricks.

As for dual shocks, they are in the cool category. They are more important for fast movers, since dual shocks tend to share the dampening load. Fast travel over bumpy ground generates heat in the shocks. In extreme cases, the shock can be cooked. The heat is reduced when there are two or more shocks on each side to share the load. Dual shocks are specially valved to be less stiff. In essence, the two shocks are valved to do the job of one, thus sharing the load. There are various aftermarket shock kits available for popular applications, but dual shocks are not necessary for most of us who move at a slower pace. If you fit in the slow category, your money is better spent elsewhere.

Steering Linkage

The two most common steering issues associated with all modified rigs are durability of the tie-rod and drag link, and bump steer. Durability comes into play with the addition of large tires and tough trail conditions. Under the wrong circumstances, these factors can produce enough force to bend a factory tie-rod like a pretzel.

From the replacement standpoint, several companies offer heavy-duty tie-rods. These start with units that are designed to replace the OE setup. First on the list are units made of larger, stronger material. Some are adapted from truck tie-rods that are more robust than the stock pieces but are still made of carbon steel. They vary in price but are usually under $100.

Next up are replacement tie-rods made of 4130 chrome-moly tubing that use the OE tie-rod ends. These vary in O.D. from 7/8 inch to 1 inch, with wall thickness from 0.188 inch to 0.250 inch. These are extremely robust pieces. The one disadvantage to 4130 is that if it does get bent, it will usually break when you try to bend it back. Ordinary carbon steel is softer and can usually be straightened. This is seldom an issue but crops up more often than you would imagine in light of 4130's superior strength.

Bump steer occurs when suspension movement tends to steer the vehicle. This occurs when the drag link is at an angle. When the axle moves up, the rod effectively gets longer and in

the dirt

High-Clearance Steering: High-clearance steering kits are available for popular trail rigs. These keep steering components out of harm's way and also reduce bump steer on the trail.

Sample Power Steering Temps

This will show the difference in power steering temps for various conditions. Test performed on a 1983 Blazer K-5.

Condition	Oil Temperature	Ambient Temperature
Freeway, high speed	oil- 134 degrees pump- 139 degrees box- 102 degrees	90 degrees
City, stop and go	oil- 130 degrees pump- 150 degrees box- 118 degrees	92 degrees
Trail, easy	oil- 153 degrees pump- 168 degrees box- 172 degrees	95 degrees
Trail, hard	oil- 193 degrees pump- 227 degrees box- 215 degrees	95 degrees

most cases makes the vehicle steer itself. Ideally the drag link should be as level as possible but lifts make the drag link reach down. This tends to increase bump steer.

The easy cure to bump steer is often a dropped Pitman arm. However, the extra leverage makes steering box damage more likely, so if a steering box brace exists for your rig, use it. This is a good idea for any advanced rig, since big tires tend to put more stress on the steering box and the spot where it mounts to the chassis. Do not bend your Pitman arm by any means, including heat. It crystallizes the metal and makes it brittle. Better to stay alive and spend a few bucks on a made-from-scratch part.

Major lifts may require a complete redo of the steering linkage. In the factory steering setups on solid-axle rigs, the tie-rod is mounted below the arms and is somewhat vulnerable to damage. Many four-wheelers are mounting their tie-rods above the arms for clearance. This has the added advantage of lessening drag link angles and minimizing bump steer. Some machine shops can redrill the tapered holes in the steering knuckles to accomplish this.

Steering Dampers

A steering damper is nothing more than a shock absorber for the steering system. It dampens the effect of tire vibration and feedback from road surface irregularities. These problems are inherent in all vehicles with large tires, 4x4s included. The effects are multiplied when you add even larger tires and lifts, so a steering damper upgrade is a vital ingredient to most buildups.

The OE damper may be inadequate, even in stock rigs, especially for fast movers. Tire size determines whether you need to upgrade your steering damper. Just as with shocks, a larger piston exerts more control, so the upgrade will be larger in diameter. A damper will not control bump steer. As discussed, this is an issue of steering geometry. Nor will it control the vibrations that come from worn-out steering components.

Many newer vehicles are already fitted with a damper. In these cases all you need to do is add the beefier unit. In older rigs not so equipped, the aftermarket supplies bracket kits to mount the damper. The key is to have the damper centered in its travel so that it does not restrict steering movement. The unit should be mounted as high out of harm's way as possible, but even then steering dampers are often front-line casualties in hard-core 4x4 circles. The damper is best mounted to the drag link.

Occasionally you will see two or more dampers mounted. For most rigs, one is plenty. The dual setups come into play with really huge tires. If one good damper doesn't stop the vibration in your mild 4x4 with 33-inch tires, you probably have other problems. If you have a full-sized truck with 44s, then twin dampers are a legitimate mod.

Power Steering

Power steering uses oil that is nearly identical to automatic transmission fluid and is subject to the same temperature frailties. If you ever wondered how hot the power steering can get, look at the nearby sidebar. Overheated power steering oil can cause a loss of power assist in critical periods and early failure of the parts. Big tires and a hard trail can push temps up fast.

At about 212 degrees, the oil in the power steering system starts to foam. The first symptoms of this will be a growling noise, which is an indication that the pump is cavitating, followed by intermittent loss of fluid pressure and power assist. Continual high temps will also degrade the internal seals and the hoses.

The answer is a power steering cooler and this is considered a necessity in many rockcrawling circles. The cooler mounts on the low-pressure (return) line between the steering box and pump reservoir. Nearly any type of cooler can be used, including small trans coolers and engine oil coolers. If you rig something up yourself, make sure to use power-steering-rated, high-temp hose.

continued on page 154

CHOP SUEY AND NO TURNING BACK

A steep drop into a bottomless pit of slime. The ramp will provide some free momentum, but prevent backing out. Plus, the momentum isn't useful here, because this is Chop Suey Mud, with sticks and old corduroy in it.

Splat! Here's the other problem. The steep entry noses the Pinzgauer deeply into the mud, creating a massive amount of drag.

The fully locked Pinzie does a bulldozer routine and manages to claw its way level.

With all four tires churning the mud into a chocolate milkshake, the Austrian rig claws along inch by inch. This is where the relative lack of power was a detriment. If the little four-banger had had a little more oomph, it could have gotten the tires spinning to sling off the cloying mud and get a bite. At 10,000 feet, that just wasn't possible. This driver did everything right but he still had to take a strap to get all the way out.

Continued from page 151

The cooler is most needed at slow speeds, so placing it in the fan's airflow can reduce temps more than mounting it just anywhere. Even a spot on a fenderwell that gets some airflow from the fan is better than a dead area. Finding a good spot may be problematic under a tightly packed hood. As with any cooler, the number one consideration is placing it in a location that is safe from trail damage.

Even if you don't mount a cooler, at least change your power steering oil once in a while if you four-wheel hard.

Just one hard trip can turn the fluid dark. Just like an automatic transmission, the fluid deteriorates and it can degrade the performance of the system even before premature wear occurs.

ENGINE

Just like in chapter 6, we're not getting into major engine mods or swaps. The majority of 4x4s are adequately powered for the trail when properly geared. What we will discuss,

the dirt

Trail Cooling Systems:
One thing you have on a slow-moving trail that's not in the big-city summer commute scenario is engine load from climbs and uneven terrain. A good cooling system is vital.

Aftermarket aluminum radiators are very efficient compared to the standard brass types. In critical cooling situations, they can mean the difference between hot and not hot. They are available in custom form or as direct replacements in a small range of applications. The electric fans on this 4x4 S-10 with a 350 V-8 conversion are a little more problematic. Obviously, these were installed because of the difficulties in the conversion. As to electric fans, there are electric fan kits available from Flex-a-Lite that are powerful enough to replace the engine-driven fan and they are available for a small range of applications. Most of the cheap electric fan kits are incapable of stand-alone operation. Most engine-driven fans are capable of high airflow. The advantage of an electric is that it doesn't run—and therefore doesn't use power—when it isn't needed.

Brakes become less effective with bigger tires for two reasons: the extra rotating mass and the increased leverage the bigger tire applies against the brakes. High-performance brake linings with a higher coefficient of friction will compensate in most cases, but sometimes a greater cure is needed. Going to larger brakes or upgrading the rear brakes to discs is a good option. Off-Road Unlimited offers this rear disc brake conversion kit for the big GM 14-bolt full-floater. Usually a new master cylinder is necessary for a rear disc conversion, as is the case for this kit. *Courtesy Off-Road Unlimited*

however, are some durability modifications to make your engine hang together better.

The most common four-wheeling scenario is the slow-speed slog, grunting along at less than 10 miles per hour at just above idle speed. What if the outside temperature is 100 degrees or more? You might answer that it's no worse than L.A. or Dallas traffic, and you wouldn't be too far from wrong.

Often the OE cooling system is adequate. If it's not, and you have an automatic, be aware that the automatic transmission has a cooler built into the radiator and four-wheeling will drastically raise trans oil temp, adding to your cooling system's burden. An external tranny cooler will help. If you live in a perpetually warm climate, you might consider bypassing the radiator cooler altogether. Transmission coolers with thermostatically controlled electric fans are the ultimate in efficiency when airflow is in short supply.

Other ways to reduce operating temps in a hot-running engine, beyond any repair or maintenance problems that should be eliminated first, include a proper mix of coolant. Higher and lower mixtures do not transfer heat as well. In reality, plain water is the best cooling medium, though we know what happens to engines without coolant. High-flow thermostats that do not restrict water flow are another easy solution. Changing the opening point usually does little.

High-efficiency and larger-capacity radiators are also available. The best way of increasing radiator size is via frontal area, but that's not often possible, so we get by with another layer of cores. Larger fans with more airflow capacity may be available for your application. Along the same lines, a higher-flow water pump may be available. There are many water pump options for the common American V-8. I recently swapped from a 66- to a 100-gallon-per-minute pump and noticed a huge difference. Sometimes speeding up the pump by reducing the water pump pulley size may be enough to improve water flow at low speeds. In some cases, an oil cooler may reduce cooling system load.

Exhaust system mods, such as headers and free-flowing exhausts, can sometimes provide a small to moderate cooling advantage, since much of the engine's heat goes out the exhaust and reducing backpressure allows more heat to escape. Most other engine mods increase engine temperatures, so if you are having heat problems, these mods may have taken away some of your reserve.

ecovery
echniques

If you four-wheel long enough, you're virtually guaranteed to get stuck. You may get a little anxious or frustrated the first time, but with experience, it becomes another part of the game and an interesting puzzle. Most recovery situations are minor events that you can handle easily when prepared and equipped. It can get more serious and difficult at times, but with the correct safety procedures in place and a clear head, you can free up your rig without injury to people or the vehicle. The recovery learning curve is usually not steep and you can learn as much from watching and helping as you can from doing it yourself. Since *somebody* always seems to get stuck on just about every group trek, you'll get plenty of opportunities to learn.

BASIC RECOVERY DOCTRINE

Obviously, the first consideration is safety. Choose whatever is the least dangerous method of recovery. It's better to leave a rig stuck for eternity than to hurt or kill someone. With safety first in your mind, determine the best way out. Is it forward or back? That decision goes beyond just finding the nearest piece of solid ground and a

Safety, or the lack thereof, is perennial. The need for recovery arose even in 1919, when a lucky Army cameraman snapped this shot just as the tow rope parted and a hapless GI was hurled aside. The fully loaded WW I–era 4x2 "Liberty" Model B military truck was on a coast-to-coast crossing of the United States designed to test the transport arm of the U.S. Army.
National Archives

A few of your shovel choices. From left to right, A) D-handle round-point blade, B) D-handled spade w/square point, C) folding GI shovel, and D) long-handled round-point. A and D are high-lift blades for shoveling; B is for digging; and the old GI shovel can be used any number of ways, but it's usually an on-your-knees job.

The difference between a digging shovel, right, and one meant to move dirt. Both are useful in the four-wheeling world, but if you have either, you can tailor what you carry to the conditions. For sand, snow, and mud, the shoveling blade is best. For piercing hard ground and making holes, the digging blade works best.

way around the obstacle. What's the trail like ahead? If a miles-long recovery slog looms ahead and a relatively easy drive back lies behind, which is best in your circumstance? If your destination lies ahead, do you have the time and equipment needed for the camel-like hours-per-mile grind?

If you are traveling in a group, let your recovery method suit the gang, within the limits of safety and common sense, of course. If you are a die-hard hand-wincher, for example, and enjoy spending hours cranking on a mechanical winch handle, the rest of the gang will either be comatose by the time you're done or they will have left you behind. It's an etiquette thing not to delay all your comrades unnecessarily.

BASIC RECOVERY EQUIPMENT

There is always a risk of carrying too much gear and getting stuck from the sheer tonnage of it! Tailor your gear to the trip. No chain saws in the desert, for example. Still, there are a few items on the "A" list that should be considered vital and we'll run though them here. Winches are covered in a separate section.

Shovel

A basic must-have. There are many uses for a shovel in the 4x4 world, from recovery to camping. First, some shovel basics. Shovels come with square, pointed, or round heads. They come with long or short handles, some with folding handles. The round or pointed heads pierce the ground better, but the square point cuts roots better. Some shovels have a rather large head and some are small. Some shovelheads are tilted and counterbalanced for shoveling rather than digging. The small- or medium-sized ones are the easiest to carry and are easier to use when digging in close quarters, such as under a vehicle. From my own experience, I prefer the round or pointed tip, as it can deal with hard ground better, and a shallow lift for digging. All types have a potential place in the four-wheeling world, but what you carry will at least partially be dictated by what you *can* carry.

The bare minimum for any rig is the ubiquitous folding GI entrenching tool. The GI shovel is convenient, easy to pack, and useful for close-in work, such as making a flat spot for a jack. Because it folds and locks, it can be used as both a shovel and a pick. The problem is the small size, which necessitates getting up close and personal with your "work." Many four-wheelers carry them along with a larger shovel.

Next up are the short, D-handle shovels. These shovels are very sturdy, but, while they take you a little farther away from your work, they still involve some stooping. It's small enough to make stowage fairly easy. It's not quite long enough to reach under the middle of a bigger rig.

Finally, the long-handled shovel is the best for frequent or serious use, but is the most difficult to stow. Get one with a beefy handle, as the extra leverage makes the long handle easy to break in hard use. People living in mud country are fond of these shovels because they use them the most.

Axes, Picks, and Saws

People who regularly travel wooded areas usually have an ax or saw along. Treefalls and hang-ing limbs make these items a necessity for the woods runner, although often a small hatchet or small saw is sufficient. There arc folding saws available that can take care of small limbs. Some folks will carry

Axes are very useful in wooded areas. With a good ax, you can cut through nearly any size timber given enough time and energy. From left to right, A) large hatchet, B) a "boy's" ax, and C) a full-sized ax. The hatchet rides with me all the time. When I lived in more wooded areas and had less space in my old rig, I carried the boy's ax because it was more compact. I seldom carry the big ax, but as you can see, it's been used as well.

If you are regularly in the woods, a saw is a very useful tool. Here is a selection of what I carry at different times. At the bottom is a small multiblade saw that is always in the vehicle's basic kit. It's useful for limbs and wood up to about 5 inches in diameter. The other two are just varying sizes of bow saws that I carry according to how big the trees may be. Some people actually carry chainsaws. That may seem to be overkill from some perspectives, but I've been around enough to see them earn their keep.

the dirt

Shovels:
A short, D-handle shovel provides the most utility in the most compact, easy-to-carry package. They're sturdy, versatile, and easily stowed.

TRAIL ENDERS

Safe Saws:
Keep your saw or ax securely stowed no matter how often a wooded stretch has you reaching for it. The same applies to your shovel. You never want tools—or any solid object—going airborne.

the dirt

Picks:
Some folks carry picks. They can be useful in rare circumstances, but most often they'll just be added weight. A particularly extended and remote trip might be one venue where a pick is justified.

The Max from the Forrest Tool Company is a multipurpose tool. The new units have a polycarbonate handle that's much stronger. The kit includes the ax, a small pointed shovel, rake, mattock, broad pick, and hoe. A leather ax sheath and canvas carrying case are included. It does just about everything, though not as well as a purpose-built tool. The ax stands up pretty well against other axes. This kit is great for all but those with specialized equipment needs.

Two ways of achieving the same thing. You can see the difference in design between the strap and the double-braided rope. Straps are more easily obtained, but in my experience, most people who have tried them like the ropes better for snatch recovery. I have both and use a strap mostly for towing, because it's a little more tolerant of chafing and is cheaper to replace when it gets worn from dragging on the ground.

full-blown axes or saws that would make a lumberjack smile. Some even carry chainsaws. Choose your weapon according to need but don't overload. If you have to pick one item, a hatchet is often more useful as a single tool than a saw.

for remote firefighters, it's a tool that has interchangeable heads that include an ax, shovel, rake, and pick. It doesn't work as well in each of its guises as the single-purpose tool would, but you can have them all at your fingertips and it's easy to stow.

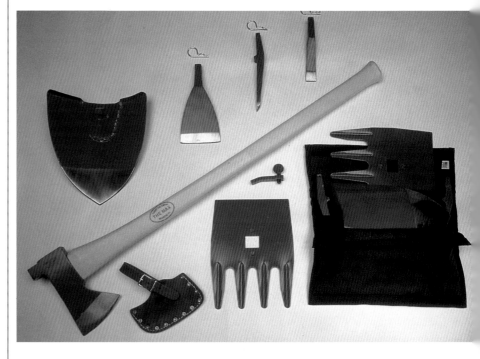

The Max

If you carry all the stuff listed above, you'll use up a fair bit of space. What if there were a universal tool that did it all? There is, and it's called the Max Multipurpose Tool. Designed

Recovery Straps and Ropes

A recovery strap or rope is another must-have that is part of trail etiquette. Recovery straps or ropes are used in most situations because they're faster and simpler than a winch. There are times when the slow, deliberate action of the winch is better and safer, but my own observations (by no means scientific) show that a recovery strap is the best option 80 percent of the time. Of course, with a recovery strap, you do need another vehicle!

At the early points of four-wheeling history, manila, hemp, or nylon hawsers (a hawser is another word for "big rope") were used. The nylon strap came into favor in the late 1960s and is now standard fare here in the United States. Elsewhere, recovery ropes (a.k.a. "K.E.R.R." – Kinetic Energy Recovery Rope) are more common. Rope is making a comeback here in the States, mostly through the efforts of a company called Master Pull.

The theory behind both types is stretch. The elasticity does two things. First, it cushions the shock, thus lessening the chance of shock loads breaking parts. The second is that it stores energy. The stored energy effectively multiplies the force applied. Recovery straps can be used for just a simple pull, or can be used for what is commonly known as a "snatch," or kinetic energy recovery. More on that a bit farther on.

Recovery Straps

Typical recovery straps are made of a woven nylon webbing, often used in cargo handling, that has eyes stitched in both ends. Strap widths vary from 2 to 4 inches, with capacity rated according to this size. A common 2-inch strap is rated for about 15,000 pounds and a common 3-inch strap at 22,000 pounds. Lengths run from 20 to 30 feet.

Most sources say that recovery straps will stretch by 15–20 percent. These ratings appear to come from the material (nylon) rating and not from tests of an actual strap. The elasticity, of course, is directly proportional to the amount of energy put into it and the strength rating of the strap. A lower-rated strap will stretch more than a higher-rated one when subjected to equal loads, but you need to make sure the strap is rated for 2–3 times the GVW of your rig.

There is a quality gap in strap manufacture. This is not so much with the strap material, which is largely generic, but with the stitching of the eye. To make the eye, the material is folded back and the two pieces are stitched together. The quality of the stitching is important, as well as the material used for thread. In some cases, ordinary cotton is used and it deteriorates with time and weakens when wet.

Recovery Ropes

Recovery ropes come in many forms historically, from the old three-strand nylon ropes to the more modern and effective double-braided rope. The double-braided material is what's on the market now. The Master Pull

If you use it for snatch recovery, start thinking about replacing a strap when it gets chafed like this. This unit is still safe for towing and perhaps even a light snatch. It may not be capable of its maximum rated performance, however.

"Super Yankers" run from 3/4 to 1-1/4 inches in diameter with 19,000 to 52,000-pound ratings. As with straps, common lengths run from 20–30 feet, but you can order longer lengths. Just like straps, the ropes are rated to stretch, in this case from 15–25 percent (even a bit more). The quality gap with ropes concerns the way the eyes are spliced, though splicing is inherently stronger than any other method of making an eye. Better ropes will have some sort of a chafing guard in the eye.

Recovery Ropes vs. Straps

Controversy is growing as to which type is better for recovery. At the moment, the people I know who have tested both prefer ropes. The consensus is that rope's increased elasticity absorbs shocks better. You can feel more of a jolt snatching with a strap than with a rope. This point was illustrated by Harry Lewellyn, the infamous "Silver Coyote" of ECO4WD. He subjected both a strap and a rope to the same pull and the strap stretched only 1.7 percent,

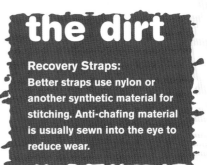

Getting out to wade for a recovery amounts to the worst of a bad situation. When there is ice in the water, double that assessment! This is pull-out recovery to aid a Jeep with a drowned ignition system. Somebody has to get out to hook up in this situation. Usually, etiquette dictates the driver of the stranded rig do the unpleasant task, but in this case the erstwhile rescuer in the Samurai does the dirty work.

the dirt

Recovery Straps:
Better straps use nylon or another synthetic material for stitching. Anti-chafing material is usually sewn into the eye to reduce wear.

The Hi-Lift jack is a very useful piece if you have the room to carry it and there are suitable places on your vehicle to use it. It can also be used as a winch. Some useful extras are the plastic base (red) from Hi-Lift, as well as some well-used homemade examples that do the same job. The ropes are useful for placement and recovery of the pieces. The yellow doodad is a Jack-Mate, which fits on either end of the Hi-Lift and provides very useful hookup capability as well as a good base for use in rocks or other irregular surfaces.

The adapter from Hi-Lift allows it to be used on certain types of bumpers.

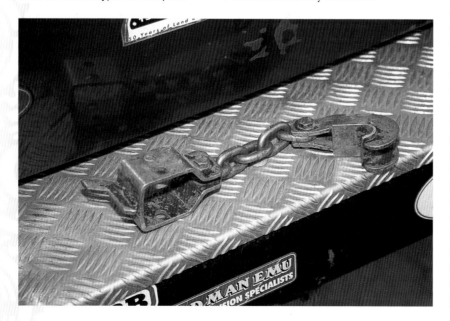

whereas the rope stretched some 14 percent. Another advantage to rope is that the spliced eyes retain the strength of the rope, whereas the stitched eyes of the strap are not as strong as the strap itself. Stitching failures are relatively common.

A Word On Chains and Wire Rope For Recovery

Some four-wheelers still rely on chains or cables for recovery but these can add greatly to the danger aspect. There is zero give in chain and very little in cable. That means every shock and jerk is transmitted to the towing points and this transfers a very high shock load that can break stuff. Many four-wheelers will not hook up to a chain to tow you out. The one good thing about chain is that when it breaks, or breaks an attachment, it's largely dead and drops immediately.

Tow Strap/Ropes

Tow straps or ropes are similar to the recovery straps and ropes, but they are usually of less capacity and have less elasticity. They are often shorter and are primarily used to tow a disabled vehicle from one point to another. They are preferable to a chain or cable in this role because their elasticity absorbs shock loads.

If you have a snatch strap or rope, there seems little need for a dedicated tow rope. Unfortunately, some people confuse snatch and tow straps and try to use the average tow strap for recovery, often with disastrous results. A quality strap may be up for some recovery work (simple tow-out rather than a snatch) if it has an adequate weight rating. The worst possible situation is encountered with those cheap, packaged tow straps that are commonly available from discount auto stores with hooks built into each end. The price is usually under $10 and while they may be capable of pulling a midsized car around on the street, they are less certain towing a heavy 4x4 up a steep slope, and much less capable of recovering a stranded rig. They break easily, sometimes with dangerous results.

Jacks

The very least you'll need is an OE-style telescoping jack to change flat tires. The problem is that if you upgrade tire size, the OE jack may not have enough lift—an embarrassing situation if you didn't think of it beforehand. Also, OE jacks run from OK to cheeseball. The old OE bumper jacks are usually dangerous, especially on a loaded rig. You can upgrade those old units with a telescoping jack as necessary, perhaps with a hydraulic unit. Many people opt for the legendary Hi-Lift jack.

The so-called "sheepherder's," or Hi-Lift jack, is a useful upgrade. Hi-Lift is the name brand that has become a noun for any jack of this type made by a variety of manufacturers. The original Hi-Lift has been in production since 1905 and has spawned many copies. Hi-Lift jacks come in a variety of heights and weight ratings. The actual Hi-Lift brand lifts 7,000 pounds and comes in four sizes: 36 inches, 42 inches, 48

inches, and 60 inches. One of these will lift your rig well free of the goo! The slick part is that they can also be used as a manual 7,000-pound winch that will pull (or push) you 3–4 feet at a time. It ain't as easy as an electric winch but it gets the job done. Storage and weight can be a problem in some rigs, but many rack and bumper manufacturers offer build in-storage brackets for them.

With any jack, you need to have a 1x1-foot piece of wood, or larger, for a base to prevent your jack from burying itself in soft ground. Marine plywood, at least 3/4-inch thick, is best because it doesn't split. The Hi-Lift Jack Company offers a base specifically for their jacks made out of molded, high-strength plastic.

NON-WINCH RECOVERY TECHNIQUES

All of these involve recovery by "armstrong," that is, they take a certain amount of manual labor. In some cases, they are alternatives to the use of mechanical devices. In others, they are the best or the only solution to certain problems.

Sometimes all a rig needs is a tiny bit of momentary help.

The wrong way to counterbalance a rig, right; and the right way, bottom. The guys hanging on the old Rover are in danger of being bucked off by sudden movement or hurled some distance if the vehicle goes over and they can't get clear. The guys helping the Samurai are much safer. If the rig goes over, they can walk forward or let go of the strap.

The Manhandle

When the original jeep was designed in 1940, one of the design criteria was that it be light and small enough to be "manhandled" out of any situation by no more than four soldiers. In WWII, there were few mechanical aids available, but even today, with all the great technology, it can still come down to human grunt. When a vehicle needs just a bit of help, the simplest solution may be for a couple of strong backs to give it a shove. In some cases, the manhandle is necessary only because some or all of those modern conveniences have been left behind. Ahem!

Simple and easy doesn't always mean safe. From the day the first jeep was manhandled out of a tricky spot, people have been getting injured doing it. It's important that the actions be coordinated and that the driver knows exactly what to do. Imagine a group running to push a rig up a slippery ledge, only to have an unaware driver decide to back out at that moment. Common sense also counsels people not to push or lift beyond their physical abilities. Don't expect four people to be able to lift the back end of a Suburban out of a hole. A Samurai, maybe.

Manhandling comes in several forms, starting with the ordinary push. A vehicle having traction problems and unable to move ahead can be given a shove by as few as one person, or by as many people as can find a spot to push. It takes very little time and the rig is on its way quickly and easily.

The next form of manhandling is the counterbalance. A rig on the edge of tipping over may need only a little extra weight on the high side to be secure. You will occasionally see people hanging all over a tilted rig. You will also see them hurled off by sudden movements of the vehicle as it tries to drive out. The safest way to counterbalance is not to hang on directly, but to attach a strap to a high point on the vehicle and have the helpers hold the vehicle secure with it. You can get more people on a rope or strap than you can hang off a vehicle, or you can

This classic Bronco needed a little help in the snow, so the little Samurai came to the rescue with a pull-out recovery. Sometimes all that's needed is just a little help for a short distance, and the strap is a fast and effective way to do it.

hook the strap to another vehicle. If the rig ultimately goes over, all they have to do is let go of the strap or walk forward. Never, *ever*, should anyone try to hold the vehicle up from the low side. Overall, it's better to let the rig go over than to get people injured in a vain attempt to save it.

A few burly souls can often roll a tipped rig back onto its wheels. Again, this is best done with bodies pulling on a strap or rope. When people are too close to a rolled rig being righted, they have a bad habit of getting hurt. The strap moves them away from the source of injury and if something bad occurs, all they have to do is let go of the strap.

Pull-Out Recovery

Pull-outs are often confused with a snatch. A simple pull-out, even if you are using a snatch strap, is not really a snatch. In that case, you are merely using the traction of another vehicle to aid one that is having difficulty. When the towing vehicle cannot generate the traction to pull the stranded rig out, that's when the snatch comes in.

Pull-outs are done slowly and gently by putting the towing vehicle on the best ground for traction and coordinating the pull with help from the vehicle in difficulty. All the stuff we talked about regarding hookup points applies. The rope is attached and the towing vehicle applies tension. At the command of a remotely sited spotter

who will coordinate the recovery, both rigs will apply power.

The towed rig needs to go lightly on the throttle, just below the point of tire spin, or just very slowly turning the tires. Spinning wildly will cause the vehicle to leap ahead when it does find traction.

The towing vehicle needs to apply a steady pull, using all the traction available, but below the point of spinning the tires excessively. The vehicle may slip a tire here and there, but if you are making progress, stick with it. If you are sitting there merely spinning rubber, it's time for another idea before something breaks. Try to keep tension on the rope until it's clear that the stranded rig is out of trouble. This prevents the stuck rig from running over the rope.

the dirt

Towing:
The towed vehicle should avoid running over the tow rope if possible. It won't hurt to have it under the vehicle, just avoid getting it under the tires. Getting it caught under the tire often breaks the rope.

Shackles are one of the universal items in winching and recovery. These are all screw-pin, or anchor, shackles. These are most often called "D" shackles, but the industry will call them "bow" shackles. Shackles are classified by the diameter of the bow. Only shackles with a working load rating on them should be used. This can be expressed in several ways: WLL (Working Load Limit), WL (Working Load), or SWL (Safe Working Load). Each of these terms reflects the safe load limits for which the shackle is rated. The breaking strength is actually higher, depending on the steel alloy used, with design factors from two to five times SWL. Here are the sizes that come into play most often. From the lower right, clockwise: the 5/8-inch has a 3/4-inch pin and a WLL rating of 7,000 pounds; the 3/4-inch unit has a 7/8-inch pin and an SWL of 9,500 pounds; the 7/8-inch shackle has a 1-inch pin and an SWL of 17,000 pounds; and the 3/4-inch has a 7/8-pin but a high WLL of 13,000 pounds. As you can see, two shackles of the same size can have different weight ratings. Buy the best!

The Hi-Lift can be used as a winch as well as a jack. Point the top end of the jack to the vehicle that needs to be moved and attach a chain or strap. The Jack Mate is a handy item that makes hookup easier. Lower the jack to the bottom of travel, and, using the special Hi-Lift attachment (see inset) that attaches to the lifting part of the jack, attach the jack to the dead-man.

Without the jack base, the jack sinks out of sight in soft ground.

This is what happens when the bumper isn't up to supporting the weight of the vehicle.

This is a tricky operation—a rock-sliced tire on a steep, maximum-performance climb. Not only that, the Jeep was wedged against the bank and couldn't back down easily. The trick was to secure the Jeep with a winch cable and use the Hi-Lift to lift the unit up enough to install the spare.

Snatch Recovery

The snatch, or kinetic energy recovery, is a tricky operation that should not be undertaken lightly. When a simple pull-out attempt will not do the job, the possibility of a snatch can be considered. At that point, the smart first step is to look around for a winch. A winching operation is always preferable to a snatch. Why? Winching is a slower, more controlled operation and therefore safer. A snatch involves vehicles at speed and requires split-second timing and coordination. There's lots of energy at work and if it goes awry, bad stuff happens. That said, the snatch is much faster, less complicated, and more appealing to people wanting to maximize fun time. In deciding on a snatch or a winch operation, ask the following:

- Do both rigs have very good towing points?
- Is the area clear? Tight quarters makes the operation trickier.
- What are the ground conditions? I am less inclined to snatch in rocky terrain because of the danger of running the rig into rocks and the wheel blocking effect. Example: Don't try to snatch a rig up a ledge unless the height of the ledge is well below the height of the hub. If the ledge is higher than the hub, it becomes a very effective wheel block.

If, in light of these questions, you determine that a snatch is safe and practical, get the rigs properly attached (see page 169) and clear the area of people. If possible, use an outside spotter, located in a safe spot that both drivers can see, to coordinate the operation. The two drivers can do it, but an outside person can do it better. The towing vehicle will back toward the stranded vehicle a few feet and the strap or rope will be set so that it will pay out cleanly and not kink. On command, the stranded rig will apply a little power and the towing rig will launch forward at a fast walking pace. The slack will come out and the strap will rapidly come to attention and stretch like a rubber band. The energy of the towing vehicle in motion is multiplied by the elasticity of the strap

and, in theory, the stranded rig leaps from its predicament like a cat that falls into a bathtub. But what if it doesn't?

The level of energy can be ratcheted up as much as the participants dare by applying more speed and distance. Backing up more and applying more speed will raise the energy level considerably. The danger is that the energy will exceed the capacity of the strap or the towing points of either or both vehicles. That's where it gets dangerous.

How much speed or energy is enough? That point is variable according to the strap rating, the towing points of both vehicles, and the relative weights of the vehicles. It's so variable that it's hard to give a number. Most experts recommend speeds of no more than a fast walking pace and backing no more than one-quarter to one-third the length of the strap. You will see people use more energy than that, but within the speed and distance limits mentioned, assuming excellent towing points and a strap in good condition, you should be safe.

Jacking Out of Trouble

This applies mostly to the sheepherder's-type jacks that were made by the Hi-Lift Jack Company and others. The techniques that you'll see listed here are commonly used on the trail, but are not always advocated by the jack manufacturer.

The Jack Mate slips onto the lower end of a Hi-Lift and provides a purchase on things such as this knob on a boulder. It's shown lifting up the heavy front of the author's rig here during a test. It works! Note the eye for a shackle and the chain slot.

Kinetic Energy Dangers:
If a stretched rope or strap breaks, it will send its loose ends and any shackle or broken attachment point flying at speeds in excess of one hundred miles per hour. Such projectiles can go through glass like air and punch through a body panel like an armor-piercing anti-tank shell. Keep yourself and other people well clear of towlines at all times and exercise equal care at the wheel.

The Hi-Lift jack is ideal for jacking a rig off a boulder, as Bill Burke demonstrates. The slick snow conditions caused the Bum-V's tires to slip off the boulder and get hung up on the axle. Jacking it clear was the easy, nondamaging cure. Note the Jack Mate getting a bite on a small knob on the rock.

Jacking:
If the vehicle is on an incline, jacking is very dangerous. Look for another way to solve the problem, such as one of the other recovery methods discussed in this chapter.

The first requirement for a sheepherder's jack is that your vehicle can safely use one without damage. Many modern rigs cannot because they don't have solid bumpers or jacking points. There are a few adapters available that can fill the gaps in some vehicle applications, but often the only alternative is a replacement heavy-duty bumper or custom-built stuff. Check on your rig's suitability before shelling out for a Hi-Lift. In some cases, you can use a worm or hydraulic jack to lift a rig out of a hole or rut, but obviously, the degree of difficulty is higher and the danger may be greater. Necessity is the mother of invention when you don't have the right tools, but think safety whatever you do.

Since Hi-Lifts come in various jacking heights, you need one that fits your rig. They all are rated for approximately the same weight capacity, but the amount of lift differs. A stock rig could use one of the shorter jacks, but a tall, big-tired rig will need the taller unit for obvious reasons. You need enough lift to reach the jacking point, account for suspension travel, and lift the rig clear of whatever is the problem.

The most common scenarios for using a sheepherder's jack are when a vehicle has sunk deeply into soft ground or is hung up on an obstacle. The jack is placed to lift one end of the rig up out of the ruts or holes, which are then filled in. On soft ground, the jack will need a base to avoid sinking into the ground. Usually a 1x1-foot piece of flat material will work, but on extremely soft ground you might need something bigger.

The danger with a rig jacked up without the safety of stands is that the jack can release (not likely with a HD unit such as a Hi-Lift, but it's possible) or the vehicle can roll off the jack. For that reason, the rig must be secured from rolling away from the jack, or off to the side. Blocking the tires will keep it from rolling away and a few well-placed bodies may be enough to hold it from going off to the side. That or a strap (or straps) from another rig or secured to a tree. Keep the jack handle in the up position, which locks the mechanism. Regardless of these precautions, *nobody* goes underneath the rig!

There is an unauthorized but useful technique called the "jack-n-drop." The vehicle is jacked up out of the holes or ruts and allowed (or encouraged) to roll off the jack to one side. In theory, the tires end up on solid ground. It works, most times at least, but it's hard on the jack. The manufacturers don't like to warrantee a jack broken this way, not to mention be liable for injuries. I've done it, but my opinion is that it's a lazy way to do the job. A responsible 'wheeler is going to fill the tire holes anyway, so why not start off that way?

Soft-Ground Support

It's one thing to get stuck in a small hole, but it's another to face an endless sea of soft stuff. One method of support on soft ground is the use of sand ladders or planks. Sand ladder is the common name for PSP (Perforated Steel Planking) or PAP (Perforated Aluminum Planking), which is used by the military for building remote airfields. This is great and useful stuff in the right venue, but few four-wheelers

Good Attachments, Bad Attachments

Good Attachment. The eye of the strap is inserted into the Class III receiver and the receiver pin is pushed through the eye. This makes for a quick, economical attachment. There is some danger of chafing at extreme angles, but an advantage is that there is no heavy metal attached to the strap end to become a cannonball if something fails at this end.

Bad Attachment. Not only is this a not-so-stout Class II receiver, the strap is hooked to a hitch ball. First off, the strap can slip off. Second, the 1-7/8-inch ball can break off due to shock loads or overloading and become a cannonball.

Good Attachment. This receiver attachment from Warn is designed for use with a 3/4-inch D-shackle rated for a safe working load of 13,000 pounds. Other manufacturers offer similar products. This is a stout setup, offset only by the remote possibility that an attachment failure at a high load could turn this hunk of metal into a dangerous projectile.

Bad Attachment. Lots to talk about here! First is that the bumper probably isn't strong enough to handle a hard pull. Second, the sharp edges at the back of the bumper could cut the strap even if the bumper held. Third, where are this guy's tow hooks?!

So-So Attachment. In the absence of other proper hookups, this would be at the bottom end of acceptable. If the ball did shear off, it would be pulled forward.

PSP (Perforated Steel Planking) or PAP (Perforated Aluminum Planking) can be useful in rare instances, but it's a pain to carry around.

the dirt

Road Building:
To cross a stretch of soft ground, you could do what the old miners did in the Colorado mountains. They paved the roads with logs and the practice was called corduroy. Some of that work is still there one hundred years later.

the dirt

Tire Chains:
Chains are truly remarkable in mud. You might even try them *before* you get stuck!

have the need or the carrying space. It looks cool if you have a place to carry it.

The idea is to pave the soft stuff with material to spread the weight of the vehicle over a larger area. A short stretch may be needed, or a long one. Given a finite length of available material, it would be necessary to keep moving the PSP planks from behind to in front in a continual motion. In some parts of the world, four-wheelers have done this for miles at a stretch.

Alternatives? Use natural building materials. This could include logs and sticks. If you do, make them relatively short so they won't flip up and cause damage. Use only deadwood, please, and clean up the area when finished.

Slippery Stuff

There are places where the ground surface will support vehicle weight but not provide traction. Ice is the usual suspect, but Greasy Mud can play the same trick. On ice, some sand, or dirt, branches thrown on top can get you moving. The branches will work in

mud, as can small rocks. For lack of anything else, your floor mats, tent, or clothing can work if you're prepared to write them off afterward.

Tire chains are probably the best bet. They bite into ice and they work like paddles in Greasy Mud. There are mud chains and ice chains; the mud units use larger-link chain. The ice chains will work OK in mud, but the mud chains aren't ideally suited to icy highways.

Towing

This usually involves towing a disabled or partially disabled rig back to civilization. Bear in mind that many states do not allow rope tows on the highway, so you can expect some attention from the local constabulary if you drag a dead rig into town on the highway at the end of a rope. Also be aware that vehicles with automatic transmissions should not be towed long distances unless they have a true neutral position on the transfer case or the driveshafts are removed to prevent the transmission from turning.

The strap needs to be long enough to leave time for the towed driver to react, but short enough to keep both rigs on roughly the same section of the road. Fifteen to twenty feet seems a workable number, but longer lengths can work as well. The shortening options are to tie a knot in the strap, which is not a good idea as they are almost impossible to undo, or to double the strap into a "Y," called a yoke. Recovery ropes are a bit more tolerant of knots—simply tie a bowline to shorten the strap. The tow strap should be moused (tape, tie, or wire the eye onto the hook) to prevent it from falling off the towing attachment. Avoid dragging the rope or strap on the ground. Chafing will weaken it. The pace? Slow. Dead slow, as conditions warrant.

Towing requires a great deal of attention from both drivers. If the towing vehicle has an operable engine, it's best to have it running to supply power steering and brakes. Otherwise, both drivers should be aware that some extra arm and leg muscle will be required to steer or brake. The goal of both drivers is to keep tension on the tow rope. That means the towed rig will be using a lot of brakes and the towing rig will be gentle with speed changes, and will signal stops and turns. Avoid running over the strap or putting abrupt tensioning on it. The towed rig driver will be too busy to want to feel like the proverbial one-armed paperhanger!

Problem situations come in very rough ground, where the terrain must be covered extremely slowly. In steep terrain, the towing rig may not have the traction to pull the dead rig up a slope. In these cases, a winch or a second vehicle attached to the towing rig can supply the extra muscle needed. Turns can also be a problem, and the towed and towing rigs must coordinate a line around tight corners. A long strap complicates turns.

WINCHES AND WINCHING

This section encompasses all types of winching, both power and manual. We'll cover most types of power winches, though the manufacturer's instructions will take precedence when they differ. We'll also show a few types of manual winches. While winching techniques are similar for all types, we'll give a few specifics on operating each kind.

Manual Winches

These run the gamut from the ordinary "come-along" that's available from the hardware store to some pretty fancy units that cost more than some power winches. Manual winches

This Warn accessory kit represents the basic winch gear. It consists of a 10-foot length of 5/16-inch Grade 7 transport chain (SWL 4,700 pounds); an 8-foot, 2-inch tree strap; a snatch block (16,000 pounds, 4-inch sheave); a couple of 3/4-inch shackles; and a handy carrying bag.

share one thing: the need for human strength. The mechanical advantage on some is such that they are not a huge strain to operate. Others will definitely get your sweat glands into operation.

There are still a number of four-wheelers who rely solely on a manual winch and their own strength for recovery. Stout-hearted souls, every one! There are other 'wheelers with power winches who use the mechanical winch as a backup to provide an additional source of power in complicated recovery situations, where pulls might be needed from more than one location.

continued on page 174

Here's an example of a snatch block winching operation. The white Wrangler has slid off the road in relatively deep snow and its driver's repeated attempts to drive it back onto the roadbed have put it farther over the edge. The green Jeep cannot get past the white one due to the slippery conditions, so the cable was run to a tree and then back to the white Jeep. This pulled the Jeep back onto the road where it could continue in the 18-inch-deep snow. The driver of the white Jeep assisted the winch with the available traction.

Winching Hall of Fame (and Shame)

Fame. There are five wraps left on the drum, just enough to carry a full load. Poly rope needs two or three more wraps.

Shame. Unless you like raw hamburger on the end of your arms, use gloves.

Fame. Checking the winch motor temp during a long hard pull will preserve the equipment. If it's too hot to touch with a bare hand, it's too hot to use. Let it cool and let the battery charge.

Shame. This wire rope is history and it shouldn't be used. It's lost a major portion of its strength at this point and a full winch load may well break it.

Fame. Using a tree strap saves the tree for later enjoyment.

Shame. Hooking a wire rope back onto itself is a sure path to ruined rope and, possibly, major failure.

Fame. Putting a damper on a highly stressed winch line is good insurance. If the cable or attachments break, the damper will help slow the cable down.

Shame. Routing a bare cable around a rock is asking for chafing damage or outright failure.

Fame. Routing the winch control wire carefully keeps it clear of the winch drum and the tires.

Shame. Using homemade or unrated gear can be risky. Some people have the engineering sense and skill to design and build something at home. Others do not. This one looked rather nicely done.

Fame. A piece of wood can be used as chafing protection.

Shame. When the spinning tires of this vintage Jeep flatfender hook up, it's going to leap far ahead of the Pierce Winch 9,000-pound unit, possibly overrunning the cable. All you need to do is give the winch a little assist. This worm gear winch is so powerful that this driver could probably stand on the brakes and still be winched out.

Fame. It's best not to cross a loaded winch cable, but if you must, step on it as Bill Burke demonstrates—but only if the cable is stationary. This way, if something were to happen, you would simply be hurled aside rather than cut in half.

Fame. The proper way to butterfly a winch cable. It's much easier than re-spooling when winching situations are frequent. The key element is to make sure the cable will stay in place.

A simple single-line pull with the Jeep attached to a tree via a strap. The Jeep wasn't seriously mired and needed only a little help, so the single line was enough. He was on the second layer of cable on the drum, so his ultimate pull would have been reduced somewhat. Had the vehicle been more seriously mired, a double-line pull would have been necessary.

3) Requires operator to be closer to cable.
4) They are slow.
5) They can be forgotten at home.
6) Those with built-in cable drums are short on cable.

Suggested Use
1) Primary recovery in low-cost situations.
2) Second source of pulling power for hard-core 'wheelers.

Power Winches

A power winch is operated by some type of motor, whether it be electric, hydraulic, or PTO (Power Take-Off) mechanical. These are the three major divisions, but ultimately they are all powered by the engine, directly or indirectly. If the engine is dead, the winch will be dead sooner or later.

Mechanical

Mechanical winches were once the standard. Some early winches were driven directly by the engine, but later ones use the transfer case or the transmission PTO drive points. They still have a place in commercial situations due to their nearly unlimited duty cycle. They are less popular with recreational users.

Because most PTO winches are powered through the transmission, they have as many speeds as the transmission has gears. The transfer case is not a factor, even if the PTO is driven from there because it draws power from the transmission output shaft. In this case, the forward gears spool the winch in and reverse spools it out. At any given engine speed, the winch is slower in first gear than it is in high gear. PTOs may also be driven from certain heavy-duty manual transmissions via an access port in the side of the case.

The choker chain in the winch kit is useful for such things as moving logs. The chain is used where chafing damage might result to a strap and where there is no worry about the chain causing damage to living or valuable things. The chain can be useful for hookups on the chassis of rigs without proper recovery points. On older winches, such as the vintage Braden PTO winch on this old Power Wagon, a section of chain was attached to the end of the cable more or less permanently. This was the sign of a winch that was used for work rather than recovery. Note the fellow playing with the winch cable, sans gloves. Ahem!

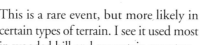

This is a rare event, but more likely in certain types of terrain. I see it used most in wooded hill and mountain country.

Manual Winch Advantages
1) Usually lower cost than a power winch.
2) Lightweight.
3) Can be used anywhere—front, rear, sides.
4) Can be left at home when not needed.
5) Good backup for power winch.

Manual Winch Disadvantages
1) They are, well, *manual!*
2) Usually they are lower capacity than power winches.

Mechanical Winch Advantages:
1) Longevity due to simple, robust construction.
2) Can be used for long periods at a stretch. Nearly unlimited duty cycle.

Stuck and unable to make the climb, Don Haynes gets the chance to test the new Qwik Winch. In reality, a little digging would have enabled him to back down, but the direction of travel was up. Note how much more deeply the rear is dug in compared to the front. This is weight transfer in action.

The manual Qwik Winch is designed to use the receiver as a base of operations. Don has receivers welded to both the front and the rear of his Wrangler TJ. The winch carries 90 feet of 3/16-inch aircraft cable and is capable of a 1,600-pound single-line pull (with three layers of wire rope), but pulleys are available to quadruple the pull to 6,400 pounds.

Because the pull was uphill and his rig was buried in deep sand, Haynes opted for the triple purchase. The line runs from the winch to one sheave of a double pulley at the anchored end then back to a single pulley at the Jeep. It runs back again to the second sheave of the double pulley at the anchor and back to the Jeep.

Haynes reported that the winch was easy to crank with the triple purchase. The towrope is there as a damper in case something comes loose.

3) Flexible line speeds according to transmission gearing and engine speed. In high gear and at up to 2,000-rpm engine speed, they are the fastest winches.
4) Often has a large cable capacity.
5) Waterproof operation.
6) Very powerful.

Mechanical Winch Disadvantages:
1) More difficult to use alone.
2) More difficult to use, period.

3) If the engine doesn't run, neither does the winch.
4) Increased maintenance, including lubing driveshaft U-joints, oil in gearboxes.
5) Increased weight of unit.
6) Few choices available, few mounting kits available, and many newer rigs cannot be fitted due to lack of PTO driving points.
7) Complicated installation.
8) Relatively high cost.

Suggested Use:
1) Owners who regularly work their winches for long periods.
2) Commercial applications.

Desirable or Necessary Improvements:
(N=Necessary, D=Desirable)
1) Synthetic oil in gearboxes to reduce friction. (D)
2) Improved engine cooling system for heavy loads at prolonged low rpm. (D)

Winching Hand Signals

1- Stop! One clenched fist could be regarded as a normal speaking voice. Double fists is a shout!

2- Winch in.

3- Winch Out.

4- A little bit. Could be combined with winch in or winch out.

5- I'm working on the cable at the drum. See the appropriate driver response in photo six.

6- The appropriate driver response to number five. The winch control lying in clear view on the dash or a pair of empty hands are also commonly used.

Hydraulic Winches

Hydraulic winches have been available for many years but had not generally been used in the recreational market until the MileMarker unit appeared in 1995. The hydraulic power needed to run the winch can be supplied by an electrically driven pump, an engine-driven pump (either a belt-driven hydraulic pump or the power steering pump), or by a PTO-driven hydraulic pump.

Hydraulic winches are known for their ability to tolerate long duty cycles. They can have as long a cycle as a PTO winch, though there's some chance of overheating the hydraulic fluid. Commercial hydraulics are generally worm gear units (essentially a PTO winch with a hydraulic motor), while the MileMarker (designed for the recreational market) is a planetary unit, essentially a planetary-drive winch with a hydraulic motor.

Operation is similar to an electric winch, with a few differences. Mile-Marker's newest two-speed has great pulling power in low, and the line speed at full load is good. When it comes to spooling in and rewinding cable or light pulls, using the high setting puts line speed near the top of the recreational winch crowd. The single-speed hydraulics aren't much faster with no load than with a full load, but while they may be slow spooling in empty, they are among the faster units with a load. Until another company comes out with a hydraulic winch for the recreational vehicle crowd, when we talk about hydraulics, we're essentially talking about the MileMarker.

The Avenair More Power Puller lives up to its name and is a popular manual winch. I used this one for a number of years as my main recovery tool. The only downside is that the 3/8-inch wire rope on the small-diameter drum tends to snarl up easily when not kept taut.

Hydraulic Winch Advantages:
1) Long duty cycle.
2) Waterproof operation.
3) Easy solo operation.
4) Simple installation.
5) Low weight.

For many years, into the 1970s, PTO winches were a big part of the market. This Ramsey Model 200 was an option for trucks in the era of Jim and Peg Marski's vintage 1969 Jeep J-2000 pickup. While these winches have an almost unlimited duty cycle, they are complicated, heavy, and difficult to use solo.

The MileMarker hydraulic winch debuted in 1994 and offered recreational four-wheelers a shot at the utility and precision of a hydraulic winch. These units are powered by the vehicle's power steering pump.

6) Low maintenance.
7) Low electrical load.
8) Relatively low cost.
9) Precise control.
10) Fast line speed under load.

Hydraulic Winch Disadvantages:
1) Slower line speed unloaded.
2) When the engine doesn't run, neither does the winch.
3) Not suitable for all vehicles. Some do not have a sufficiently powerful power steering pump.

Suggested Use:
1) Vehicle recovery or work where a long duty cycle or precise control is needed.

Desirable or Necessary Improvements (MileMarker):
(N=Necessary, D=Desirable)
1) Flush power steering fluid. (N)

2) Power steering cooler on return line. (D)
3) Improved engine cooling system for prolonged low-speed operation. (D)

Electric Winches

Electrics have all but taken over the recreational four-wheeling market and for good reason. They are light-weight, easy to operate, and easy to install. For the four-wheeler who needs occasional help out of sticky situations, they are a good choice. Currently, a wide variety of choices are available in terms of mounting systems, winch ratings, and winch performance.

There is a wide range of durability in the electric winch world. Most are best suited for occasional recovery use and have a short duty cycle. The short duty cycle isn't a problem as long as you give the motor time to cool and the battery time to recharge. The upper-echelon electric winches have a longer duty cycle in terms of the motor's capacity to endure heat, but the electrical system drain can still be a problem without extra mods.

Electric Winch Advantages:
1) Light weight.
2) Easy installation.
3) Easy operation.
4) Lowest cost.
5) Will run for a short while without the engine running (up to 5 minutes at a full load, depending on battery[ies]).
6) Widest range of applications.

Electric Winch Disadvantages:
1) Short duty cycle.
2) Severe loads on electrical system that can cause battery or alternator failure if duty cycle is exceeded.
3) Motors subject to overheating and failure if duty cycle exceeded.
4) Can be ruined by water.

Desirable or Necessary Improvements
(N=Necessary, D=Desirable)
1) Increased-capacity battery. (N)
2) Dual-purpose marine-type battery. (D)
3) Dual batteries, one being an isolated deep cycle. (D)
4) High-output, continuous-duty alternator. (D)

The perennial favorite in recreational four-wheeling is the electric winch. They are inexpensive, lightweight, and come in a huge variety of weight ratings up to about 15,000 pounds. Winches under 6,000-pound rating should not really be considered, except for extremely light vehicles. The "average" 4x4 should have an 8,000-pound winch, or more, depending on vehicle weight. This is a Ramsey planetary-drive electric with a few years and miles on it.

Electric Winch Drivetrains

Three basic types of drivetrains have withstood the test of time—spur gear, worm gear, and planetary. Each has some particular advantages and disadvantages. The only spur gear unit to remain on the market is the venerable and legendary Warn 8274-50. Spur gear winches are very fast but are usually at the high end of the full-load amp draw spectrum. On the downside, they are bulky (mostly tall) and will not fit on every vehicle.

Worm gear winches go back as far as spur gear types at least, but there have been few worm-only-type electric winches, none in the recreational market. To remain compact, the worm drive part of the unit is connected to the motor via two or more spur gears. The motor lies under or alongside the winch gear housing. The spur gears offer some extra gear reduction as well and reduce the size of the gear needed to drive the drum shaft. The advantages of a worm gear setup are that they are very good at holding a load and need very little in the way of a braking mechanism. On the downside, they are bulkier, heavier, and slower.

Electrical Considerations

If you choose an electric winch, give some thought to your electrical system. If your winch is destined for occasional, relatively light-duty use, you can get by with your OE charging system and battery by taking care to keep winching duration short. Normal starting–type batteries do not like being deeply discharged, so winching at "five-on-five-off" intervals will allow the motor to cool as well as letting your charging system pump some amps back into the battery. Bear in mind that permanent magnet motors, as fitted to many lower-rated winches, draw some 10–15 percent fewer amps than the heavier-duty series wound motors, but they are less tolerant of abuse and heat.

Your first upgrade would be to install a dual-purpose, or marine, battery. A marine battery can withstand repeated discharges much better than a starting battery. You can make this change when you replace your current starting battery when it tires out. Also, buying the biggest, highest-rated battery that will fit your application will extend winching capacity.

the dirt

Winches:
The most recent addition to the winch lineup is the planetary gear winches. They use a small planetary gear, similar to what's used in automatic transmissions. Their best features are compact size and low cost. They're in the middle between the spur and worm gear types for friction and amp draw.

A winch mount bumper need not be ugly or clunky. This stylish ARB unit is sharp enough to work well even with a Grand Cherokee. This one has been painted to match. Look for a bumper that doesn't adversely affect approach angle.

The Basic Winch Operations

You're stuck! Step one is to release the clutch on the motor so that the cable will freespool. How this is done varies from winch to winch. Once you've determined what you will use as a dead man, freespool the winch cable to that location. Gauge the difficulty of the pull and, if it will be a difficult pull, either spool out to the last layer on the drum for maximum power or use a snatch block to double the power.

Make a secure hookup to a solid object that won't move or be uprooted. If it's a living object, use a strap so it won't be harmed.

Disengage the freespool on the winch and plug in the winch control. Route the wire so that it won't be caught in the drum, a tire, or anywhere else. Take up the slack in the cable and add a blanket, coat, or purpose-built kinetic-energy damper to the cable.

The safest location to winch from is the cockpit. If you are solo, you will have to stop periodically to make sure the cable spools correctly on the winch drum. If you use poly rope, this is less important because it cannot be damaged by crushing.

Battery voltage and winch motor life are interrelated. The farther down battery voltage goes, the hotter the motor gets. Ideally, keep battery voltage above 10 volts when winching, but never run it below 7.5 volts. Unless you have a big battery or a big alternator, the only way to meet these conditions on a long pull is by stopping periodically to let your battery build up juice. The motor will then get a cooling-off period as well.

Some owners install a second battery just for the winch. A true deep-cycle battery can supply more amps over a longer period of time than either a starting or even a marine battery. If the second battery is isolated from the starting battery, you don't have to worry about being able to start the engine after a long winch pull.

Some owners also install a larger alternator to help with winch use. Industrial alternators rated at over 200 amps are available for many 4x4 engines. An example would be the Premier Power or the Wrangler Power Products line of HD alternators. Bear in mind that your OE alternator may not be up to extended use at full output. Most OE alternators have a short duty cycle at full output. Like a winch motor, they can overheat and go up in smoke when worked too hard.

Choosing Winch Capacity

The most important consideration is winch capacity. The manufacturers all come pretty close to each other in terms of recommended capacity. The minimum capacity to look for is your gross vehicle weight (not curb weight) plus about 15 percent. If your pickup's GVW is 8,600 pounds, add 15 percent and you get 9,890 pounds, rounded up to 10,000 pounds.

Choosing Line Capacity

It stands to reason that more line will allow you to reach out farther. True, but more line is a mixed blessing. To start with, your winch's maximum rated pull is on the first, or innermost, layer of wire rope (see nearby chart). The rating decreases with each succeeding layer. The more

line you have on the drum, the farther you are away from that maximum rating. The other consideration is that more line on a drum is easier to get snarled up, jammed, and kinked. Many winchers prefer less line on the winch but carry an extra 50-foot length as an extension.

Choosing Line Speed

Line speed is really only an issue when spooling in after a recovery. Many winches are extremely fast unloaded, but all will slow down to between 1 and 8 feet per minute under a full load (most are 3–5 feet per minute), thus putting them all in the same general ballpark. Some people think line speed is an important issue, and others don't care. A winch that's very slow will take an eternity to re-spool, but then we can all benefit from learning to take the time to properly re-spool our winches each time. Generally, PTO winches are the fastest, followed by spur gear electrics, planetary (electric or hydraulic two-speeds), and worm gear types.

Those who compete in rockcrawling competitions have an issue with line speed. Since they are negotiating tough rockcrawling situations on the clock, they want a fast winch that will spool in fast under load or not. They use the winch to get them over a bad spot, but they don't want to lose more time stopping to unhook, so the winch must come close to keeping up with the vehicle. The old standby is the Warn 8274, but recently Warn

Winch Safety:
Always wear gloves when working with wire rope. Broken strands can hook the skin and really tear up your hands.

the dirt

Winch Pull:
Spooling out more cable is both easier on the winch and generates more pull. It's the same situation as big tires vs. small tires. The smaller "tires" (the wraps closest to the drum) offer a "lower" effective gear ratio, making it easier on the motor, lowering amp draw, and reducing heat.

Winch Line Speeds

Line speed and rated pull are determined by the layers of cable. The principle is similar to how tire diameter affects axle ratios. The first layer, like the shortest tire, offers the lowest overall ratio and speed, and the most power. The last layer, like the tallest tire, provides the highest ratio and highest speed, but is least powerful.

Line Pull and Speed vs. Layer
MileMarker 10,500-pound unit, low gear

Layer	1	2	3	4
Line Speed	6.42 FPM	7.3 FPM	8.42 FPM	9.75 FPM
Rated Pull	10,500 lbs	8,500 lbs	7,400 lbs	6,400 lbs

introduced the HS line, which combines a high-power motor with tall gears for blistering-fast line speed.

Choosing a Mounting System

First, I won't tell you anything about looks and style. Beyond that, obviously, the mount must be able to handle the pulling capacity of the winch. After that, the weight of the assembly (winch and mount) becomes an issue. Too much weight may cause your front suspension to sag lower and possibly bottom out on rough terrain taken at speed. Some rigs are more tolerant of this extra weight than others, pickups over SUVs, for example. How far the unit hangs out will also dictate how much the unit is affected by weight. The farther it hangs out, the more leverage it exerts. All this can be compensated for by stiffer front springs, but that adds to the overall cost.

Two other important considerations are how the winch mount affects your approach angle and the accessibility of the winch cable. A mount that seriously impairs your approach angle may be a net loss in the performance department, perhaps causing you to *need* your winch more.

Free access to the winch cable is both a cost and safety issue. If you can't properly re-spool your cable, it will get damaged. If it gets damaged, it may part and hurt you or someone else. Also, if the cable is difficult to access, the owner is more susceptible to hand injuries if trying to re-spool properly.

Portable winches are fairly popular and useful in many arenas. They have some inherent disabilities and a few great advantages. The main advantage is that they can be used front or rear. Most plug into a Class III–type receiver, but a few hook up via shackles, cables, and such. Most are electric, using special high-amp plug-in electrical connectors. A few use a small gasoline engine, but they reduce approach and departure angle and do not tolerate side angles well.

Wire Rope

Wire rope is the heart of the winch. The two things that kill wire rope are abrasion and fatigue. Crushing also causes damage. Wire ropes with more wires per strand, such

Receiver winches can be handy, especially when you can put them in the rear. They can be left at home when not needed. On the downside, they are not tolerant of side pulls, and may be difficult to install on a rig mired to the bumper. If left in place, it seriously degrades departure angle. They are the most viable option on rigs without good, or good-looking, bumper mounts available. On many rigs, the receivers can be installed behind those plastic valances so popular these days, with only the actual 2x2 receiver protruding.

as 6x37, are more resistant to fatigue because they bend more easily, but they are less resistant to abrasion because of the thin wires. On the other hand, 7x19 ropes are more resistant to abrasion but less to fatigue. The 7x19 is pretty universal, but some owners replace theirs with 6x37 WSC for more flexibility and a slightly higher breaking strength, and the cost is nearly double per foot.

Wire rope can be made of various grades of steel, but most are carbon steel or stainless steel. The steel type used is directly related to the rope's overall strength, flexibility, resistance to abrasion, and resistance to fatigue. Commonly, Improved Plow Steel (IPS) and Extra Improved Plow Steel (EIPS) are used. Most recreational winches use galvanized cable. The galvanizing reduces the strength of the wire rope by as much as 10 percent, but that's usually calculated into the nominal breaking strength listed for the particular rope.

Breaking strength, or nominal breaking strength, is the commonly shown specification for wire rope. Nominal is the key word. That spec does not include any manufacturing defects from the factory or wear and tear from use. Though made of steel, typical wire rope is relatively fragile. It can be damaged by chafing, kinking, crushing, and normal wear and tear. Every tiny strand that breaks weakens it, and if enough of these tiny strands break, the entire rope will go. By the way, these broken strands (sailors call 'em "fishhooks") can rend flesh. Snip them off with wire cutters as they appear.

The "cardinal sins" of wire rope use are to hook it back onto itself, allow it to chafe against hard objects such as rocks and especially sharp edges, and allow it to get wadded onto your drum and crushed during a winching operation. All of these situations contribute to shortening the working life of the cable and decrease your safety margin. Replace the cable when it gets damaged. There's no point hauling the winch around if it's not at full, safe pulling capacity.

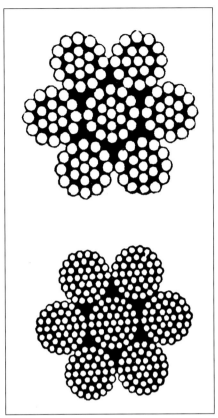

The two common types of wire rope used for 4x4 winches are 7x19 (top) and 6x37 WSC. Most winches come standard with 7x19 WSC galvanized aircraft cable in assorted diameters. The 7x19 designation refers to the number and configuration of the strands that make up wire rope, in this case seven strands (or bundles) of 19 wires each. Seven-strand wire is made up of six strands around the seventh, hence the WSC (Wire Strand Core) designation. This wire rope is also sometimes known as 6x19 SC (Strand Core).

UHMWPE

UHMWPE stands for Ultra High Molecular Weight Polyethylene Fiber (just call it "poly") and it's a new form of winch rope. It's stronger than wire rope of the same diameter (13,700 pounds vs. 9,800 for 5/16 inch) and much lighter. A 120-foot roll of 5/16 cable, for example, weighs nearly 28 pounds with a hook attached. A 120-foot roll of poly weighs 5 pounds with a hook. The other advantage to the poly rope is that it's "dead," that is, it does not stretch and store kinetic energy. Unlike wire rope, if poly breaks, it drops dead onto the ground and does not snap back much, if at all. It also floats and you can tie a knot in it. Gloves are not necessary using poly rope.

The poly ropes have been in service for two or three years in the four-wheeling world but have been used for many years in the commercial fishing industry. The service record is good in both venues. Four-wheelers were worried most about abrasion, but the outer sheath of the rope is very resistant. It seems likely in a chafe-to-the-death competition that wire rope would win,

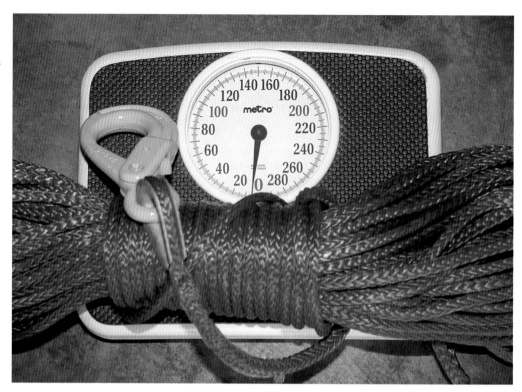

This is what the first-generation 5/16-inch Master Pull UHMWPE poly rope looks like. It now comes in a couple of other colors. Note the reading on the scale. It's stronger than wire rope of equivalent size, but it's less than a fifth the weight.

Top Five Winching Safety Tips

Replace damaged cable and hardware.

Hands off the winch controls while someone is working around the winch or winch cable.

Hook up only to solidly mounted anchor points. This doesn't include most bumpers, spring shackles, and so on.

Keep spectators well clear of the danger area.

Always wear gloves when working with winch cable.

but in day-to-day, moderately careful use, I put them on equal terms.

One potential problem has to do with poly's compatibility with certain winches. The common planetary winch has a one-way brake built into the center of the winch drum. When spooling out under power, that is, lowering the vehicle under power, the brake will generate some serious heat. The manufacturers caution against this lowering practice and advise doing it only in short spurts, but as with many manufacturers' recommendations, they are ignored and the extra heat is not beneficial to the poly rope. It isn't good for wire rope, either (above 400 degrees), but if you don't smoke the winch lowering a rig down a long slope, you may cook the poly rope and weaken it. Basically, if you follow the winch manufacturer's recommendations, you won't have problems.

Winch Techniques

Here we are near the end of the book and I've got to warn you again about the double-edged nature of an aspect of four-wheeling—in this case, the winch. It can be a convenience, a boon, and a lifesaver. It can also be a pain in the butt (or somewhere else)

and a life-taker. (Which is usually up to the operator.) Use it wisely and you can have a four-wheeling career free of winching accidents.

The "Average" Winch Pull

A few years ago, I purchased a line dyno. This is essentially a very-high-capacity scale with rings on each end that can be used to measure winch pull. I used it to measure winch pulls every chance I got and then compared my information with two other fellas with the same equipment. Based on that information, I have come to the conclusion that the average winch pull is between 2,500 and 3,500 pounds. I make no claims that this is scientific, but even situations that had the winch groaning in agony were only 3,500 pounds.

My test illustrates a point. You will see a lot of damaged and abused winch cables out there and, like me, wonder what's been keeping those people alive. It's equipment overkill. Even a thrashed 5/16-inch cable, originally rated for 9,000 pounds, maybe up to a third of its original capacity—or maybe not. And you never know when your winch will be called upon for a full load—and there you are holding a grenade with the pin out.

Dead Men That Don't Smell

Though not a huge rock, this sliver was ideally placed and wedged to provide a great dead man. The choice of a strap instead of a chain might result in some chafing, but some folks have an aversion to chain. It's acceptable as long as the strap is not allowed to deteriorate to an unsafe condition.

Neither the tree nor the boulder was quite solid enough on its own, but together, they were ideal. How convenient!

Though the dead juniper was more ideally placed for a straight pull, the live one was deemed stronger and Bill Burke prepares the tree strap for use in the recovery.

Two lengths of transport chain were needed to make a secure dead man out of this boulder. A shackle can be used to attach the hook, or the hook can be attached directly.

With no ground anchor in sight, what can you do? If this is a common occurrence, consider the Pull-Pal ground anchor. It folds up to the size of a Hi-Lift jack and comes in 6,000-, 11,000-, and 14,000-pound capacities. It holds well in most sorts of soft ground and sometimes will dig itself out of sight. A simple kick to the side and a pull to the rear will pull it out of the ground. After using the Pull-Pal, fill in and tamp down the hole.

This line dyno proved useful in testing winch pulls over the past few years and led to my observation that few pulls are more than 3,500 pounds. With all the worn-out and abused winching gear out there, this accounts for the fact that there are few serious accidents. The other observation is that many electric winches are fed an inadequate amount of amps, which results in decreased performance.

the dirt

Re-Spool Correctly

Take the time to re-spool correctly after each operation. If you make it a habit, you'll never forget and damage the cable by crushing it. During a winching operation, if the cable starts to collect on one end of the drum, stop, secure the vehicle or load, unload the winch, un-spool a few feet of cable, wind it onto the drum properly, and start winching again. In a real emergency, of course, do what you gotta do.

If the trail is a nightmare, and you are winching every hundred yards or so, it's acceptable practice to butterfly the cable around your front bumper or brush guard. This is nothing more than a tight figure eight. It saves a good deal of time.

Side Pulls

With a roller fairlead, you can safely pull about 15 degrees to either side, or up and down. Beyond this, you put the winch and cable at risk. The most obvious problem is that the cable will all wind onto one side of the drum. This can damage the cable by crushing it, and if enough cable gets built up on one side of the drum, it can break the winch. There may be times when an extreme side pull is necessary and worth the risk. If you stop and re-spool before the cable gets wadded too badly, the odds are much better that you can get away with it.

Maximum Pulling Power

Maximum rated pulling power comes from the layer of cable closest to the drum. Every layer after that decreases the pulling power of the winch by about 10 percent per layer.

Electric Winch Tips

Keep all hands off the winch control when people are working around the cable or winch. That way you can't accidentally engage the winch when people are vulnerable. Route the winch control carefully wherever you are working so it doesn't get caught by the winch cable, a tire, or someone's foot.

When spooling in without a load, many electric planetary gear winches will continue rolling via inertia, and will spool in as much as 2 or 3 feet of cable. It's controllable when you know about it. When spooling in, especially that last foot or so, spool in with short spurts on the control so as not to get fingers caught or strain any components.

An 8,000-pound electric winch will draw well over 400 amps at full load, and bigger winches draw even more. Even with the engine running, that kind of draw will pull a battery down in just a few minutes. If you have a voltmeter, watch it carefully, and when it stays below 10 volts while winching, wait a few minutes and let the battery build back up. To be on the safe side, don't shut your engine off after a long winching operation. There may not be enough amps left in the battery to crank the engine.

On a hard winch pull, the electric winch motor will get hot and this heat can cook it to death. Periodically check the motor with your bare hand—keeping clear of the line—and when it gets too hot to hold your hand against comfortably, stop and let it cool.

Mechanical Winch Tips

Using a mechanical winch is best and most safely done with two people—one to operate the PTO, transmission, clutch, and throttle from the cab, and the other to watch the drum and direct the situation. If you are outside watching the cable spool in, you can't easily stop the winch in an emergency, and if you are inside, you can't make sure the winch is spooling properly or that there isn't some unseen problem occurring.

A mechanical winch won't stall like an electric winch when it reaches its load limit, because you have what amounts to engine power behind it. Instead, something breaks. This could be the cable, the hook, or some part of the drivetrain. Fortunately, there's a shear pin built in somewhere between

the gear drive and the drum. Make sure you have an extra pin or two on hand. If you have an old winch that's out of production and parts are scarce, a machinist can make a shear pin. Don't be tempted to use an ultra-strong pin, because that may overstress some other, less easily replaced part.

Hydraulic Winch Tips

There's really only one hydraulic unit to talk about here: the Mile-Marker. It uses the power steering pump to supply hydraulic pressure. On installation, it's vital to thoroughly flush the power steering fluid and replace it with new fluid—doubly so if you have an older vehicle. Power steering fluid breaks down with age and heat, and old fluid will not permit maximum winch performance, which may even harm the winch. On older rigs with lots of miles, it might be advisable to have the pump pressure tested at a competent shop. A small power-steering cooler, which mounts on the return line, can help keep the fluid cool.

Using a hydraulic winch is very much like using an electric winch. Unlike the electric planetary winches, the hydraulic does not roll on while

Here are two common types of so-called snatch blocks, also known as pulley blocks. The upper unit is one from Superwinch and is a common and easily used two-piece type. They come from various manufacturers in ratings of 6,000 to 16,000 pounds and with assorted sheave sizes. The orange one is a heavy-duty locking unit rated for 24,000 pounds with a 5-inch sheave. In general, the larger the pulley the better, because wire rope is weakened at every bend. The larger the drum on the winch or the sheave on the pulley, the more strength is retained.

the dirt

Winch Pull:
A snatch block, or pulley, is a useful tool because it effectively doubles the pulling power of your winch while slowing line speed by 50 percent. In cases where a hard pull is needed, and you can only run out a short length of cable, use a snatch block to both run out more cable and double the line pull.

the dirt

Winch Motor Heat:
The winch motor will get hotter as the battery draws down, so taking a winch break periodically is a good idea on two counts: it lets the winch cool and your battery recharge.

Common Winch Specs, 6000 lbs. and Up

Manufacturer	Model	Capacity in lbs	Rope Dia/Len.	Motor Type/HP	Amp Draw Max Load	Max Load Speed, FPM	Drive/Ratio
MegaWinch	MW-12000	12,000	3/8-125	SW/2.5	425	1–3	W/468/133:1 (1)
MileMarker	MMW-7000	7,000	5/16-100	Hyd.	2	8.92	P/8:1
MileMarker	MMW-9000	9,000	3/8-100	Hyd.	2	7.1	P/6:1
MileMarker	MMW-10500	10,500	3/8-100	Hyd.	2	6.42(1)	P/6:1
Pierce	PS654	9,000	5/16-150	SW/1.5	400	3.0	W/460:1
Pierce	PS-654-M	12,500	5/16-150	SW/1.5	400	2.0	W/720:1
Ramsey	REP-6000	6,000	1/4-100	PM/1.6	230	6.0	P/294:1
Ramsey	REP-8000	8,000	5/16-95	PM/1.8	280	4.5	P/210:1
Ramsey	REP-9000	9,000	5/16-95	SW/1.9	400	2.0	P/138:1
Ramsey	ProPls6000	6,000	1/4-1000	SW/1.4	250	2.5	P/210:1
Ramsey	ProPls8000	8,000	5/16-95	SW/1.9	350	4.0	P/210:1
Ramsey	ProPls9000	9,000	5/16-95	SW/1.9	405	4.0	P/138:1
Ramsey	RE 8000	8,000	5/16-150	SW/1.9	345	3.0	W/360:1
Ramsey	RE 10000	10,000	3/8-100	SW/1.9	330	2.5	W/470:1
Ramsey	RE 12000	12,000	3/8-100	SW/1.9	390	2.0	W/470:1
Superwinch	S6000	6,000	5/16-100	PM/1.6	400	2.5	P/253:1
Superwinch	S9000	9,000	5/16-100	SW/2.0	435	2.0	P/253:1
Superwinch	X6CD	6,000	5/16-100	PM/1.6	400	2.5	P/253:1
Superwinch	X9	9,000	5/16-100	SW/2.0	435	2.0	P/253:1
Superwinch	Husky 8	8,500	5/16-100	SW/2.1	405	1.5	W/229:1
Superwinch	Husky 10	10,000	3/8-90	SW/2.1	450	1.5	W/294:1
Warn	HS9500i	9,500	5/16-125	SW/4.6	425	6.67	P/156:1
Warn	HS9500	9,500	5/16-100	SW/4.6	425	6.67	P/156:1
Warn	M8000	8,000	5/16-100	SW/2.1	423	3.0	P/216:1
Warn	X8000i	8,000	5/16-100	SW/2.1	423	3.0	P/216:1
Warn	M8274-50	8,000	5/16-150	SW/2.5	435	3.0	S/134:1
Warn	XD9000	9,000	5/16-100	SW/2.5	400	5.0	P/156:1
Warn	XD9000i	9,000	5/16-125	SW/2.5	400	5.0	P/156:1
Warn	M10000	10,000	3/8-125	SW/2.5	475	3.0	P/199:1
Warn	M12000	12,000	3/8-125	SW/2.5	400	3.0	P/261:1
Warn	M15000	15,000	7/16-90	SW/4.6	460	2.48	P/315:1

1) A two-speed unit.
P = Planetary, S = Spur Gear, SW = Series Wound, PM = Permanant Magnet

spooling in, but it might very slowly spool out while holding a heavy load. This occurs in high-time units where the control valves might leak slightly. A new unit shouldn't do this.

On MileMarker high-capacity winches that use 3/8-inch, 7x19 cable, the small diameter of the drum makes for a bit of a snarl on the last layer of cable, because the cable isn't flexible enough to stay wrapped. Keeping tension on the cable prevents this, but swapping to a more flexible 6x37 wire rope or the poly rope would solve this minor problem

Portable Winch Tips

Avoid hard pulls beyond a few degrees to either side on the Class III receiver-type portables or risk bending the winch mount or tow hitch. If your rig has sunk into terra firma, you may have to dig to get the winch plugged in and hooked up. In the case of the rear mount, because the electrical cables are so long, expect some loss of power due to line loss. This can be compensated for by using larger-diameter, 00-gauge ("double-ought") cables.

Basic Hookups

There are two basic hookups: the single-line pull and the double-line pull. The single line is just that. You run out enough line to hook up and start winching. As discussed earlier, if the pull is a hard one and you don't have enough cable out, you may overtax the winch. In this case, you would use a double-line pull. With the double-line pull, a snatch block is attached to the vehicle being recovered, or the dead-man you are winching from. The winch cable is then routed through the block and back to the winching vehicle and secured to a solid (preferably chassis-mounted) anchor point. Look to the nearby photos for "thousand-word" pictures and more info.

Advanced Hookups

The number of advanced hookups available is limited only by your imagination and equipment. Usually, the advanced hookups are needed to change the direction of the pull. With

enough snatch blocks, cable, and dead-men, you can pull yourself out sideways or backward. You can also lift the vehicle to pull it out of a hole. If you have enough equipment, you can perform some amazing feats. In the case of advanced hookups, look to the illustrations for a few ideas.

Winch Assist

Using your vehicle's motive power in self-recovery will ease the strain on the winch and reduce the likelihood of breaking something. You usually have a little traction and it can be used to lessen the winch pull.

Signals and Safety

Often, someone outside the vehicle and in a position to see the big picture will direct a winching operation. This is good practice. The best way for the driver/winch operator and the director to communicate is by hand signals. Spoken or shouted words can often be misinterpreted or drowned out by loud noise. Before you start winching, review the hand signals the director will use to be sure you both have the same understanding of what means what.

A cable loaded with several tons of weight stores kinetic energy. If the load is suddenly released by the failure of a cable or a hookup point, the cable can snap back, up, or to the side with enough energy to cut a person in half. Kinetic energy dampers can be placed on the cable. These can be nothing more than a heavy coat, blanket, or tarp placed on the end of the cable that's most likely to come loose. That's usually at the hook-up end. There are also some purpose-built winch cable dampers on the market. Keep spectators well clear of the operation for their safety.

Natural Dead-Men

In the winching world, a dead-man isn't the mortal remains of some poor four-wheeler. Rather, it's a solid anchor to winch from, or for securing the winch vehicle. You may be winching another vehicle that outweighs yours, or the ground conditions

the dirt

Helping the Winch:
When helping the winch with your drive wheels, match the winch's speed. Overrunning the winch causes slack in the line and allows for a snarled cable. Lurching forward and sliding back against the cable can cause a jerk forceful enough to break the winch.

Winch Safety:
The operator of the winch vehicle is usually in the most danger if the cable breaks, because it often snaps directly back. There are two things you can do to decrease injury to the participants. First, lay a blanket, tarp, or coat over the winch cable to dampen the kinetic energy if the cable gets loose. Second, raise the vehicle's hood—this will protect those inside more than safety glass alone.

TRAIL ENDERS

Winch Safety:
If you are using a dead-man to recover yourself, choose one that is solid enough to take the weight of your pull. Some four-wheelers have pulled logs, rocks, and trees down upon themselves.

increase the pull to the point where your vehicle is dragged toward the stuck one. Sometimes, all you need to do is to block the wheels of the winching vehicle. Sometimes you need extra help. If the weight of your vehicle isn't enough to hold, a more solid anchor is needed. In these cases, you need a dead-man.

A dead-man can be another vehicle, a log, a rock, a tree, or whatever. It just needs to be something solid, heavy, and safe. You then back your rig up to the dead-man, secure the vehicle with the appropriate chain or strap, and winch away.

Incidentally, when winching with an automatic-equipped vehicle, always use the parking brake in conjunction with Park. Using Park only may either break the Park pawl (as mentioned in chapter 4) or jam it. Sometimes a solid foot on the brake pedal, locking all four wheels, is needed. Some four-wheelers actually install brake system line locks, which lock the brakes in the same manner. Other means of securing the vehicle could be as simple as rocks or wood blocks in front of the tires, or using terrain features such as large rocks, logs, or gullies as natural wheel blocks.

Manmade Dead-Men

Over the years, there has been a succession of devices built to provide a portable dead-man. The Sand Spike, the Gopher, the Kro-Built, and others have come and gone. Some, like burying the spare tire or adapting the Danforth boat anchor, are adaptations of equipment designed for other purposes. Others, like the Pull-Pal ground anchor, are purpose-built. Many of these ground anchor products have disappeared, but the Pull-Pal has withstood the test of time. It is truly a remarkable tool that outperformed all the others and has survived.

So there you are, stuck and out of reach of any dead-men, with no vehicles to provide a handy tow. Assuming you also don't have a Pull-Pal, what can you do? The age-old cure has been to bury the spare. It works, though only if the digger is

dedicated. Dig a deep hole, at least as deep as the tire is tall, also digging a slit trench for the cable that gradually drops to the level of the center hole of the rim. Leave one side of the hole as perpendicular and solid as you can. Run the winch cable through the center hole and hook it to the stoutest—I mean the *stoutest*—bar, or bars, you have. A spare axle shaft will do it, as will a Hi-Lift jack's beam (though they could be bent, so be prepared to sacrifice them), but a jack handle or a breaker bar alone probably will not be strong enough. Bury the whole thing again, with as many rocks and as much solid material as you can find. How well this will hold depends on the type of ground and how well you did your work. If you make the winch job easier by digging the rig out as much as possible and assisting with the tires, it may hold sufficiently to get you free. Be sure to fill in your hole when done.

The easier solution is the Pull-Pal. It works like an old-fashioned plow and in most types of ground but rock. It requires only soft enough ground to get a bite into, and the right angle to work. The heavier the load, the deeper it will dig in. How much it will hold depends on the ground, but I've used it in snow, sand, and various types of dirt and it has seldom failed to hold. Look at the pics on page 185 for some tips on how to use it.

Manual Winch Recovery

Many of the tips you've read above apply to manual winches. Some of the differences include the fact that it's more difficult and potentially dangerous to assist the winch with the vehicle. The manual winch is simply too slow to keep up, and since people are in close proximity to the cable and winch, you don't want sudden slack and retensioning. The manual equipment usually isn't as durable as the powered stuff, so it needs more care.

The great advantage to the manual portables is that they can be hooked up anywhere—front, rear, side, corner, bottom, or top. They can be used

the dirt

Tree Straps:
When a living tree is your dead-man, always use a tree strap to protect it from damage. A winch cable or chain will cut through the bark of the tree and "girdle" it, which can kill the tree. Chains are useful in winching from rocks, dead logs, or rough surfaces that would damage a strap or cable.

anywhere they are needed. For hard-core types, they make an ideal #2 winch. They are useful in case the main power winch gives out, but more important, they offer another option and dimension for complicated recoveries. If you have snatch blocks, you can perform the same kind of complicated "round-the-corner" hookups as with a power winch.

I was once firmly entrenched in manual winching. This was mostly due to being semi-destitute, as opposed to being a tough guy. I *was* younger, stronger, and better able to endure in those days, but here are a few observations that might be useful. I learned that the fatigue of a long recovery led to stupid mistakes. I also learned that patience was required to avoid shortcuts. The slow pace of a manual recovery is an asset and a boon to clear thinking and a safe recovery. Use it!

Winching Effort

Because your vehicle is rolling on wheels, the effort required to move it is less than the same weight lying flat on the ground. That's why a single person can move a 5,000-pound truck by pushing and not a 5,000-pound crate. On a flat, hard surface, the person is only required to generate the grunt equal to about 4 percent of the truck's total weight (about 200 pounds). Ditto for the winch.

Ground conditions will increase the effort. A truck mired to the hubs in goo will require more effort than a truck on pavement. In addition, the slope, if any, will increase the pull. Here is some information on how ground conditions and slope will affect winch pulls. These figures are averages taken from various winch manufacturers' information

Ground Condition	Effort Required (as a percentage of total vehicle weight)
Pavement	2–4 percent
Grass	8–14 percent
Hard-Packed Sand	10–17 percent
Wet Sand	15–20 percent
Gravel	10–20 percent
Soft, Dry Sand	25–30 percent
Shallow Mud	30–35 percent
Deep Mud	40–60 percent
Deep Clay Mud	50–70 percent

A slope will have its own factor, to which you will add the above ground condition factor. Calculating the effect of slope is simply done by approximating the slope in degrees, and then multiplying it by the loaded weight of the vehicle and dividing that by 60. Whatever figure emerges, add this to your loaded weight to determine the approximate pull required. Then add the appropriate percentage of that weight that the ground condition will account for.

$$\frac{\text{slope (in degrees) x loaded wt (lbs)}}{60} = \text{winch pull}$$

Winch Pull x Ground Factor (in percent) = Additional Load

Additional Load + Winch Pull = Total Load on Winch

Let's use an S-10 Blazer as an example. It weighs about 4,500 pounds with all the gear we've installed and we've added 300 pounds of gear and supplies, making it 4,700 pounds total. We're trying to winch it up a 50-degree slope consisting of shallow mud.

$$\frac{50 \times 4,800}{60} = \text{4,000-pound pull}$$

4,000 x 35 percent = 1,400 pounds additional pull from mud

4,000 + 1,400 = 5,400-pound winch pull

CHAPTER 9

BRING 'EM BACK ALIVE

Navigation and Field Repairs

Breakdowns are avoidable to some degree by good maintenance, but when they do occur, they may come at the most inopportune times. The middle of an off-camber, maximum-performance climb with a 50-foot drop-off is not the best place, but a broken U-joint halts the ride.

HERE WE'LL COVER:

Basic compass operation
•
Basic map reading
•
GPS tips
•
Field repairs
•
Tools and spare parts

It isn't wise to venture out, especially alone, without knowing something about the area where you are going and how to get back. That requires a rudimentary knowledge of map reading and land navigation. In a similar vein, what you carry in the way of vehicle emergency and breakdown supplies, as well as the basics of how to repair a broken or ailing rig far from the nearest mechanic or shop, become more important the farther out in the boonies you go.

NAVIGATION

The basics of navigation will enable you to read a map, use a compass and GPS (Global Positioning System) receiver, and generally have an idea of where you are in the outback. This section is not intended to turn you into another Frank Worsley (legendary navigator for arctic explorer Ernest Shackleton), but to give you an overview of the procedures and equipment necessary for backcountry navigation. There are many good books on the topic, should you want more detail.

Maps and Guides

It makes sense to have a map of the areas where you will travel. If you are going on an organized run, you could let that slide, but it's kinda fun to track the route anyway. No matter where you go in the United States, there's no good excuse not to have a map if you need it. Maps of every spot in the country are available. Between the USGS (U.S. Geological Survey), states, and even county governments, maps are available that cover almost every square inch of our proud country. There are private purveyors of traveling knowledge as well, offering road atlases, highway maps, and trail guides.

Available Maps

The USGS office has maps of virtually any location in various scales. Some are old; some are quite new. You

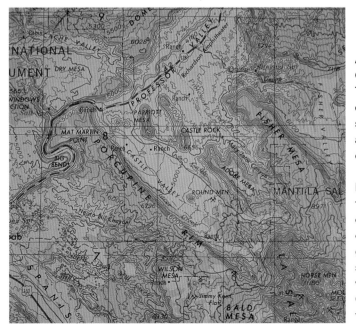

A typical USGS (U.S. Geological Survey) map. This is one of the more detailed maps in 1:24 scale, which shows roads and even buildings. The entire map illustrates about 70 square miles of ground. Note the contour lines in this area, indicating lots of elevation changes. Close contour line indicate steep grades and, as you can see, there's a lot of near vertical around here. Contour interval on this map is 40 feet.

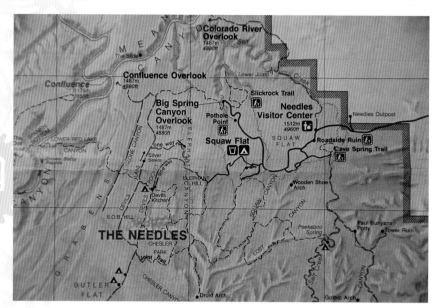

Here is a typical National Park map. It's less detailed than the USGS Topo maps, but it has most of what you need to find your way around. You may find some of the 4x4 roads missing from these maps.

can order them from one of the branch offices of the USGS and can sometimes find them at state or federal park headquarters. The U.S. Forest Service and the Bureau of Land Management both have their own maps, though they will only show lands under those jurisdictions. Most parks, whether federal, state, or county, will have their own maps available and these may also serve to guide your way, though sometimes with less detail than the USGS maps. They may be more current, however.

Another option is DeLorme's Gazetteer series. These are books that contain an entire state divided into grids. California, for example, is divided into two books (north and south) and 127 grids. This is detailed enough to see most roads and trails as well as terrain contours. DeLorme covers a good part of the United States state by state—certainly all the places where the best four-wheeling exists.

Electronic maps are available that can used in conjunction with a GPS or a laptop computer. Programs are available from DeLorme and others that contain very complete maps of the United States on CDs or disks. Many USGS maps have also been put onto CD-ROMs.

Trail Guides

As the popularity of four-wheeling grew, a market also grew for the creation of trail guides. These started out as quite simple and crude, but have developed into very accurate and sophisticated materials. They come in the form of individual maps of a trail or a popular four-wheeling spot, such as those available from Rick Russell, or books, such as those available from Charles Wells, Tony Huegel, and others, on four-wheeling in states or

At the bottom of USGS Topo maps are the important distance scales. This one shows it in miles, feet, meters, and kilometers. Contour interval is also shown.

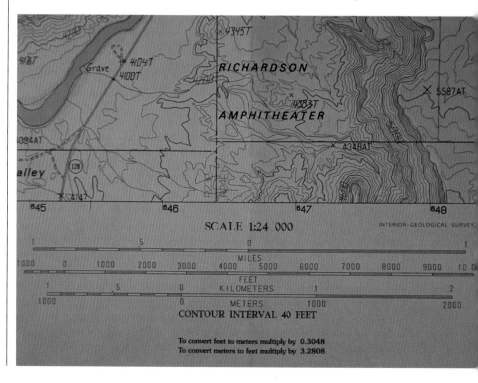

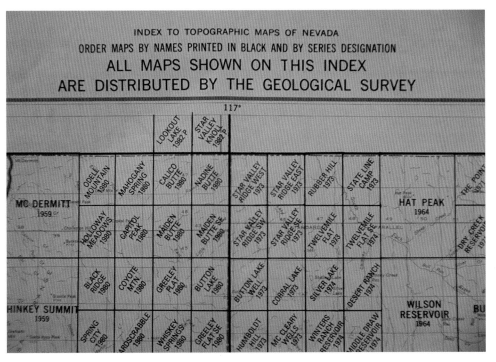

INDEX TO TOPOGRAPHIC MAPS OF NEVADA
ORDER MAPS BY NAMES PRINTED IN BLACK AND BY SERIES DESIGNATION
ALL MAPS SHOWN ON THIS INDEX
ARE DISTRIBUTED BY THE GEOLOGICAL SURVEY

This is a portion of the USGS maps available for the state of Nevada. The USGS has a map index for every corner of the United States. These same maps are now available on CD-ROM as well, so you can have the entire United States available on your laptop computer. The smaller maps shown here are 1:24000, and the larger ones are 1:62500. Four of the smaller will fit into one of the larger ones. Another section of this index shows 1:100,000 and 1:200,000 maps.

regions. These publications are usually incredibly detailed.

Map Reading: Scales

Every map has a scale that indicates the area it covers and the details it provides. Think of the scale as the difference in view between the naked eye and binoculars when viewing the ground from high above. They are precisely scaled so you can measure distances accurately. You will commonly see three scales on USGS maps, with the 1:250,000 covering the widest area and having the least amount of detail. It represents an area 1 degree of latitude by 2 degrees of longitude, or about 4 miles per inch as measured on the map. Next up are the 1:62,500 maps that "zoom" in to about four times the magnification of the previous maps and cover an area of about 1/4 degree each of latitude and longitude, or 1 inch to the mile. Finally, the 1:24,000 maps are the most detailed, covering about 1/8 of a degree of latitude and longitude, or about 2,000 feet per inch. The detailed maps cover about 70 square miles and are finely detailed. Other scales are seen on maps from various sources, so the first place to look on any map is the legend.

Map Reading: Topographical Features

Topographical, or "Topo," maps show contours that will give you an indication of the terrain features. The contour lines (see the nearby illustration) represent elevation above or below sea level and are marked with broad lines in evenly spaced intervals

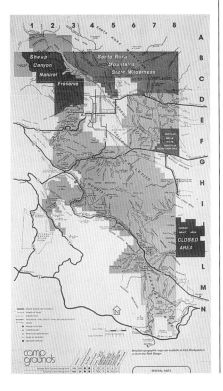

Here's a sample of a state park map, in this case an older map from the lovely Anza-Borrego Desert State Park in southeastern California. Most of the trails are listed with enough info to navigate around the park. Since the actual roads are clearly marked in most cases, there's little need for more detail.

Here are just a few of DeLorme's many state Gazetteers. They give you a detailed view of an entire state, both the paved and unpaved roads. The scale is large enough that some details are left out, but I've navigated plenty of trails using only these and simple common sense. DeLorme offers the same items in more detail on a CD that can be integrated with a laptop and a GPS.

Here are three excellent representatives of trail guide books. These encompass much of Colorado and the hotspots of Moab. Author Charles Wells travels the country, running virtually every trail in his books, recording directions, obstacle locations, and GPS coordinates (which you don't need to use, but are handy). This is the highest standard for this type of book. There are many others by other authors for various places around the country. Some meet Wells' high standard and some do not. All can be useful if they are accurate. Wells debuted an Arizona guide in late 2001.

that give the elevation at that line, with dividing lines in between that can be either at 40- or 100-foot intervals. Peak elevations are also shown. The grade can be determined by how close the lines are to each other. Lines that are very far apart indicate a very shallow slope. Lines close together indicate a very steep slope. These contours can give you an almost three-dimensional look at where you are going.

Compass

Every driver who ventures off-highway should have a compass. Not all of us are Dan'l Boone, able to calculate accurate directions by looking at moss on trees (assuming there are trees or moss where you are!). There are two basic types: the magnetic compass and the electronic compass. One reads magnetic

north and the other true north. A GPS (more below) can be used for this purpose, too, but it will eventually run out of battery power; the small handheld compass will work just as well today as 100 years from now.

The handheld compass must have a calibrated dial (showing 360 degrees) for taking bearings. It can be used in survival situations or for routine navigation.

You may also want a vehicle-mounted compass *in addition* to the handheld (which stays in the survival kit or is used for taking bearings). It's convenient and useful for "quick and dirty" navigation on the go. The GPS can replace the vehicle compass, but not the emergency handheld.

Using the Handheld Compass

Two important factors that affect navigation by compass are *deviation* and *declination*. Deviation is the error imposed by outside sources, including ferrous materials (anything with iron), magnets, or electricity. Your 4x4, belt buckle, power lines, and electrical devices can all interfere with the magnetic compass and cause it to read inaccurately.

Declination is the difference between true north and magnetic

Maps are available from a great many sources, three of which are shown here. From left, is a BLM map, a National Forest map, and a privately produced map. All three are excellent examples with detail similar to USGS maps.

north and changes according to whether you are east or west of the "zero" line where they briefly align. True north is located at the north pole. Magnetic north is somewhere in Canada and still moving. Each Topo map will have the declination from true north listed for that location, but older maps will be inaccurate because of the continual changes. There are isogonic charts available that can show you up-to-date declinations from any locale, but with a handheld compass,

accuracy to that degree is impossible in most cases.

Take magnetic compass readings away from all sources of deviation, including your rig, belt buckle, pocketknife, and power lines. The main thing to remember is that the needle *always* points north. The part of the needle that always points north is usually tipped in red. The most common use of a compass is to determine the direction of travel or to determine your position by triangulating from

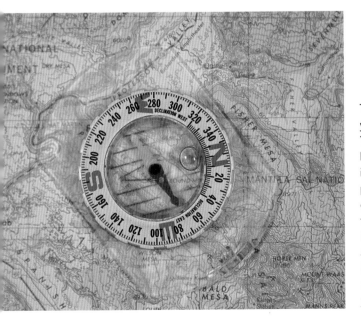

This simple compass and a good map are all you need to find your way around. That doesn't mean you can't upgrade to a GPS. You can use the compass to determine a course from the map. Lay the compass on the map and use the body to mark an imaginary line from where you are to where you want to go, pointing the compass direction arrow toward where you want to go. You can draw a line from where you are to the destination, but the edge of the compass is usually good enough. Once the body is aligned, rotate the compass dial so that "N" points north, and align the orienting lines in the compass dials with the meridian lines on the map. If you then pick the compass up and turn around until the red needle aligns with the red mark on the dial, you have your course. Be sure not to rotate the compass dial.

Special four-wheeling maps are available for select areas. These are a few of Rick Russell's Sidekick maps. The common element in these maps is that the they are geared toward the needs of four-wheelers, so they show such things as degree of difficulty for the trails, the location of areas of interest, camping areas, and other useful stuff, not the least of which is how and where to get local help.

two visible landmarks. The body of the compass is designed with an indicator arrow that you point in the direction you want to measure. Remembering that the needle always points north, the rotating dial has a red indicator that must be aligned with the red-tipped needle and once done, the direction of travel will be shown in both degrees (0-359) and direction (N, E, S, W). If you want to navigate on that bearing, you just need to keep the needle and the indicator aligned.

The vehicle-mounted compass can only be used to indicate direction of travel. A vehicle-mounted compass is useful at those moments when you face a fork in the road and aren't sure which way to turn, but you know the general direction you need to go. The problem with a vehicle compass is that all the metal creates a massive deviation. Even the magnetic effect of the ignition coil when the engine is running can throw the compass off. For that reason, the compass needs to be adjusted for the deviation. This is done by pointing the vehicle in known, accurate bearings, engine running, and adjusting the compass to match. The ideal is to use your handheld compass to find these bearings, but you can use streets that are known to run in a true direction.

GPS

The Global Positioning System (GPS) is the new, high-tech kid on the block. It's simple, easy to use, and deadly accurate. The military used it publicly for the first time to send cruise missiles into certain people's latrine windows during the Gulf War, and today they are even more accurate.

GPS relies on 24 satellites in various orbits around the earth. They transmit on two frequencies and the GPS units need to receive signals from at least four of them to determine a position accurately on both the horizontal and vertical plane. Along with locating a position, they can measure speed and estimate time of arrival. Most GPS units can do that to within 60 to 100 feet on a horizontal plane, with vertical (altitude) readings to within 250–500 feet. That's assuming the government hasn't turned on a system called *selective availability* (SA) that makes pinpoint accuracy available only to American or allied military units with the required decoders. With SA on, accuracy deteriorates to about 300 feet horizontally (or worse) and 1,000 feet vertically (or worse). Unfortunately, or perhaps fortunately in light of our enemies, SA is on most of the time.

GPS comes in many levels of performance. The newer models are 12-channel parallel units, meaning they can continually track up to 12 satellites simultaneously. In a clear area, an average of eight satellites are above the horizon and available for tracking. Older GPS units were serial (tracking only one satellite at a time) and could track only two to five satellites. Most newer GPS units take 3–5 minutes to start, locate satellites, and begin giving you information. If you are in a closed area where mountains, trees, or buildings block satellite signals, the wait could be longer. You do need a certain amount of clear sky. Sometimes even being in the inside of a vehicle is enough to disrupt the signal, though external antennas are available for many GPS models to cure that problem.

Until you've used a GPS and discovered the magic, you may be hesitant. A basic model such as this E-Trex from Garmin is just above a hundred dollars and is worth the money for entertainment value alone. Given coordinates, you can find your way to or from anywhere. I find it most useful for mapping unknown areas so I can avoid getting lost. By marking waypoints at critical intersections, I can easily find my way back. They are useful even in non-four-wheeling situations. I recently located the long-lost corner marker for our farm that was first settled in 1864!

Most GPS receivers fit into one of three categories—basic units, point-of-interest units (POI), or mapping units. They vary in price according to features. The basic units can find positions, store routes and waypoint information but cannot download maps or point-of-interest databases. They can connect to a laptop computer and upload or download waypoints in conjunction with map software.

In addition to the basic capabilities listed above, POI units have more memory and can store the locations of parks, amusement parks, fishing locations, racetracks, or whatever interests you. Dads can look like real heroes, navigating the family right to the doorstep of whatever attraction is desired. These POI databases are available from various sources and can be updated. Specialized databases according to interest are also available, such as fly-fishing spots in Montana.

Using the GPS

Once you turn the unit on, it will immediately start tracking satellites. In a few minutes, it will have your position located to within the error margin. Some units will give you an idea of the amount of error probable. You can have the unit display coordinates in several ways, but only standard latitude and longitude (in degrees and minutes) and UTM (Universal Transverse Mercator) are useful. UTM is a coordinate system that's a little easier to plot on a map than latitude and longitude. Most newer Topo maps have both. Older ones only have Lat/Lon.

Before using the GPS in conjunction with a map, you must enter the map datum onto the GPS. Map datums are simple mathematical formulas that convert the earth's surface from round to flat. You must have the correct datum entered to get an accurate location on the map. All Topo maps show this information and GPS can match almost all the newer ones.

If you were starting off on a trip and wanted to find a particular spot, you could use the "Go-To" feature by entering the coordinates, select go-to, and the unit will direct you there. If the unit has mapping capability, it will show you the map, where you are on it, and perhaps even give you directions. Otherwise, you will just get the "thataway" arrow showing you the "as-the-crow-flies" direction to the destination and the approximate trip time. You have to correlate these directions

the dirt

GPS:
The top-of-the line mapping units can upload and download complete maps to and from map programs on laptops. They usually are equipped with higher-resolution screens and other features. They can record your route automatically as you drive and later allow you to print out a detailed map of your travels.

GPS:
Many GPS units will make you a route map, whether it's a rudimentary squiggle on the screen or a detailed route superimposed on a real map that can be printed out.

with maps of the existing road systems to find your route.

If you set off on an unfamiliar trip, you can mark a waypoint at the start and waypoints along the way at critical turns, thus plotting your return trip. Waypoints are marked positions you can store on the unit. You can then use the go-to to find your way back to any of your en-route waypoints, or the first waypoint.

FIELD REPAIRS AND SPARE PARTS

Overall, current vehicles are much more reliable day to day than they once were, though perhaps more fragile and less tolerant of abuse. Because of the modern complications of sophisticated electronics, the days of bubble-gum and bailing-wire repairs are gone for many types of problems. Diagnosis is also more difficult. In the old days, when the engine quit, you checked for fuel and spark. No spark? Probably the points closed up or the condenser failed. No fuel? Probably the fuel filter was plugged or the fuel pump went bad. Today, if the engine quits, you can still look at the fuel pump or the filter, but it could be a fuel injection problem. An ignition failure usually comes from a module or another electronic part. In some cases, you can do more harm than good by tinkering.

Tools

The All-the-Time Kit

This is the crawling-on-the-ground minimum for any vehicle. Most of this kit will fit into one 19x9x9-inch plastic tool box. Beyond major overhauls, nearly every sort of repair could be performed with this kit.

1) Service manual.
2) A jack large enough to lift your fully loaded vehicle to change a tire. Make sure it has the reach to lift your rig if it has big tires. Include a 1x1x3/4-inch plywood base for the jack to keep it from sinking into soft ground. Also include wheel blocks or determine something in your existing kit that will serve. If you have one of those short, wimpy lug wrenches, scrap it and buy one with some leverage (or use a breaker bar and socket).
3) Two flashlights: one small for the glove box and one larger for working. A 12-volt light with a long cord that connects to the battery is ideal as a work light.
4) Work gloves to avoid cut hands.
5) Three-pound sledgehammer for "persuasion."
6) Eight- or 12-ounce ball peen hammer.

7) Combination wrenches 1/4 inch to 1 inch (or metric 8mm–24mm). Add or delete as necessary to cover your vehicle's specific sizes.
8) Tubing wrench(es) (if applicable) to fit tricky fittings on your rig.
9) Socket set in 3/8-inch drive with six-point sockets as listed for wrenches; spark plug socket; 12- , 6-, and 3-inch extensions; swivel and long-handled ratchet. Optionally, a 1/2-inch-drive socket set could be substituted or a few of the larger sizes could be included with a breaker bar for those big, tight bolts.
10) Allen wrench set (if applicable).
11) Torx bit set (if applicable).
12) Test light for electrical circuits.
13) Wire cutters and/or combination wire cutter/stripper/crimper.
14) Pliers, both combination and needle-nose.
15) Large channel locks.
16) Vice grips, small and large sizes.
17) Wire terminal crimping tool.
18) Large adjustable wrench, 12 inches or better.
19) Small, medium, and large punches; center punch; and a cold chisel.
20) Screwdrivers–large, medium, and small in both standard and Phillips.
21) Hacksaw and extra blades.
22) Crowbar or pry bar.
23) A spindle nut wrench to fit your front axle and/or rear full-float rear axle (if applicable), with appropriate adapters to fit your ratchet or breaker bar.
24) Files, including a good-sized bastard file (coarse) and a couple of smaller, less coarse ones.

25) A siphon hose and funnel (suitable for ATF fill).
26) Jumper cables and/or "jumper" battery box.
27) Tire pressure gauge.
28) Valve core removing tool.
29) Scissors or utility razor blade/Xacto knife.
30) Air transfer hose.
31) Any specialty tools applicable to minor repairs on your particular rig.

For Severe Conditions, Add

32) Twelve-volt air compressor, portable or hard-mounted, suitable for your tires. Chassis-mounted air tank a good option.
33) Battery-powered or hand drill with a selection of bits.
34) One large and two small C-clamps.
35) Assorted wood blocks, 2x4, 4x4, and so on.
36) Tire breakdown tools, including bead breaker and "spoon" bar.
37) Large pipe wrench.
38) Torque wrench.
39) Tire rod removing tool ("pickle fork").
40) Small grease gun w/cartridges.
41) Underhood welder, w/welding mask, rod, and so on (very optional, but useful).
42) U-joint installation tool (easier for novice wrenchers, but not necessary for experienced).
43) Any specialty tools applicable for repairs on your particular rig.

What about broken stuff? Drivetrains are still fairly simple, as are suspensions. You can still limp home on just the front or rear axle, or replace a broken axle shaft on the trail. Automatic trans repairs are no easier to fix than they ever were and a grenaded transfer case strands you just as much as it did 30 years ago. At least a few things haven't changed.

Some of what you read below in the nuts and bolts sections may be beyond your current knowledge. It's up to you to bring that level of knowledge up to where those procedures are understandable—otherwise, they won't be much help when you break down.

BASIC FIELD REPAIR STRATEGY

Think strategically about what you do and the likely emergencies for which you might need to prepare. There is such a thing as carrying too much. By overloading a rig with too much gear, you are inviting major

breakage and decreasing performance. Tailor a breakdown kit according to your particular vehicle's weaknesses, how far in the boondocks it will be, the severity of the terrain, and how easily help could reach you. The nearby "Tools and Essential Spare Parts" sidebars outline some ideas of what to carry and will answer many questions this section may generate.

To keep weight down, I vary the items in my own kit. A basic kit is always with the vehicle, but when I'm going in harm's way on a very tough and remote trail, I load up with hard parts including spare axle shafts, universal joints, a spare driveshaft, and other heavy parts. I make it easy to add or remove items from the kit, tailoring it to the severity of the terrain and the likelihood of certain types of damage. If I pile in everything, which happens only rarely, I've got 500 pounds of extra equipment. Yes, I can feel the difference in performance!

The first defense against breakdowns is a well-maintained vehicle. Routine maintenance helps you find and address serious problems before they become an issue out on the trail. There is really no excuse for a maintenance-related problem stranding you in the wilderness. That said, fate is not always kind. Some breakdowns are largely unpredictable until they manifest themselves. Remember that the harder you work your vehicle, the more TLC it needs and the more breakdown preparation you have to do.

The second line of defense is a well-prepared vehicle. That includes a common sense breakdown kit, but also common sense modifications to suit the terrain. Taking a vehicle onto a tough terrain with a known weak link is almost as bad as a maintenance problem. An example would be a generally acknowledged weak axle assembly that you have put in further peril by saddling with big tires and low gears. It's like rolling dice you know are loaded in favor of the house and then putting a big money bet down.

When breakdowns occur, judge the safety of the jury-rig repair you have to make against the availability of

Mechanical problems can occur anywhere, anytime, even halfway up a steep climb. In this case, the alternator belt failed just as a winching operation began. Without the alternator, the winch would have quickly drawn the battery down, so step one was to install a spare. The vehicle was carefully secured before work began.

The Bum-V's storage box pretty much loaded for bear. The goal is to have the commonly needed items readily at hand. For me, that means the winch kit, strap kit, snatch rope, air hose, GI shovel, sledgehammer, and a selection of recovery hookup items. The foam rubber lays over the top of the load to keep it in place.

the dirt

Spare Parts:
The main trick is not to be stranded by small, easy-to-carry stuff. Think in terms of little things that will completely stop your rig. People have spent cold nights in the boondocks for the lack of a fuse, or the knowledge to work around that fuse failure.

help. Some field repairs make the later permanent repair more complicated and expensive. Don't double your repair bills with a draconian jury-rig if you are within easy reach of a tow or other help.

Overall, the most vulnerable part of any 4x4 is the tires, so a few common sense items in the tire repair area make a lot of sense. First is a fully inflated, serviceable, full-sized spare tire. If your rig has a space-saver or temporary spare, I would heartily recommend upgrading to a full-sized

spare to match the rubber on the ground. That may not be easy if there is no built-in storage for it. It could come down to installing an externally mounted carrier.

Tools and Spares Strategy

Regardless of your technical expertise, dealing with vehicle repairs in the field is a far cry from dealing with them in a shop or even your driveway. Imagination and ingenuity carry the day. You can't carry *every* tool and *every* spare part with you wherever

Storage trays similar to this are available from a variety of sources and make tools and spares stowage neat, clean, and safe. In the case of this Jeep CJ, it leaves useful stowage space on top.

you go. The first tool you need is knowledge. A basic understanding of how vehicles work and a little wrench-twisting experience is necessary if you expect to be of any use in a breakdown situation. You can gain this knowledge by taking night classes on auto repair in a local college or trade school. There are also numerous books written for beginners in bookstores and libraries to help you along. Once you gain a little confidence via knowledge, get some practical experience with maintenance chores on your own rig.

Once you have some basic skills, a selection of tools becomes your next priority. First on that list would be a repair manual for your vehicle. Consider keeping a small paperback Haynes or Chilton manual, available in most auto parts stores and book-stores, in the vehicle at all times. While these "pocket" manuals can't compete with a factory manual in terms of detail or scope, they are often easier to use and certainly less bulky to keep in the vehicle.

In terms of hand tools, the idea is to be able to do "the mostest with the leastest." The list in the sidebar and the photos shows a sample kit, but each vehicle is a little different. By careful observation and checking, you might eliminate some things that aren't applicable and add a few that aren't covered. As far as quality goes, let your pocketbook be your main guide. Avoid the "X" brands. These tools are generally of very poor construction and often jam or break when put to the test. The best bets in cost-effectiveness are midpriced, made-in-the-USA brands, such as Sears Craftsman or SK Tools, which combine availability and quality.

How you carry your tools is another good topic. Avoid metal toolboxes because they are heavy and can damage items stored near them. Plastic boxes don't rust, won't scratch anything else, and are 80 percent lighter. You could also consider tool bags as an alternative for the same reasons. Another good idea is to have a small selection of very commonly used tools in a small roll near at hand to the driver. Who wants

to dig for the toolbox through piles of gear for a pair of pliers to pop the carburetor linkage back together?

Spare parts is an area that requires thought and judgment. Choosing the right parts depends on how long you expect to be out of the normal maintenance and repair loops. Obviously, a weekend trip into the mountains requires less preparation than a Sahara expedition. You can base some of your decisions on the repair records of your type of vehicle. Magazines such as *Consumer Reports* publish frequency-of-repair lists for the various components of many cars and trucks. You can also get a feel based on your own experiences with the vehicle, and have a talk with some local mechanics. Exclude major items such as internal engine, transfer case, and transmission parts and evaluate the rest. Some

This hard-core Grand Cherokee owner carries around spare front axles and CVs, as well as a spare tie-rod in lieu of a beefed-up front axle. These were parts chosen based on previous failures and the handsome carrying case was removable for easier trips.

weaknesses can be eliminated by upgrades or conversions to more reliable parts. Some faults are unimportant or easy to work around.

We've talked in general terms, but let's get to some specifics. What follows are some down-home "fixits" for problems ranging from extremely minor to full-gonzo major. Many of these fixits are avoidable by the means already discussed, but are worth talking about because a) parts can fail regardless of care and do so without warning, and b) you're a human being and as such, brain flatulence is always a possibility.

TIRE REPAIRS

Many people have been in the situation of having two flats on one run. The only option was a repair of the least damaged tire. There are a number of tire repair kits on the market, including the Safety Seal kit, which I have demonstrated for you on page 209. These kits can safely and permanently repair certain types of damage, and can also make temporary repairs adequate

to get you out of the woods but not back on the highway.

In addition to a tire repair kit, a more extended trip may dictate carrying a tube and some tire patches and vulcanizing compound. A huge tear may not be repairable by normal means, but you can stitch the sides together with fishing line or even baling wire, then put a big patch inside over the stitches and install a tube to hold air. A tire repaired in this manner is not safe for the highway or even safe for speeds much higher than 10 miles per hour, but it will get you to, or closer to, civilization

MINOR ELECTRICAL REPAIRS

Blown fuses are a fairly common failure. Step one is to determine if the failed circuit is vital. If not, and a simple fuse replacement isn't a cure, let it go and continue your trip. If a new fuse blows and no obvious short is found, try a fuse one or two sizes larger. For example, if a 10-amp fuse blows, a 15-amp may hold, but don't

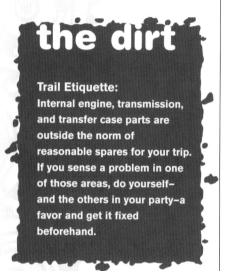

the dirt

Essential Spare Parts

The Weekend Kit
This kit will cover your behind in most circumstances, especially if you are meticulous in keeping your vehicle in good repair. Many spare parts can be good used pieces that have been tested to work.

1) Inflated, serviceable spare tire; matches tires on ground.
2) Duct tape.
3) A selection of spare fuses, at least two of every size used in your vehicle.
4) At least 1 gallon of water over and

above basic human needs.
5) Assortment of zip-ties, from tiny to huge.
6) Water pump, power steering and alternator belts.
7) Radiator stop leak, heavy duty.
8) WD-40 for frozen bolts and drying out wet electrical systems.
9) One quart motor oil, one quart auto trans fluid (can be used in power steering also), one pint brake fluid. Substitute one quart 90wt gear oil for ATF on manual trans vehicles, in squirt-type bottle, but add one pint power steering oil. Motor oil can be used in place of 90wt in an emergency.
10) One spare spark plug (if applicable), one spare spark plug wire long enough to work on any cylinder, points and condenser (if applicable), distributor cap and rotor.
11) Fifteen feet of 10-gauge wire (this wire is large enough to work nearly any circuit) and a few shorter lengths of smaller wire. A selection of crimp-

on electrical connectors, 18 to 10 gage.
12) Roll of baling wire and small roll of plumber's tape.
13) Rags or HD paper towels.
14) Hand cleaner.
15) Tube of high-temp silicone sealer.
16) Loctite thread restorer.
17) Small can of wheel-bearing grease.
18) Extra tire valve cores, caps, and at least one new valve stem.
19) Spare set of keys.
20) Small can of misc. hardware, including nuts and bolts, screws, washers, hose clamps, cotter keys, and so on.
21) Quick-set epoxy (JB Weld).
22) Fuel tank repair kit (epoxy type).

Heavy-Duty Kit, Add
This kit is in addition to what is listed above and should cover you for extended periods in primitive conditions or in areas with more breakdown potential. Variable according to your past history and how well the rig is built up.

get carried away. Putting a 40-amp fuse in place of a 10-amp may fry wiring. Often, there is more than one electrical item on a single fuse. If one is vital and the other not, you may be able to separate the two at the fusebox. If not, bypass the damaged circuit by running a wire directly to the important item from another power circuit. Make sure you use a fused circuit to power it and that the fuse is of sufficient capacity. If you have to eliminate some non-vital items to make the vehicle run, don't hesitate. Your mechanic and your pocketbook may suffer if you go wire-cutter happy on a main wiring harness, but if it's a matter of a survival or a long wait in the wilderness, you'll know what to do. You can also balance the cost of a tow against the cost of a repair if you are close enough to call for help.

If you suffer a blown fuse with no spare, use a non-vital fuse of the same or similar capacity to replace it. If there is no major short involved, a piece of wire or a bolt or anything conductive that will fit can be made to work. Just be aware that repairs such as these are your last-ditch,

crawling-on-the-ground solutions and result in what amounts to an unfused circuit.

Dead batteries are another fairly common failure. Obviously, jumper cables or a "jumper" battery pack are on the vital list and will get you moving again; but what if you are camping alone with your family without either and someone leaves the stereo on all night? If the battery is not stone-cold dead, putting it in a warm place for several hours (4–6) will help it regenerate. Depending on how far it was drained, it may come back enough to give you one more try.

A stone-dead battery would prevent any success at push-starting a manual transmission vehicle. Alternators need a little bit of field voltage to energize them and a battery with less than 2 volts won't do it. A 9-volt alkaline battery or a lantern battery applied to the "Field" terminal of the alternator (+ term. of the battery to the field, - term. to alt. case) could be enough to get the alternator energized for a push start, but be quick, as the small battery will drain fast. Remember that all alternators are a little different, so consult your

23) A tire plugging and/or patch kit and at least one inner tube so that a very damaged tire can still be made to hold air. Extra valve stems. Several extra lug nuts and wheel studs.
24) An extra fuel filter.
25) Brake cleaner spray.
26) Hose repair sleeves to fit your hoses, plus hose clamps.
27) Spare locking hub (used OK).
28) Spare front axle U-joint or CV joint.
29) Gasket-making paper.
30) Fuel line hose and clamps.

Super-Heavy-Duty Kit, Add
This is for hard-core 'wheelers in harm's way. Variable according to situation and level of buildup. It's simpler, more reliable and lighter, for example, to upgrade to "unbreakable" status rather than carry a load of spares for a marginal unit.
31) Three quarts 90wt (in squirt bottles), three quarts ATF, three quarts motor oil.
32a) For fuel injected gasoline engines:

spare control unit, spare fuel pump, and necessary installation pieces.
32b) For carbureted gasoline engine: carburetor gasket set, needle and seat, and spare float. Spare mechanical fuel pump or repair kit (low-pressure electric in-line pump acceptable substitute).
33) Electronic ignition module and/or coil.
34) Wheel bearings. One each inner and outer, front and rear axles. Include one spindle bearing, axle seals, hub seals, and knuckle seals.
35) Starter or repair kit (mostly for manual trans rigs that regularly start in gear).
36) For manual trans vehicles: repair kits for hydraulic clutch, or spare clutch cable.
37) Spare rear axle shaft. If offset axle, short shaft is most likely to break first. If c-clip axle, spare c-clips(s).
38) Spare spider and side gears, shims, cross-shaft, and lock-pin (if applicable).
39) Diff cover gasket.
40) Complete spare front axles, both

(delete spare U-joint). Alternate, one outer stub shaft and spare U-joint (usually the first to break and fits both sides).
41) ARB Air Locker air hose fittings, solenoid valve, and air hose (if equipped with ARB).
42) Larger selection of nuts, bolts, and hardware. Include specialty items, such as extra spindle nuts, shock bolts, spring bolts, driveshaft U-joint bolts and straps, fill plugs, engine drain plug, tire rod nuts, and so on.
43) Spare tie-rod, w/ends.
44) Spare driveshaft (most vulnerable one). Alternate or additional spare universal joints, one of each type. Include bolts, caps, or straps as needed.
45) Anything vulnerable or that has broken more than once (time for an upgrade?).

Bent tie-rods or drag links are relatively common across the range of vehicles and terrain, but few are as spectacular as this one. As bad as this one is, it can be removed and straightened. The initial bend can be removed by prying against a large rock or in the receiver hole of a hitch. The final bit of straightening can be done on a hard, flat surface with a sledgehammer. Once bent and straightened, the rod will never be as strong as unbent, so it shouldn't be trusted beyond getting back to civilization. Solid tie-rods or aftermarket tie-rods made of alloy steel may be more difficult, or impossible, to straighten.

Suspension Trail Repairs: Suspension, chassis, and steering field repairs are designed to get you to the pavement where a tow truck can carry you the rest of the way for a proper repair. Your life is at risk with many temporary repairs, so don't count on them for high-speed driving, where a failure could be deadly.

manual for specific information on the location of the field terminal. Old-style generators produce power regardless of the battery condition.

In conclusion, when you get down to it, in a survival situation there are only a few priority electrical items on the vehicle—the engine electricals, perhaps the headlights, and maybe the heater. The rest is superfluous. If a major electrical meltdown occurs, rip wiring out of anywhere and get those vital pieces to work. You can do without the rest.

SUSPENSION, CHASSIS, AND STEERING

Most suspension damage is a result of pilot error. If it happens, bent tie-rods, or any other steering or suspension link, can be straightened enough to get by. Remove the offending part, find a rock, get the biggest hammer you have, and John Henry that part straight. Most steering rods are tubular steel and can be straightened without losing a great deal of strength. If they break, a rod can be inserted into both broken ends of the tube and welded, pinched, clamped, or bolted into place. Beware of solid or cast pieces. Cast parts may break as they straighten and solid pieces may become fatigued and bend again very easily. Heating a cast part over a fire may prevent breakage when putting it straight, but the part will become brittle and may break under stress. By splinting the weakened part with steel rods and wire (or clamps) you can add a margin of strength.

Broken leaf springs can be splinted with a flat piece of metal and wire, hose clamps, or a c-clamp. Broken anchor pins on a leaf spring can be replaced by a regular bolt with the head filed to fit the receptacle on the axle. A broken coil spring can be overcome by using a piece of wood in its place to support the weight of the vehicle. A similar trick can work on leaf springs by jacking the vehicle up and putting a block between the axle and the chassis and chaining the axle down. Either way the ride will be brutal, so take it slow.

The new underhood welding units, such as the Premier Power Welder system, are very useful for emergency repairs of all types, including suspensions. The system combines a high-output, industrial alternator (useful for electric winch systems as well) with a welding box that uses high-frequency current instead of massive amounts of amps. You can actually get pro-quality welds with it, but perhaps more important, it's an easy system for amateurs to use.

DRIVETRAIN

Drivetrains are another area where a controlled right foot makes for 98 percent fewer problems. Beyond that, wheel bearings can fail through lack of maintenance, or if water enters the hub. With water, the grease can fail rapidly and bearing failure can come soon after that. The key is to stop before the bearing gets really bad and you lose the wheel and hub altogether. If the bearing completely disintegrates, you're hurting unless you have a spare. If the bearing remains in one piece, you can nurse it a long way by cleaning out all the metal and goop, repacking it in fresh grease, and taking it easy.

Manual transmissions can have failures but often will have at least one gear left to limp home on. If something does fail, stop and drain out as much metal as you can before you proceed. The metal floating around could kill it quickly and completely. The most common manual transmission system failure is in the clutch area, specifically, the release mechanism. Linkages can break and hydraulics can fail. If no repair is possible, the vehicle can be started in low gear and shifted carefully without disengaging the clutch by matching engine speed to gear speed. If the

clutch assembly itself fails and the vehicle won't move, there's very little to do but lace up your boots.

Automatic transmissions usually give lots of warning before they fail. If the auto box starts to slip, stop ASAP and check the fluid level. The most common causes for auto trans failures are overheating, low fluid, or lack of maintenance. A leaking trans cooler line, for example, is not a problem in itself until the fluid gets low and the tranny starts to slip. It grinds itself up very quickly once slipping begins.

Broken rear-axle shafts are possible and not uncommon in harder-core realms. The only people that need worry about safety are people with semi-float axles. Full-float axles, as

Broken front-axle U-joints are one of the more common drivetrain ailments in difficult terrain with rigs that have big tires. I have dozens of shots like this one, with industrious owners popping in a new joint or axle assembly. At least half the time, the ears of the axle yoke (either the outer stub or the inner axle) are damaged as well, so I like to carry a complete axle unit rather than a spare joint. It's a faster exchange too. Good used pieces are OK. Note that this vehicle is not supported by jack stands, which are not practical to carry. The removed tire, placed in a strategic location, can prevent the vehicle from falling all the way if the jack lets go.

Below: Found on road dead! Universal joint failures are not uncommon. The number one cause is lack of maintenance. The so-called "lifetime lubricated" U-joints are a major factor in this. If the grease breaks down (after 80,000 miles) or if water gets in, there's no way to know or to prevent failure except by periodically dismantling the joint and relubing it. Replace any failed or worn joints with a greaseable type and lube them regularly. There's old trail lore that says nongreaseable joints are stronger than greaseable, but some destructive test done by Warn Industries a few years back that I included in a Four Wheeler magazine story a few years back showed them to be essentially equal in strength. Beyond the maintenance issue, there are some rigs with extraordinarily small U-joints or weak straps and yokes. Jeep Wrangler YJs and many Cherokees are well-known culprits that need upgrading.

This is what happens to a driveshaft that hits a rock while under a heavy torque load. Unless you have a spare, there's not much to do here. I have seen resourceful and skilled 'wheelers with underhood welders cut and section damaged driveshafts such as this. That's beyond most of us normal folks. One cure for future failures is to have the new driveshaft built of heavier wall tubing to resist damage.

This broken axle will make a nice stake! No fixing this puppy. Unless you have a spare, this is probably where you are stopped. This shaft was from a Dana 35 axle, which appeared on a large number of Jeep Wranglers and Cherokees. It's fine for street use but is well known for being one of the weakest axles ever to appear on a 4x4. It's not safe for more than medium-duty four-wheeling or a moderate tire size increase.

seen on many 3/4-ton rigs and all 1-tons, are safe to drive with a broken shaft. The obvious cure for a broken shaft in a semi-float unit is to replace it, and if you frequently venture into "axle-snappin' territory" you may (and probably should) carry a spare. Bear in mind that axles can break either at the outside or at the inner splined end. If they break on the inside, the broken stub will stay in the carrier and the twisted splines may wedge it there. It may come down to disassembling the diff, or removing the other axle and pounding the stub out from the opposite side with a long rod and fishing it from the axle tube.

If you don't have a spare shaft, whether you can limp to civilization or not depends on whether you have a c-clip–retained axle or a pressed bearing type. A c-slip–type is a definite no. With the shaft broken, the remaining parts of the axle and the hub, complete with wheel, will part ways with the vehicle. You can sometimes move a few feet before this starts to happen. One exception is c-clip axles that have rear disc brakes. The caliper will hold the axle in place to some degree. Many newer Dana and corporate axles are c-clip types.

A pressed bearing axle can usually be driven a bit, though they will not always stay pressed in place. I wouldn't drive the highway with a broken pressed bearing shaft, but some people do. If the axle has been replaced, the mechanism holding the axle in the bearing may be damaged and not hold as well as it should. The bad result would be losing a wheel and hub at highway speed.

Grenaded differentials, lockers, or ring gears are usually fairly hopeless without lots of spare parts. I have seen people with underhood welders weld up broken spider gears and limp home. Since you have another driving axle, you can usually get back to civilization on the remaining unit. If you have a c-clip–type axle, broken spiders and some types of carrier failures will release the axles. This often precludes

Tire Repair in the field

Tire damage is a relatively common occurrence; the likelihood increases as the terrain difficulty increases. It makes sense to carry some tire insurance in the form of a good spare and a tire repair kit. This Safety Seal kit will repair the ordinary nail hole and can be used to temporarily repair worse damage. I used it to demonstrate the ordinary nail repair as well as something worse. The "worse" is not a good or safe repair for the street, but it will get you off the trail in the event of sidewall damage.

For your edification, I took a knife and made a 3-inch slash in the sidewall of a 31x10.50 tire. I used three Safety Seal self-vulcanizing plugs to fill the slit. As an experiment, I mounted the tire and drove five miles at up to 30 miles per hour and then let the tire sit for a month. It did not lose a single pound of air from the 35 psi I originally installed. I would not drive at freeway speeds with this tire, but having been faced with more flats than I had spares, this option could have been a trip saver, if not a lifesaver. I must protect Safety Seal here by saying these sorts of repairs are not authorized or advocated by them, but I have seen them done countless times on the trail. The tire is obviously trash afterward, but it will have gotten you to a place where a new tire can be procured.

The Safety Seal kit comes in a nice carrying box. These kits do not use a cement or vulcanizing compound, which is a plus. I have carried plugging kits previously and found that the compound had a short shelf-life that always seemed to have expired by the time I really needed it. The self-vulcanizing plugs in this kit are ready for use and are good for at least six years.

Oh no! A nail! Actually, you wouldn't believe how hard it is to get a nail into a steel-belted tire by hand.

Step one is to use the special lubricant and ream the hole with the probe tool.

Only for you, dear readers, would I plunge a butcher knife into the sidewall of a serviceable tire.

Three plugs filled the 3-inch slash nicely. I like to jam in as many as will fit. I put 35 psi into this tire immediately. As a test, I put about five miles on it at speeds up to about 30 miles per hour (faster than you should go!) and it held fine. I later let the tire sit in my garage, and it did not leak a single pound of air over a 30-day period.

After threading the plug through the slot in the insertion needle and lubricating it with the lubricant provided, push the plug into the hole until the sleeve touches the tire. Next, push the sleeve against the tire to hold the plug in place as you withdraw the needle. The tire is repaired!

the vehicle even being towed, because the axles will not be retained. Desperate 'wheelers with underhood welders have welded the c-clips to the axle buttons to retain the rear axles long enough to limp to the highway.

If the vehicle will still roll safely, you will probably need lots of help from a towing rig or from your winch to get through on a tough trail. Don't overstress that remaining axle. The front, especially, is very weak compared

> **In Case of Vehicular Drowning:** Repeated attempts to start a waterlogged engine may cause serious damage. In fact, the engine may already be damaged from ingesting water if it was running when the water entered the combustion chamber.

The chassis flex that results from difficult off-highway travel is a primary cause of broken engine mounts. It usually happens to vehicles with particularly flexy chassis, such as older Jeeps, most pickups, and long-wheelbase SUVs. A broken mount can allow the engine to slide forward a couple of inches and the fan to contact the radiator. In this shot, the damaged tubes are being pinched shut below the top and bottom tanks. It will effectively seal the leaks but reduce cooling capacity. Heavy-duty engine mounts, often made of polyurethane, are available for many 4x4s.

to the rear. Once you discover that one of your diffs is "outta there," do what you can to isolate it. If it's the front, unlock the hubs and go into two-wheel drive. In the rear, it might be advisable to remove the driveshaft if you don't have a slip-yoke–type rear output on the transfer case. Slip-yoke t-cases will puke oil without the driveshaft in place.

Broken front universal joints can be repaired some of the time if you carry a spare U-joint. If you get off the throttle quickly when you hear the ominous "snap," the yokes on the axle can sometimes be saved. I have seen a good number of front-axle U-joints replaced on the trail. A good portion of the time, however, the yokes are damaged too badly and a new axle shaft, or shafts, will be needed. I carry a spare pair of front shafts, inner and outer both sides, for really rough terrain. Broken locking hubs are not uncommon. I carry a spare as well as a solid drive flange (not available for all axles).

Driveshafts and driveshaft U-joint failures are uncommon except in the most extreme circumstances. In rocky terrain, the most likely failure is if one or the other gets hit and damaged. You get off easy if the unit is merely bent. Often, after a major impact, the tube will collapse and be twisted in half by

torque. No cure here but a spare shaft, which is not on many spare-parts lists.

ENGINES

Most engine failures relate to ancillary parts. Seldom does the actual engine fail, or fail to the point where it can't run. That depends on how you drive. If you're a high-revving throttle jock, of course, your odds for major engine problems increase.

Cooling System

Cooling system ills probably top the list of engine failures. Hoses are the main weak link and that's why they should be replaced every few years regardless of how they look. If a failure occurs at the end of the hose near its fitting, it can often be shortened and reinstalled. Assuming you don't have a spare, hoses leaking near the middle can be repaired with duct or electrical tape, though this is often a so-so repair. A severely split hose can be sewn closed with fishing line and taped. The best hose repairs come from temporary sleeves that are manufactured in various sizes. You can cut out the damaged section and install the sleeve with a couple of clamps. This makes for an almost permanent repair and the sleeves are easier to carry than spare hoses.

The important step to remember with hose repairs, and many other cooling system repairs as well, is that most jury-rigs will not hold pressure. This means leaving the radiator cap loose. A pressurized system raises the boiling point of the cooling water by holding as much as 18 psi. This kind of pressure will blow a tape job all to heck. Another consideration is cooling system efficiency after emergency repairs. Combine an unpressurized system with a loss of coolant that further raises the boiling point (which you replaced with plain water, soda, beer, even urine), and you have very diminished cooling capacity, perhaps up to 30 percent. This could be a problem in hot weather, making temp gauge monitoring of vital importance.

Radiator damage is a possibility. Minor leaks can be stopped with the can of radiator stop leak in your spare parts kit. I like the aluminum-based products such as Alumaseal best, but the gloppy stuff (such as Bars-Leaks) works also. If you have time, epoxies such as JB Weld can make a semi-permanent radiator tank repair. Major radiator repairs usually involve the core, which is composed of tubes connecting the upper and lower tanks (or left and right on a sideflow radiator) and a large number of cooling fins to radiate heat. When some of the tubes become damaged, the trick is to snip away the cooling fins around the damaged area of the tube, cut it, pinch off both ends of the tube, and roll the ends much like you would a tube of toothpaste.

Water pump seal leakage can be slowed by reducing cooling system pressure. When a water pump shaft seal leaks, the fluid drains through a weep hole on the pump housing near the shaft area. As long as you have extra water, you can keep adding and driving.

As part of my cooling system emergency tools, I carry a 5-psi cap to fit my radiator. I have found this to be a good compromise between the original 18-psi unit and no pressure. This proved a very useful addition a couple of years ago when I nursed a blown head gasket home.

Belts

Drive belt failures are avoidable by regular changes. Belts drive a number of engine ancillaries, many of which are not absolutely vital to its operation. You can do without air conditioning, the smog pump, and even power steering if you must. The vital areas, in order of importance, are the water pump and alternator. Without the water pump, the engine will quickly overheat. Though the battery can run the engine several hours without the alternator, sooner or later it, too, will die. If one of the vital belts fails and you haven't a spare, one of the non-vital belts may fit. Even if it's a bit too loose, it will spin that vital pump or alternator enough to keep you

going. Rope, leather belts, or even pantyhose can be used as temporary belts to get you a few miles farther down the road.

Engines with serpentine belts use one to run everything. I've seen problems when the belt tensioner or the bearing on one driven item fails. There seems to be no way to corncob these setups back into operation in this case. It might be possible to figure out a way to reroute the belt around such a failure, but in the ones I've studied, this did not appear to be possible. If I had a serpentine system, I might be tempted to carry a spare (new or used) tensioner assembly for some journeys. Whatever type of belt system you have, ask for the old ones for spares when having them replaced during normal maintenance.

Fuel System

Plugged fuel filters are common. Bouncing around may cause the fuel pump to slurp up debris in your tank and restrict fuel flow when it reaches the filter. If the engine lacks power but runs more or less normally at low speeds, the fuel filter is a likely suspect. Carry a spare filter or two. Without a spare, plugged filters can be partially cleaned by blowing through them in reverse flow and tapping out the debris. Remember that with EFI, the system will be under high pressure, so don't just crack open the fuel filter lines without following the depressurizing procedure in the shop manual. Usually, pulling the fuel pump fuse and cranking the engine over for a minute will release most of the pressure, but your manual's instructions take precedence. Take appropriate fire precautions and put a rag over the lines as you remove them to reduce spraying.

Mechanical fuel pumps on carbureted engines usually fail because the neoprene diaphragm in them leaks or ruptures. If the pump can be disassembled (not common these days), a piece of rubber inner tube can be used as a temporary replacement. It won't last long in the fuel, but it might get you where you need to be. Another

option for a failed fuel pump on a carbureted vehicle is to gravity-feed it. If you start a gravity feed from a fuel can held several feet above the carburetor through a hose leading down to the carb, the engine will run almost normally at slow speeds.

Fuel-injected engines are a class in themselves and a lot harder to nurse home. If the engine suddenly shuts off, look at the main EFI system fuses or for a major connection that has come adrift. This includes the fuel pump fuse. Most EFI fuel pumps are mounted inside the fuel tank. Have someone cycle the key on and off a few times while you press your ear to the fuel tank. You should hear the pump buzzing away. If not, check power to the pump (fuse or connections). Without fuel pressure, you are stopped.

A minor problem may cause the engine to run poorly and give you an EFI warning light. In this case, the system goes into "limp-home" mode. It may run poorly but it will run. Have a look under the hood for loose vacuum lines or wiring connectors. Sometimes letting the unit sit, keying off, or disconnecting the battery for a few minutes will temporarily or permanently clear a fault. If the engine starts running rich (too much fuel) and blowing black smoke, there is some danger of overheating the catalytic converter. In some cases, it can overheat the floor of the vehicle, possibly even setting undercoating or carpeting on fire. Correct the problem if you can, but otherwise take regular cooling-off periods to reduce the danger.

A leaking fuel tank can sometimes be repaired using an ordinary bar of soap. Seam leaks or small tears can be sealed by rubbing a bar of soap over the wound or cutting slices to push into it. Gasoline reacts with the soap, causing it to harden. Regular, old-fashioned soap is what works. Deodorant or scented bars may not do the job, but pure soaps such as Ivory will. The only problem with the soap trick is that on modern rigs, the tank is partly pressurized, so the fuel cap may need to be left loose for the soap to hold. The best option is one of the commercial tank repair preparations available in auto parts stores. It's a fuel-resistant epoxy and I've used it with great success and always carry two packages. It can also work on oil pans and transmission cases, as I have also found out personally.

Engine Internal

Internal engine failures aren't common. Catastrophic failures such as thrown rods and sudden, complete loss of oil pressure are fatal. Knocks or noises can often be nursed quite a way. Again, gauge the ease of an outside rescue against the potential of increasing the repair costs. An engine with an internal problem may still run, but it most often is grinding itself up inside. The key elements are cooling and oil pressure. If the oiling system retains at least 10-psi pressure per thousand rpm, you have a chance.

Loud knocks with an accompanying loss of oil pressure usually indicate bearing problems in the lower end (crankshaft, connecting rods). A higher-pitched tapping could be the valve train and usually does not come with a loss of oil pressure. If accompanied by a miss, it could be a valve problem, a broken valve spring, a pushrod, or rocker arm that has come loose or broken. The key element to an engine with sick innards is to run slow and easy. High speed or stress can put it the rest of the way out of its misery.

IN CASE OF VEHICULAR DROWNING

The usual scenario is that the vehicle was submerged deeply enough to kill the engine. That could happen from one errant splash in the engine compartment or complete or nearly complete submersion of the vehicle. Step one is to get the vehicle onto dry ground. Unless you are absolutely certain that it was only a splash onto the

ignition that killed the engine, it's better not to crank it over until you make some checks. If you try, and the engine won't turn over, STOP! This is usually an indication that water has entered the engine cylinders and hydrolocked it. If water gets into the combustion chamber of the engine, it effectively stops it from turning because water does not compress as air does.

Once the vehicle is on dry land, remove the air cleaner. If the air filter is wet, or there is water in the filter housing, the odds are good that the engine has ingested water. In that case, remove the spark plugs (or the glow plugs or injectors from a diesel), ground each spark plug wire to the block, and crank the engine over with the key. This will pump the water from the cylinders, sometimes quite violently, so stand clear. Clear any water from the air intake system as needed and if the air filter is wet, lay it out in the sun or on a hot engine to dry. A wet air filter will not flow air well, so get it as dry as possible before installing it and running the engine.

Before you reinstall the spark plugs, check the engine oil level. If there is obvious water in the crankcase, usually indicated by the oil level being over full, the best idea is to change the oil and filter on the spot. You may not have the oil and filter available for this, so if you let the oil and water separate (it may take half an hour, but eventually the oil will be on top and the water below), you can loosen the drain plug and let the water out. When clear oil begins to flow, reinstall the plug. Drain this oil/water into a container and not onto the ground. Check the oil level and add whatever is needed.

The ignition system may also be wet, so remove the distributor cap. WD-40 sprayed in and around the distributor will help it dry. In lieu of that, wiping out the excess water and allowing some air-dry time will also serve. Fuel-injected engines may stop

when the electronic pieces are soaked. First, check to see if the fuel-injection control unit (ECU) has been immersed. Some are quite water-resistant; others are not. If the unit has been drowned, you are faced with removing it and emptying the water. If the unit has a removable cover, it can be opened for better draining and air-drying. Other fuel-injection components may also require drying out. You may be able to get these components operating in some fashion right away, but the majority of the time they are write-offs in the long term because of corrosion.

With the spark plugs reinstalled, the engine should restart normally. There will probably be a great gout of water from the tailpipe and some steam for some minutes afterwards. Time and heat will dry out the rest of the underhood components, though you may encounter electrical problems down the road due to wet connections or resulting corrosion.

Other places to look for water are the transmission, transfer case, axles, and all the other stuff mentioned earlier. The cure is a complete change of all fluids. While you may be able to limp to civilization with water-contaminated oil in the diffs or transfer case, automatic transmissions are very vulnerable to water contamination. Running an automatic with more than a tiny bit of water contamination can result in total failure.

If the vehicle has been in deep water, there are a multitude of other potential problems. There's a good reason why flood-damaged vehicles are usually totaled! If yours goes in so deep that you get into these worst-case scenarios, unless you are stranded alone and have the expertise to solve all the problems, you are probably better off getting the rig hauled out and taken care of by pros. The general rule of thumb for modern vehicles is if water was high enough to reach into the dashboard in a significant way, you have a very hurting unit and a possible total.

APPENDIX I
Glossary of Terms

A-Arm—A triangular suspension component used on independent suspensions. Also could be called a control arm, upper or lower. It pivots on the chassis at two points, the wide end of the "A," and the pointy end attaches to the spindle.

ABS—Anti-Lock Braking System. An electronically controlled system that prevents skidding under hard braking by controlling and equalizing wheel speed. A two-channel system controls only two wheels, the rear; a four-channel system controls all four wheels.

Add-a-Leaf—An inexpensive method of lift where an additional leaf is added to the leaf spring pack to provide a small amount of lift at the cost of ride quality.

Aftermarket—Vehicle parts or equipment not manufactured by the OE manufacturer.

Amp Draw—The number of ampere-hours (amp-hours) needed to run an electrical device.

Approach Angle—The maximum angle of climb that a vehicle can surmount without hitting some part of the body, chassis, or mechanicals in the front.

Arch—See *Camber*.

Articulated—When one tire is at its upper travel and the other at its lowest travel and the axle is at a severe angle in relation to the body. See also *Cross-Axled* and *Articulation*.

Articulation—The ability of a suspension to combine compression and droop on one axle. If a suspension articulates well, the body will stay relatively level but the axles will operate at severe angles.

Aspect Ratio—The ratio between the tire's width and height. Expressed as a percentage, it represents the tire's profile or the distance between the tread and the rim versus its section width.

Axle Wrap—See *Spring Wrap*

Backspacing—Another term for wheel offset. It's the distance from the inside edge to the mounting flange.

Bead—The area that mates the tire to the wheel. This area is a critical part of the tire's construction and consists of a hoop of high-tensile steel wires to which the belts are attached. This anchors the belts as well as providing a firm grip on the rim.

Bead Seat—This is the smooth face on the bead area of the tire that seals against the rim to hold air.

Bead Filler—A solid rubber wedge built into the lower sidewall designed to stiffen the area near the bead.

Beadlock—A type of wheel rim that clamps the outer bead of the tire to the rim and is used for tires that are operated at low pressures. It prevents rolling the tire off the rim and suddenly deflating it.

Beater—A 4x4 in rough condition. Usually one that looks bad but runs well.

Beef—Strength. Also adding strength to a part: upgrading.

Belts—Rubberized woven fabric that runs around the circumference of the tire under the tread. Polyester and steel in combination is the most common construction material.

Binder—Short for "Cornbinder." Slang for vehicles built by the International Harvester Company.

Blip—A quick stab of the throttle.

Bogger—A vehicle built for running mud. Also another term for an aggressive mud tire.

Bolt Clips—A device used to keep the spring leaves lined up atop each other. This is the preferred method because it does not restrict the movement as the "cinch"-type clamps may do.

Bottom—Compressing the suspension to the point where it reaches the bump stops.

Boxing—Usually refers to chassis modifications, where it is reinforced by closing the open part of a "C" or "U" section with additional material. It adds considerably to the strength.

Built—Short for built-up, or heavily modified.

Bump Steer—Where a bump or movement of the suspension forces the steering system to steer to one side or the other. Accompanied by movement of the steering wheel. Can occur at low speeds as the suspension moves up or down, or can occur at speed when bumps are encountered. It occurs to most 4x4s to a certain degree at low speeds, but at speed, it can be dangerous.

Bump Stop—A rubber or polyurethane bumper that limits the compress point or upward travel of the wheel.

CAD—Center Axle Disconnect. A device that disconnects one front axle shaft (usually the long one) from the differential via a splined, sliding collar. It's commonly actuated by engine vacuum, but can also be cable or hydraulically operated. The idea is to reduce the parasitic drag of the front axle, prevent the driveshaft from turning in two-wheel drive, and was conceived as an alternative to locking front hubs. This system only works with open diffs and it still allows the differential side and spider gears in the differential to rotate. If a limited slip or locker is installed, the left axle will then drive the ring, pinion, and driveshaft, usually causing a vibration at higher speeds.

Camber—The built-in curve or arch in a leaf spring. Also a steering term indicating the inward or outward tilt of the tops of the front tires. Positive camber tilts them out (as viewed from the front) and negative camber tilts them in.

Chafer—Rubber-coated fabric added to the bead area for strength.

Cardan Joint—The original name for the common universal joint, named for the sixteenth-century Italian mathematician, Jerome Cardan, who established their basic principle of operation.

Casing—The body of the tire, built up from cords and belts of material. Also known as the "carcass."

Caster—The forward or backward tilt of the steering axis. Positive caster tilts the top pivot from the vertical toward the rear of the vehicle and negative is the opposite.

Center of Gravity—The point of a vehicle where it balances on all planes. On most rigs, that point is somewhat forward of center and 1 to 2 feet off the ground, when viewed from the side, and slightly off to one side when viewed from the top. A lower center of gravity makes for a vehicle that is resistant to rolling over.

Chunk—When a tire throws off small pieces of tread. The result of heat and friction, but can occur when a tire is siped.

Compression—The amount of upward travel of a suspension above the static ride height.

Contact Patch—The part of the tire that makes contact with the ground and provides traction. The patch varies according to the tire size and the tire pressure used.

Cord—The stranded material incorporated into the belts and plies that are made into the casing of the tires.

Compound—The mixture of material that is the "rubber" part of the tire. There are five basic ingredients: rubber, carbon black, plasticizers, a curing ingredient, and an ozone retardant.

Crown—The center of the tire tread.

Cross-Axled—When the front and rear axles are articulated opposite each other.

Crawl Ratio—Also known as final drive ratio. The maximum multiplied lowest gear ratio, to include first gear, transfer case low range, and axle ratio. If there is another gearing device, that ratio is also added.

CV Joint—Constant-velocity joint. Several types exist, including the six-ball Rzeppa (pronounced "Cheppa") joint, the similar Birfield type, the four-ball Bendix type and the Herrington type consisting of two Cardan or U-joints. The result is the smooth transmission of power with no vibration. They are used on driveshafts and steering axles.

Dead-Man—An anchor point to winch from. It can be just about any solid object capable of supporting the weight applied against it.

Declutching—Usually pressing in the clutch to uncouple the engine from the drivetrain. It can also refer to the neutral position of items such as the transfer case, PTOs, winches, CADs, and other items that use a mechanical-type disconnect.

Deep Gearing—See *Low Gearing*.

Deflection—Movement or compression of a spring. Also the amount the tire "gives" under load. Essentially, the difference between its free and unloaded radius and its fully loaded radius.

Departure Angle—An imaginary line or angle at the rear of a vehicle between the contact point of the tires and the lowest part of the rear overhang. This angle dictates the height and steepness of the obstacle that the vehicle can descend, as well as the angle of the climb the vehicle can make without dragging tail.

Directional Stability—The ability (or lack thereof) of a tire (or vehicle) to maintain a straight line rather than following irregularities in the road.

Drag Link—The steering rod that connects the steering box Pitman arm to the tie-rod.

Dragging Tail—a.k.a. butt-dragging, tail dragging. When the rear of the vehicle makes contact with the ground, especially on a climb or descent.

Droop—The amount of downward suspension travel below the normal ride height of the vehicle. a.k.a. jounce.

Drop Pitman Arm—A special type of Pitman arm that is lower than stock. This reduces drag link angularity and bump steer.

Duty Cycle—The period over which a device can be operated before damage or undesirable effects occur. A cycle of on-time vs. off-time.

Eye—The loop in the end of the spring into which a bushing is installed and the spring is mounted. Also the eye in a rope or cable end.

Eye-to-Eye—The measurement of a leaf spring from the center of one eye to the other. Usually taken unloaded.

Fairlead—A guide for the winch cable. Can be a hawse type, which is a simple opening with smooth radiused edges. A roller fairlead has rollers on the top, bottom, and sides to guide the cable.

Free Arch—The distance between the top of the inside of a leaf spring to an imaginary line drawn between the center of the two eyes. The spring is unloaded.

Free Length—The unloaded length of a coil spring.

Full-floater—A full-floating axle, which is one where the weight of the vehicle is borne by a separate stub axle and bearings rather than the axle itself.

GCVWR—Gross Combined Vehicle Weight Rating. The maximum weight for a vehicle, its cargo, and its towed load.

Gnarly—Either some part that pegs the heavy-duty meter, or a tough obstacle or section of trail.

Granny—Low gears. First gear, low range, for example, is sometimes called "granny-granny."

Green Tire—This is the uncured tire, complete with all of its other components and awaiting being put into a mold and heated.

Grenade—When applied to four-wheeling, to destroy a mechanical part in a spectacular way.

Grip—A term used to describe the traction, or friction coefficient, of a tire on the ground surface.

Gusset—A reinforcing component used to strengthen a place where two structural members join.

GVWR—Gross Vehicle Weight Rating. The maximum weight for a vehicle and its cargo.

Hammered—Beaten, abused, trashed.

High-Centered—Hung up at the center of the vehicle. Can also be used when hung up on the axle.

Hook Up—To gain traction.

High Gearing—Numerically low gear ratios. Generally speaking, ratios from 2.50:1 to 3.54:1 are considered "high." See also *Tall Gearing.*

Hydrolocked—An engine that is prevented from turning by water in the cylinder. Water does not compress. Sometimes also called "hydro'ed" or "hydrauliced."

IFS—Independent front suspension.

Lift—The raising of a vehicle to gain trail clearance and clearance for tires.

Limited Slip—A traction-aiding differential that will supply a preset amount of torque to the tire with the most traction.

Line—A path through or over an obstacle that provides traction and clearance.

Line Pull—How much pull the winch can generate. This is variable because there are several ways to measure it. Most winch ratings are taken from the first layer of cable. Winch ratings assume an adequate battery.

Line Speed—How fast the cable spools onto the drum. Line speed varies according to load, gearing, motor power, and which layer of cable is in use.

Locked Up—A vehicle with a locker or lockers.

Locker—A traction-aiding differential that will provide 100 percent of the torque to one axle or both.

Low Gearing—Numerically high gear ratios, a.k.a "deep" gearing. Generally speaking, from 4.10:1 to about 6.13 (pretty near as low a ratio as you can find for light-duty truck and SUV axles) are considered low gears. Lower than 4.88:1 is considered "super" low. Ratios from 3.54 to 4.10 are regarded as moderately low.

Low-Lock—Low range.

Main Leaf—The first or primary leaf of a leaf spring. Often this is the only leaf with an eye, though the second leaf may also have one that wraps around the outside of the main leaf.

Meats—Tires, especially big ones. a.k.a. "Zapatos," "skins."

Military Wrap—This is where the second leaf of a leaf spring loops loosely around the main eye. As the name implies, this was originally mandated by the Army so that the vehicle was operable with a broken main leaf.

Multilink—A coil spring suspension with multiple locating links.

Nail—To fully depress the accelerator pedal. To "punch" it.

Nerf Bar—A rocker guard.

NOS—New old stock. Old parts but never used and still in their original boxes.

OEM—Original Equipment Manufacturer. Also "OE." A term sometimes used to describe a stock vehicle.

Off-Camber—Tilted sideways on a slope. Sidehill.

Overwound Cable—Where the cable spools off the top of the winch drum.

Panhard Rod—The transverse link that locates the axle laterally on a coil spring and some leaf spring suspensions. a.k.a. "track-rod."

Part—To break, refers to the cable.

Permanent Magnet Motor—A simple motor that uses two magnets instead of energized field coils. The advantages are compact-size and a lower-amp draw than *series wound* motors. Power and performance characteristics are similar to the *series wound.* The disadvantages are that they generate more heat at high loads, and have an increasingly shorter duty cycle as the load increases. *Permanent magnet* motors may also produce less power at below-zero temperatures, because the magnets lose magnetism. These motors are most often used in the lower-capacity or lower-priced winches.

Pin Offset—Describes a situation when the anchor pin that locates the axle onto a leaf spring is not centered on a spring. Specifically, it is the distance the pin is off-center.

Pinion—The input drive for the differential, or a shaft with a small gear attached. The "spider" gears in an open differential are also called pinions.

Pinion Angle—The angle of the differential input pinion in relation to the horizontal position.

Pitman Arm—An arm that attaches to the output shaft of the steering box. It converts the rotating motion of the steering box into lateral motion for steering.

Pitch—Also called ramp. Refers to how tightly a spring has been wound. Close-together coils have less pitch than coils that are farther apart.

Planetary Gear—A multipiece gearset that consists of the sun gear in the center, the planet gears (two, three, or four of them) that rotate around the sun, and a ring gear around them all.

Posi—Slang for a limited slip differential. Named after GM's "Posi-Traction" unit, which was built by Eaton.

Prerunner—In reality, a truck designed to prerun a desert race course. Also a style of truck devoted to going fast in the dirt. Can be 4x4 or 4x2 but has very compliant, long-travel suspension that's built for frequent flying.

Progressive Rate—Springs with rates that increase as they are compressed.

Proportioning Valve—A device in the braking system that apportions brake pressure front and rear.

PTO—Power Take-Off. A mechanical device that uses engine power, either directly or through the drivetrain, to power the winch or some other device. Many winch PTOs drive off the transfer case and some drive off the transmission.

Pumpkin—Slang for the removed part of removable carrier differential, aka Hotchkis design, such as a Ford 9-inch or a Toyota.

Radius Arms—Fore and aft locating arms for multilink suspensions. a.k.a. trailing arms.

Ramp Breakover Angle—An angle formed from the contact area of the tires and the lowest part of the vehicle's midsection. A measurement of clearance.

Rate—The amount of weight it takes to deflect a spring. Expressed in pounds per inch. It takes 200 lbs to deflect a 200-lb/in spring 1 inch, 400 pounds for 2 inches, and so on.

Rebound—The action of a spring returning to its natural ride height or preset "memory" position.

Ring Gear—A circular gear in the axle housing that provides the axle gear ratio in combination with the pinion gear.

Road—Any path over the ground designed for motor vehicle travel.

Roll Angle—The amount of body angle, or lean, the vehicle experiences on rough terrain.

RTI—Ramp travel index. A measurement of articulation and suspension travel calculated by driving one wheel up a 20-degree ramp until one rear wheel lifts, measuring the distance up the ramp level with the hub center, and dividing that measurement by the vehicle's wheelbase.

Static Ride Height—The normal ride height of the vehicle at rest, with no dynamic forces working on it, such as cornering.

Scrag—a.k.a. "Presetting." A method of setting the position "memory," or the permanent height or camber of a spring. After assembly, the spring is placed in a press and deflected a predetermined amount. This is usually past the normal deflection the spring will encounter in use.

Semi-Float—An axle that supports the weight on the axle shaft as well as driving the wheel with it.

Section Width—The sidewall-to-sidewall width of the tire. Not to be confused with tread width.

Series Wound Motor—The motor has field windings that consist of copper wire wound over an iron core. A series wound motor is larger than a *permanent magnet* motor and has a much longer duty cycle (more resistant to heat). It draws more power than the *permanent magnet* type with nearly the same performance characteristics. These motors are most often used in the higher-capacity, higher-priced winches, or winches designed for commercial applications.

Shackle—Either a D-shaped connector used for winching or recovery, or the pivoting link at one end of a leaf spring that allows the spring to "grow" longer or shorter as it flexes.

Shear Pin—A carefully designed pin in a PTO winch that is designed to break before something else does. Because PTO winches are driven by engines 100 times the power of an electric motor, the shear pin is calibrated to break before the winch or winch cable does. If you have a PTO winch, you should have a couple of extra shear pins just in case.

Shotpeening—Referring mainly to leaf springs. Steel shot is sprayed at high pressure on the surfaces of the leaves to compress the surface of the steel and surface-harden it. The technique is also used to surface-harden other metal parts, such as connecting rods.

Siping—Slits or cuts in the tread blocks that allow the blocks to move and grip. Sipes can be built into the tire by the manufacturer or added later. Siping usually enhances the wet and icy performance of the tire.

Slushbox—Slang for automatic transmission.

Snatch Block—A high-capacity pulley used for winching.

Snatch Strap—A kinetic-energy recovery strap.

Spool—The careful laying of the cable onto the drum, with the wraps wound tightly on the drum, tightly beside each other and tightly atop each other in succeeding layers.

Spool In—To bring cable in on the winch.

Spool Out—To let cable out on the winch.

Spotter—A person outside the vehicle who guides the driver over tricky obstacles.

Spring Wrap—Torque and traction combine to twist the axle (pushing the nose of the differential up going forward and down going backward) by twisting the spring into an "S" shape. The energy is stored in the spring until the tire slips, and at that point the spring snaps back violently. Sometimes this results in a hopping sensation, hence the other common term, "axle hop." It can be very hard on driveshafts and U-joints.

Stall Point—The point at which the winch stops under a load. This is often shortly past the unit's maximum line pull.

Stock—As delivered from the manufacturer; unmodified.

Suspension Travel—The total up-and-down movement of the suspension with the axle on a level plane.

T-Case—Short for transfer case. Some parts of the world use the term "transfer box."

Taco'ed—Bending some component into a "u" shape, or nearly so.

Tail Gunner—The captain of last vehicle in a group on a trail ride whose primary job is to make sure nobody gets left behind.

Tall Gearing—Numerically low gear ratios. Generally speaking, ratios from 2.50:1 to 3.54:1 are considered "high." See also *High Gearing*.

Taper—Some manufacturers taper the ends of each leaf of a leaf spring. This allows for a softer rate spring—as compared to a dimensionally similar untapered leaf—and reduced friction.

TBI—Throttle Body Injection. A fuel injection system that injects fuel into the airflow at the throttle butterflies atop the intake manifold.

Tie-Rod—The steering rod that connects the two wheels together.

Threshold Braking—A technique of applying the maximum braking pressure short of the tire lockup point.

Toe-In/Out—A steering geometry adjustment. Toe-in is where the front edges of the tires point in toward each other; toe-out is the opposite.

Torque—Measured in pounds-feet (lbs-ft). Force times distance. One pound of weight on a 1-foot bar produces 1 pound-foot of force.

Torque Converter—A fluid coupling/clutch used in automatic transmissions. It consists of three main parts: the impeller, which is driven by the engine; the turbine, which is connected directly to the transmission; and the stator, which lies between the two. The spinning impeller pushes the transmission fluid against the blades of the turbine, which forces it to spin in the same direction. The stator directs the flow of the oil.

Torsion Bar—A type of spring. One end is solidly attached to a chassis member and the other end is attached to one of the control arms. This converts the up-and-down movement of the suspension into twist on the torsion bar.

Toylet—A Toyota powered by a Chevy engine. a.k.a. "Chevota."

TPI—Tuned Port Injection. A GM high-performance, multiport, fuel-injection system.

Traction—The conversion of engine torque into motion.

Trail—Four-wheeler slang for an unimproved road.

Trailer Queen—Usually a show rig that travels by trailer. Can also be used for rigs that are trailered to and from four-wheeling spots. For some, this is a derisive term.

TTB—Twin Traction Beam. A Ford semi-independent front suspension for 4x4s used from 1980 to 1997.

U-Bolt—The u-shaped bolt used to attach the axle to a leaf spring.

U-Joint—Universal joint (aka Cardan joint).

Underwound Cable—Where the cable spools off the bottom of the winch drum.

Viscous Coupling—A device used either to lock a center differential or to transmit power. It consists of a number of plates in a sealed case full of silicone gel and an input and output. Half the plates are attached to one shaft and the other half are connected to another, but they are alternating. When there is a difference in speed from one side, the silicone gel thickens and couples the unit together.

Void Ratio—The ratio of open areas in a tire tread versus the parts that actually contact the ground.

Wheel Travel—The total amount of up-and-down movement of the suspension as measured at the hub.

Wire Rope—The most correct term for the winch cable on your winch.

Wire Size—The coils of a coil spring are made from a bar of metal that is wound and tempered. Wire size refers to the diameter of this material.

APPENDIX II
Sources

Bibliography

ASM Metals Handbook
1981 American Society for Metals
American Society for Metals
0-87170-134-0

Auto Math Handbook
1992 John Lawler
HP Books
1-55788-020-4

Automotive Electrical Handbook
1986 Jim Horner
HP Books
0-89586-238-7

Bosch Automotive Handbook
1993 Ulrich Adler, Editor
Robert Bosch GmbH
3-1-419115-X

Brake Handbook
1985 Fred Puhn
HP Books
0-89586-232-8

CB Radio
1976 Leo G. Sands
A. S. Barnes
0-498-01969-1

Chevy & GMC Pickup Performance Handbook
2000 Jim Allen
MBI Publishing Company
0-7603-0798-9

4-Wheel Freedom
1996 Brad DeLong
Paladin Press
0-87364-891-9

Handbook of Off-Road Driving
1990 Julian Cremona/Keith Hart
Ashford, Buchan & Enright
1-85253-211-4

How to Make Your Car Handle
1981 Fred Puhn
HP Books
0-912656-46-8

Jeep 4x4 Performance Handbook
1998 Jim Allen
MBI Publishing Company
0-7603-0470-X

Land Rover Experience
1994 Tom Sheppard
Land Rover Ltd.
0-9514493-4-6

Machinery's Handbook
1978 Oberg/Jones/Horton
Industrial Press
75-1962

Mark A. Smith's Guide to Safe, Common Sense Off-Road Driving
1991 Mark A. Smith
Mark A. Smith's Off-Roading, Inc.
Pamphlet

Performance With Economy
1981 David Vizard
S-A Design
0-931472-09-1

Power Secrets
1989 Smokey Yunick
S-A Design
0-931472-06-7

Shifting Into 4WD
2001 Harry Lewellyn
Glovebox Publications
0-944781-02-2
Why Skid
1995 Bridgestone Winter
Driving School
Rally-Art
Booklet
Winching In Safety
1989 Peter Hobson
Land Rover Ltd.
0-9512235-1-8
Wired for Success
1995 Randy Rundle
Krause Publications
ISBN: 0-87341-402-0

Magazine Web sites
Four Wheeler
www.fourwheeler.com
Jp Magazine
www.jpmagazine.com
Off-Road
www.off-roadweb.com
Truck Trend
www.trucktrend.com
4-Wheel Drive & Sport Utility
www.4wdandsportutility.com
4-Wheel & Off-Road
www.4wheeloffroad.com

Clubs and Enthusiast Organizations
Most of these are associations of clubs from which you can find or choose a local group.

Arizona State Association of Four-Wheel Drive Clubs
PO Box 23904
Tempe, AZ 85285
(602) 258-4BY4
www.asa4wdc.org
Blue Ribbon Coalition
4555 Burley Drive, Ste A
Pocatello, ID 83202
(800) 258-3742
www.sharetrails.org
California Association of Four-Wheel Drive Clubs
8120 36th Ave.
Sacramento, CA 95824-2304
(800) 4X4-FUNN
www.cal4wheel.com
Colorado Association of 4-Wheel Drive Clubs
PO Box 1413
Wheat Ridge, CO 80034
(303) 343-0646
www.cohvco.org/ca4wdci/index.html
East Coast 4-Wheel Drive Association
101 S. Miami Ave.
Cleves, OH 45002
(800) ECS-T4WD
www.ec4wda.org
The Four Wheel Drive Association of British Columbia
PO Box 284
Surrey, BC V3T 4W8 Canada
www.4wdabc.ca/contact.asp

Grand Mesa Jeep Club
3281 F 3/10 Road
Clifton, CO 81520
(970) 523-5443
Great Lakes Four-Wheel Drive Association
www.glfwda.org/admin.htm
Mile Hi Jeep Club
PO Box 8293
Denver, CO 80202
www.mhjc.org
Large club that hosts the annual All-4-Fun Week
Minnesota 4-Wheel Drive Association
PO Box 2081
Maple Grove, MN 55311
mn4wda.com/contact.htm
Red Rock 4-Wheelers
PO Box 1471
Moab, UT 84532-1471
(435) 259-7625
Large club and hosts of the annual Moab Easter Jeep Safari
Rocky Mountain Pinzgauer Club
1021 Steele St.
Denver, CO 80206
(303) 377-1528
www.pinzgauer.org
Southern Four-Wheel Drive Association
PO Box 50726
Knoxville, TN 37950-0726
www.sfwda
Southwest Four-Wheel Drive Association
10818 Lands Runs
San Antonio, TX 78230
www.swfwda.org
Tread Lightly!
298 24th St., Ste 325
Ogden, UT 84401
(800) 966-9900
www.treadlightly.org
United Four-Wheel Drive Association
4505 W. 700S
Shelbyville, IN 46176-9678
(800) 44-UFWDA
www.ufwda.org
Virginia Four-Wheel Drive Association
PO Box 722
Mechanicsville, VA 23111
www.geocities.com/od4wdc

Driving Instruction and Guided Trips
Bill Burke's 4-Wheeling America
307 N. Ash St.
Fruita, CO 81521
(970) 858-3418
www.bb4wa.com
Individual, group, or corporate-level instruction, guided trips
Bridgestone Winter Driving Schools
PO Box 774167
Steamboat Springs, CO 80477
(800) 949-7543
www.winterdrive.com
Individual and group instruction

BSR Inc.
PO Box 190
Summit Point, WV 25446
(304) 725-6512
www.bsr-inc.com
Individual and group instruction specializing in corporate accounts
Ecological 4-Wheeling
PO Box 12137
Costa Mesa, CA 92627
(949) 645-7733
www.eco4wd.com
Classroom instruction, group instruction, and group trips
Esprit de Four
16 Dorchester Dr.
Mountain View, CA 94043
(800) 494-3866
www.espritdefour.com
Safety clinics and driving instruction for drivers with little experience
First Time Out Off-Road Adventures
PO Box 4283
Georgetown, CA 95634
(925) 560-9541
www.firstimeout.com
Guided instruction trips
4x4 ABC
Harald Pietschmann
PO Box 1269
Georgetown, CA 95634
(530) 333-2696
4x4abc.com/contact.html
Individual and group instruction, guided trips, and adventure vacations
The 4x4 Center
740 Marshall Ave.
Williston, VT 05495
(800) 864-9180
www.the4x4center.com
Individual and group instruction, corporate and team-building programs
The Hummer Driving Academy
408 S. Byrkit St.
Mishawaka, IN 46546-0728
(2i9) 258-6622
www.hummer.com
Individual and group instruction
Jeep Jamboree USA
PO Box 1601
Georgetown, CA 95634
(530) 333-4777
www.jeepjamboreeusa.com
Guided trips in various locales within the United States
Jeep 101
(800) 825-JEEP
www.jeep.com
Basic course offered at the annual Camp Jeep event held in various U.S. locations
Land Rover Adventures
(866) 766-6881
www.lrabrochure.co.uk/USA
Guided instructional adventure vacations in various places around the world

The Land Rover Driving School
The Greenbrier
300 West Main Street
White Sulphur Springs, WV 24986
(800) 453-4858
www.greenbrier.com/docs/landrover.html
Individual and group training
Off-Road Experience
190 Airway Blvd.
Livermore, CA 94550
(925) 606-8301
www.offroadexperience.com
Individual and group training, guided trips
Overland Experts
112 Hemlock Valley Rd.
Hadlyme, CT 06423
(877) 931-3343
www.overlandexperts.com
Individual and group training
Rod Hall Performance Off-Road Driving School
1360 Kleppe Ln.
Sparks, NV 89431
(775) 331-4800
www.rodhall.com
Group and individual instruction
United Four-Wheel Drive Associations' 4wd Awareness Program
1504 Philadelphia Rd.
Joppa, MD 21085
(410) 671-7186
www.ufwda.org/awareness
Awareness clinics are held in various locations around the United States
Western Adventures 4x4 Driving School
PO Box 2451
Ramona, CA 92065
(760) 789-1563
www.westernadventures.com
Group and individual instruction, guided trips

Guidebooks, Maps, and Navigation
Adventure GPS Products
1629 4th Avenue SE
Decatur, AL 35601
(888) 477-4386
www.gpsfn.com
GPS and mapping products, web site has good instructional info
DeLorme
Two DeLorme Plaza
PO Box 298
Yarmouth, ME 04096
(207) 846-7000
www.delorme.com
Gazetteers, mapping software, USGS maps on CD-ROM, GPS, GPS products, and more
4x4 Now
(308) 381-4410
www.4x4now.com
Vast array of GPS and mapping tools, as well as 4x4 books, trail guides, and atlases

Fun Treks, Inc.
PO Box 49187
Colorado Springs, CO
80949-9187
(719) 536-0722
www.funtreks.com
Colorado, Utah, and Arizona guidebooks

Sidekick Off-Road
PO Box 727
Chino, CA 91708-0727
(909) 628-7227
www.sidekickoffroad.com
Trail maps, guidebooks, instructional and trail videos

USGS
U.S. Department of the Interior
807 National Center
Reston, VA 20192
www.usgs.gov
Topo maps, online ordering, general USGS map info

Parts and Accessories
Body and Related
Bolt-On Body Accessories
All Custom Fabrications
Grand Junction, Colorado
(970) 245-5686
www.acf4wd.com
Heavy-duty and high-clearance bumpers for jeeps, plus skidplates

Go Rhino!
2097 Batavia Street
Orange, CA 92865
(714) 279-8300
www.gorhino.com
Bumpers, running boards, sport bars, and more

Grizzly
700 Allen Avenue
Glendale, CA 91201
(818) 247-2910
www.grantproducts.com
Bumpers, running boards, sport bars, and more

Smittybilt, Inc.
Dept. 4x4
395 Smitty Way
Corona, CA 91719
(800)-2-SMITTY
www.smittybiltinc.com
Bumpers, running boards, sport bars, and more

Xenon
2891 E. Via Martins
Anaheim, CA 92806
(800) 999-8753
www.teamxenon.com
Fender flares, running boards, air dams, and more

Body Coatings, Paint
Arma Coatings
1551 Pearl Street
Eugene, OR 97401
(504) 484-5915
www.armacoatings.com
Urethane coatings; local dealers in many areas

Duraback Bedliner
Cote-L Distribution Co.
4064 S. Atcheson Way, Ste. 301
Aurora, CO 80014
(303) 690-7190
DIY polyurethane coating

Eastwood Company
263 Shoemaker Road
Pottstown, PA 19464
1-800-345-1178 or
610-323-2200
Equipment for powder coating at home and restoration supplies

Rhino Linings
9151 Rehco Road
San Diego, CA 92121
www.rhinolinings.com
(619) 450-0441
Spray-on bed liners and body coating

Fuel Tanks
Aero Tanks
1780 Pomona Road
Corona, CA 91720
(909) 737-7878
Replacement and oversized fuel tanks

Northwest Metal Products
3801 24th Avenue
Forest Grove, OR 97116
(503) 359-4427
Replacement and oversized fuel tanks

Seats
Corbeau USA
9503 S. 560 W
Sandy, UT 84070
(801) 255-3737
High-performance seating

Flowfit
127 Business Center Drive, Unit B
Corona, CA 91720
(800) FLO-FITS
High-performance seating

Steel Horse Automotive
601 W. Walnut Street
Compton, CA 90220
(800) 533-7704
www.steelhorseautomotive.com
High-performance seating

Wet Okole
1727 Superior
Costa Mesa, CA 92627
(714) 548-1543
Waterproof seat covers

Storage
Tubb Bedliner
PO Box 18069
Louisville, KY 40261
(502) 266-8953
www.tubbbedliner.com
Bedliners with built-in storage boxes

Tuffy Security Products
25733 Road H
Cortez, CO 81321-9119
(800) 348-8339
www.tuffyproducts.com
Locking consoles, storage boxes, and more

Tops
Can-Back
9649 Remer Street
South El Monte, CA 91733
(626) 442-0739
www.can-back.com
Rear truck canvas, bikini tops, and more

Kayline Mfg.
200 E. 64th Ave.
Denver, CO 80221
(800) 525-8118
www.kayline.com
Tops, interior parts, and racks

Napier Enterprises
2315 Whirlpool Street, Ste 161
Niagara Falls, NY 14305
(800) 567-2434
Truck bed tents

Brake Performance Improvements
Conversions and HP Brakes
Hawk Performance
920 Lake Road
Medina, OH 44256
(800) 542-0972
www.hawkperformance.com
High-performance brake items

Performance Friction
PO Box 819
Clover, SC 29710
(803) 222-2141
Composite high-performance brakes and brake products

Praise Dyno Brake
1061 S. Munson Rd.
Royse, TX 75189
(972) 636-2722
Composite high-performance brakes and brake products

Stainless Steel Brakes
11470 Main Road
Clarence, NY 14031
(800) 448-7722
www.stainlesssteelbrakes.com
Disc brake conversions and brake performance items

Stillen
3176 Airway
Costa Mesa, CA 92626
(714) 540-5566
www.stillen.com
Big-brake kits, high-performance brakes, and brake products

Stop Tech
3015 Kashiwa Street
Torrence, CA 90505
(310) 325-4799
www.stoptech.com
High-performance brake items

TSM
Dept. 4x4
4321 Willow Creek Rd. #4
Castle Rock, CO 80104-9766
(303) 688-6882
Disc brake conversions and brake performance items

Other Brake Components
Classic Tube
80 Rotech Drive
Lancaster, NY 14086
(800) 882-3711
www.classictube.com
Stainless replacement brake lines

Earl's Performance Products
189 W. Victoria St.
Long Beach, CA 90805
(310) 609-1602
Steel braided brake lines

Wilwood Engineering
461 Calle San Pablo
Camarillo, CA 93012
(805) 388-1188
High-temp brake fluid and other brake supplies

Electrical
Batteries
Optima Batteries
17500 E. 22nd Ave.
Aurora, CO 80011
(303) 340-7440
www.optima.com
Optima batteries and electrical products

Trojan Battery Company
12380 Clark St.
Santa Fe Springs, CA 90670
(800) 423-6569
Deep-cycle and marine batteries

Lighting
Hella North America
201 Kelly Drive
Peachtree City, GA 30269
(877) 224-3552
www.hellausa.com
Performance lighting products

IPF
1425 Elliot Ave. W.
Seattle, WA 98119
(206) 284-5906
Assorted performance lights and lighting products

KC Hilites
PO Box 155
Williams, AZ 86046
(800) 528-0950
www.kchilites.com
Assorted performance lights and lighting products

PIAA
15370 S.W. Millikan Way
Beaverton, OR 97006
(503) 643-7422
Assorted performance lights and lighting products

Starters, Alternators, and Welders
MG Industries (Mean Green)
PO Drawer 336
Laughlintown, PA 15655-0336
(412) 532-3090
High-torque starters and high-output alternators

Powermaster
2410 Dutch Valley Drive
Knoxville, TN 37918
(423) 688-5953
www.powermastermotorsports.
com
High-output alternators, high-torque starters, and more

Premier Power Welder
PO Box 639
Carbondale, CO 81623
(800) 541-1817
www.truckworld.com/pullpal/
High-output alternators, underhood welders, and more

Wiring
Centech Wiring
7 Colonial Dr.
Perkiomenville, PA 18074
(610) 287-5730
www.centechwire.com
Replacement wiring harnesses and power steering kits

M.A.D. Enterprises
15180 Raymer St.
Van Nuys, CA 91405
(818) 786-5725
Wiring kits and electrical products

Painless Wiring
9505 Santa Paula
Ft. Worth, TX 76116
(800) 423-9696
www.painlesswiring.com
Wiring kits and electrical products

Phoenix Gold International
PO Box 83189
Portland, OR 97283
(503) 288-2008
Power flow products, mega alternators, isolators, and so on

Sure Power Industries
10189 S.W. Avery
Tualatin, OR 97062
(503) 692-5360
Battery controlling devices, isolators, and cable

Wrangler Power Products
PO Box 12109
Prescott, AZ 86304-2109
(800) 962-2616
Megapower alternators, plus wiring and electrical products

Engine
Air Filters
K&N Engineering
PO Box 1329
Riverside, CA 92502-1329
(800) 858-3333
www.knfilters.com
High-performance air filtration systems

Camshaft and Valvetrain
Comp Cams
3406 Democrat Road
Memphis, TN 38118
(901) 795-2400
www.compcams.com
Cam, valve train, and performance parts

Crane Cams
530 Fentress Blvd.
Daytona Beach, FL 32114
(904) 258-6174
www.cranecams.com
Cam, valve train, and performance parts

Crower Cams & Equipment
3333 Main St.
Chula Vista, CA 91911-5899
(619) 422-1191
Cams, valve gear, custom crankshafts, and engine performance

Erson Cams
10601 Memphis Avenue #12
Cleveland, OH 44144
(216) 688-8300
www.mrgasket.com
Cam, valve train, and performance parts

Cooling System
Flex-a-Lite
7213 45th Street
Fife, WA 98424
(800) 851-1510
www.flex-a-lite.com
High-performance mechanical and electric fans and more

Flowcooler
289 Prado Rd.
San Luis Obispo, CA 93401
(800) 342-6759
High-flow water pumps and thermostats

Griffin Racing Radiators
100 Hurricane Creek Rd.
Piedmont, SC 29673
(864) 845-5000
Custom and high-performance radiators

Hayden Inc.
1531 Pomona Rd.
Corona, CA 91720
(800) 854-4757
Fans, oil coolers, and cooling accessories

Modine Manufacturing
1500 De Coven Ave.
Racine, WI 53403
(414) 636-1641
Replacement and high-efficiency radiators

U.S. Radiator Corp.
PO Box 30227
Los Angeles, CA 90003-0227
(323) 778-5525
www.usradiator.com
Replacement and high-efficiency radiators

Diesel
Advanced Turbo Systems
PO Box 547
5919 South, 350 West
Murray, UT 84107
(800) 688-8726
www.atsturbo.com
Turbo kits and diesel performance parts galore

BD Performance
33733 King Road, Unit A10
Abbotsford, BC
V2s 7M9 Canada
(800) 887-5030
www.dieselperformance.com
Exhaust brakes and diesel performance parts

Diesel Services Group
2924A Miners Avenue
Saskatoon, SK, S7K 4Z7
Canada
(800) 667-6879
www.dieselservices.com
Gear-type cam drive and other diesel performance parts

Gale Banks Engineering
546 Duggan Avenue
Azusa, CA 91702
(800) 438-7693
www.getpower.com
Turbo kits and diesel performance parts galore

Peninsular Diesel
805A Taylor Street
Jenison, MI 49428
(616) 457-2121
www.peninsulardiesel.com
6.5L performance engines and parts

Stanadyne Automotive
Power Products Division
92 Deerfield Road
Windsor, CT 06095
(800) 842-2496
Diesel fuel performance additives

Turbo Technology
6211 S. Adams
Tacoma, WA 98409
(253) 475-8319
www.turbotechnologyinc.com
Diesel intercoolers, exhaust, and other parts

U.S. Gear
9420 Stony Island Avenue
Chicago, IL 60617
(800) 874-3271
www.usgear.com
Exhaust brakes, gauges, diesel performance

EFI and Carburetor Performance
Carburetor Shop
1459 Philadelphia Street, Unit A
Ontario, CA 91761
(909) 481-5816
www.customcarbs.com
Performance carbs, trail-modified carbs

Edelbrock
200 California Street
Torrance, CA 90503
(800) 16-8628
www.edelbrock.com
Bolt-on EFI, performance carbs, induction systems, and more

Electromotive, Inc.
9131 Centreville Road
Manassas, VA 20143
(703) 331-0100
www.electromotive-inc.com
Bolt-on fuel-injection and ignitions

Holley Performance Products
PO Box 10360
Bowling Green, KY 42102-7360
(270) 782-2900
www.holley.com
Performance carbs, TBI, and port injection systems

Howell Fuel Injection
6201 Industrial Way
Marine City, MI 48039
(810) 765-5100
www.howell-efi.com
Bolt-on fuel-injection kits

Hypertech
3215 Appling Road
Bartlett, TN 38133
(901) 382-8888
www.hypertech-inc.com
Performance chips and reprogramming tools

Jet Performance Products
17491 Apex Circle
Huntington Beach, CA 92647
(714) 848-5515
www.jetchip.com
Performance EFI modules, performance carbs, and more

Street & Performance
Electronics
304 Smokey Lane
North Little Rock, AR 72117
(501) 945-0354
Performance chips for GM vehicles

Superchips
134 Baywood Avenue
Longwood, FL 32750
(407) 260-0838
www.superchips.com
Performance chips and reprogramming tools

Turbo City
1137 West Katella Ave.
Orange, CA 92867
(714) 639-4933
www.turbocity.com

Engine Swaps
Advance Adapters
PO Box 247
Paso Robles, CA 93446-0247
(800) 350-2223
www.advanceadapters.com
Engine, transmission, and transfer case swapping products

Forced Induction/Nitrous
Edelbrock Corp.
See contact information under
EFI and Carburetor Performance
Supercharger kits

Holley
See contact information under
EFI and Carburetor Performance
Supercharger kits

Nitrous Express
4923 Lake Park Drive
Wichita Falls, TX 76302
(940) 767-7694
www.nitrousexpress.com
Nitrous oxide injection systems

NOS
2970 Airway Avenue
Costa Mesa, CA 92626
(714) 545-0580
www.nosnitrous.com
Nitrous oxide injection systems

Powerdyne
104-C East Avenue K-4
Lancaster, CA 93535
(661) 723-2802
www.powerdyne.com
Supercharger kits

Turbonetics
5400 Atlantis Court
Moorpark, CA 93021
(805) 529-8995
www.turbonetics.com
Performance turbocharging specialists

Vortech Engineering
1650 Pacific Avenue
Channel Islands, CA 93033-9901
(805) 247-0226
www.vortecheng.com
Street and race superchargers and more

Ignition
Accel
10601 Memphis Avenue, #12
Cleveland, OH 44129
(216) 688-8300
www.mrgasket.com
Performance ignitions and performance products

Jacobs Electronics
500 N. Baird St
Midland, TX 79701
(800) 955-3345
wwwjacobselectronics.com
Performance ignitions and electrical systems

Mallory Ignition
10601 Memphis Avenue, #12
Cleveland, OH 44144
(216) 688-8300
www.mrgasket.com
Performance Ignitions

MSD Ignition
1490 Henry Brennan Drive
El Paso, TX 79936
(915) 855-7123
www.msdignition.com
Performance ignition systems

Performance Distributors D.U.I
2699 Barris Dr.
Memphis, TN 38132
(901) 396-5782
Performance and water-resistant distributors and ignition stuff

Pertronix
440 East Arrow Highway
San Dimas, CA 91773
(800) 827-3758
www.pertronix.com
Points to electronic ignition conversion and other products

Induction and Exhaust
Clifford Inline Performance
PO Box 2620
Corona, CA 91720
(909) 734-3310
www.cliffordperformance.com
Four- and six-cylinder performance specialist

Edelbrock Corp.
See contact information under
EFI and Carburetor Performance
Engine performance specialist

Flowmaster
2975 Dutton Avenue
Santa Rosa, CA 95407
(800) 544-4761
www.flowmastermufflers.com
Performance mufflers and exhaust systems

Flowtech
2605 West First Street
Tempe, AZ 85281
(480) 966-1511
www.flowtech.com
Performance mufflers and exhaust systems

Gale Banks Engineering
See contact information under
Diesel
Performance exhaust and intake systems

Gibson Performance
3780 Prospect Ave.
Yorba Linda, CA 92886
(714) 528-3044
www.gibsonperformance.com
Performance exhaust systems

Hedman Headers
9599 W. Jefferson Blvd.
Culver City, CA 90232
(562) 921-0404
www.hedman.com
Headers and exhaust system products

Holley
See contact information under
EFI and Carburetor Performance
Engine performance specialist

Offenhauser
Dept 4x4
5300 Alhambra Ave.
Los Angeles, CA 90032
(213) 225-1307
Induction systems specialists

Pierce Manifolds
Dept 4x4
8901 Murray Avenue
Gilroy, CA 95020
(408) 842-6667
Weber carb conversions

Performance Exhaust & Undercar
1087 Valentine SE
Pacific, WA 98047
(800) 437-2969
www.performanceexhaust.com
Performance exhaust systems

Performance Engines and Parts
Jasper Performance Products
815 Wernsling Road
Jasper, IN 47547-0650
(800) 827-7455
www.jasperengines.com
Performance engines and performance parts

Jegs
751 East 11th Ave.
Columbus, OH 43211
(800) 345-4545
Performance engine parts

Lingenfelter Performance Engineering
1557 Winchester Road
Decatur, IN 46733
(219) 724-2552
Performance engines and performance parts

Manley Performance Products
1960 Swarthmore Avenue
Lakewood, NJ 08701
(732) 905-3366
www.manleyperformance.com
Performance engine parts

PAW
21001 Nordhoff Street
Chatsworth, CA 91311
(818) 678-3000
www.pawengineparts.com
Performance engines and performance parts

Summit Racing Equipment
PO Box 909
Akron, OH 44309-0909
(800) 230-3030
www.summitracing.com
Performance engines and performance parts

Suspension and Related
Suspension Bushings
Daystar Products
841 S. 71st Street
Phoenix, AZ 85043
(800) 595-7659
Performance suspension bushings

Energy Suspension
1131 Via Callejon
San Clemente, CA 92673
(949) 361-3935
www.energysuspension.com
Performance suspension bushings

Custom Springs
Alcan Spring
2242 Hwy 6 & 50
Grand Junction, CO 81505
(970) 241-2655
Custom springs

Eaton Detroit Springs
1555 Michigan Avenue
Detroit, MI 48216
(313) 963-3839
www.eatonspring.com
Custom leaf and coil springs

National Spring
1402 N. Magnolia
El Cajon, CA 92026
(619) 441-1901
Specializes in thin leaf springs, also has suspension kits

Valley Spring Works
340 Industrial Way, Building B
Dixon, CA 95620
www.valleyspr.qpg.com
(916) 678-3944
Custom coil springs

Driveshafts
Denny's Driveshaft Service
(716) 875-6640
www.dennysdriveshaft.com
Custom driveshafts

Six States Distributors
1112 W. 33rd South
Ogden, UT 84401
(800) 453-2022
Custom driveshafts

Tom Wood's Custom Driveshafts
Dept. 4x4
306 E. 31st Street
Ogden, UT 84401
(877) 497-4238
www.4xshaft.com
Custom driveshafts

Handling and Street Performance
Addco
715 13th Street
Lake Park, FL 33403
(800) 338-7515
www.addcoindustries.com
Front and rear sway bars

Con-Ferr Products
733 Victory Blvd.
Burbank, CA 91502
(818) 848-1011
www.con-ferr.com
IFS front sway bar and other products

Hellwig
16237 Avenue 296
Visalia, CA 93292
(559) 734-7451
www.hellwig.net
Front and rear sway bars and other suspension components

Sway-A-Way
20755 Marilla Street
Chatsworth, CA 91311
(818) 700-0947
www.swayaway.com
High-performance suspension and sway bars

Lift Kits and Suspension Hardware
AOR
Advance Off-Road Research
725-B West Grand
Grand Junction, CO 81501
(970) 263-4300
www.aor4x4.com
High-performance suspension upgrades and more

AutoFab
10996 N. Woodside Avenue
Santee, CA 92071
(619) 562-1740
www.autofab.com
Steering box brace and other hardware

BF Goodrich Aerospace
Engineered Polymer Products
6061 BF Goodrich Blvd.
Jacksonville, FL 32226
(904) 696-4116
Velvet Ride Shackle

Dick Cepek
301 California Avenue
Beaumont, CA 92223
(800) 992-3735
www.dickcepek.com
*Suspension kits and frame
reinforcement kit*

Explorer Pro Comp
2758 Via Orange Way
Spring Valley, CA 91978
(800) 776-0767
www.explorerprocomp.com
Suspension systems and components

Off-Road Design
0134 County Road 110
Glenwood Springs, CO 81601
(970) 945-7777
www.offroaddesign.com
HD shackles, shackle flip

Off-Road Unlimited
40 E. Palm Ave.
Burbank, CA 91502
(818) 563-1208
www.offroadunlimited.com
*Crossover steering conversion, IFS-
to-leaf-spring conversion*

Rancho Suspension
500 N. Field Drive
Lake Forest, IL 60045
(888) 467-2624
www.gorancho.com
Suspension systems and components

Skyjacker Suspensions
PO Box 1678
West Monroe, LA 71294-1678
(800) 821-2985
www.skyjacker.com
Suspension systems and components

Superlift
211 Horne Lane
West Monroe, LA 71291
(800) 551-4955
www.superlift.com
Suspension systems and components

Trailmaster Suspension
420 Jay Street
Coldwater, MI 49036
(517) 278-4011
Suspension systems and components

Tuff Country Suspension
4165 W. Nike Drive
West Jordan City, UT 84088
(800) 288-2190
www.tuffcountry.com
Suspension systems and components

Power Steering Improvements
AGR Inc
2610 Aviation Parkway
Grand Prairie, TX 75052
(972) 641-2090
www.agrsteering.com
*Super Saginaw steering boxes and
high-volume pumps*

Lee Mfg. Power Steering
Systems
11661 Pendelton St.
Sun Valley, CA 91352
(818) 768-0371
*Custom power steering hoses, power
steering boxes, and pumps*

Shocks
Bilstein
8845 Rehco Road
San Diego, CA 92121
(800) 537-1085
www.bilstein.com
*Performance shocks and suspension
products*

Doetsch Tech
9402-A Wheatlands Court
Santee, CA 92071-2831
(800) 8-SHOCKS
www.doetsch-shocks.com
*Performance shocks and suspension
products*

Fox Shox
3641 Charter Park Dr.
San Jose, CA 95136
(408) 269-9200
*Performance shocks and suspension
products*

Koni North America
1961-A International Way
Hebron, KY 41048
(606) 586-4100
www.koni-na.com
Performance shocks

KYB Gas Shocks
901 Oak Creek Drive
Lombard, IL 60148
(630) 620-5555
www.kyb.com
Performance shocks

Tokico Gas Shocks
1330 Storm Parkway
Torrance, CA 90501
(310) 534-4934
Performance shocks

Tires and Related
Compressors, Tire Tools, and Tire Accessories
Advanced Air System
5901 Southview Dr.
San Jose, CA 95138
(800) 641-3206
CO-2 tanks for tire inflation

Automatic Controls Technology
480 N. Main St.
Brewer, ME 04412
(800) 982-0409 ext 002
High-output 12-volt compressors

Extreme Outback Products
3069 Alamo Drive, Ste 327
Vacaville, CA 95687
(707) 447-7711
Compressors, trail tire repair tools

Mattracks
202 Cleveland Avenue East
Karlstad, MN 56732
(218) 436-7000
www.mattracks.com
Tracked conversion systems

Performance Wheel and Tire
1096 West Hampton Avenue
Englewood, CO 80110
(303) 762-1595
Wheel spacers and adapters

Oasis Off-Road Manufacturing
PO Box 674
Lake Forest, CA 92630
(888) 966-2747
www.oasis-off-road.com
Fast air-down accessories

Onboard Air
1847 N. Keystone St.
Burbank, CA 91504
(818) 848-2900
www.onboardair.com
AC compressor conversions

Safety Seal
North Shore Laboratories Corp
PO Box 568
Peabody, MA
(800) 888-9021
Tubeless tire repair kits

Sun Performance
17 Musick
Irvine, CA 92618
(949) 588-8567
www.sunperformance.com
*A variety of compressors, tanks,
and inflation devices*

Custom Wheels and Repairs
Stockton Wheel
648 W. Fremont St.
Stockton, CA 95203
(800) 395-WHEEL
Steel wheel fabrication and repair

Tires
BF Goodrich
PO Box 19001
Greenville, SC 29602-19001
(864) 4458-5000
www.bfgoodrichtires.com

Big O Tires
12650-E. Briarwood Ave., Ste
2D
Englewood, CO 80112
(800) 321-2446
www.bigotires.com

Bridgestone/Firestone
1 Bridgestone Park
Nashville, TN 37214-0991
(800) 465-1904
www.bridgestone-usa.com

Cooper Tire
PO Box 550
Findlay, OH 45839
(800) 854-6288
www.coopertire.com

Dick Cepek
43455 Business Park Avenue
Temecula, CA 92590
(909) 587-0190

Goodyear Tire and Rubber
1144 E. Market St.
Akron, OH 44316
(800) GOODYEAR
www.goodyear.com

Interco Tire Company
PO Box 6
Rayne, LA 70578
(318) 334-8814
www.interco.com

Kelly Springfield Tire Company
12501 Willow Brook Rd. S.E.
Cumberland, MD 21502
(800) 638-5112
www.kelley-springfield.com

Michelin
PO Box 19001
Greenville, SC 29602
(803) 458-5000
www.michelin.com

Mickey Thompson Performance
Tires
4670 Allen Rd.
Stow, OH 44224
(800) 222-9092
www.mickeythompsontires.com

National Tire and Wheel
PO Ox 391
Wheeling, WV 26003
(800) 847-3288
www.ntwonline.com

Pirelli Tire Co
500 Sargent Dr.
New Haven, CT 06536-0201
(203) 784-2200
www.us.pirelli.com

ProComp Tire Company
2360 Boswell Rd.
Chula Vista, CA 91914
(800) 776-0767
www.procomptires.com

Yokohama Tire Corp
PO Box 4550
Fullerton, CA 92631
(800) 423-4544
www.yokohama.com

Wheels
Alcoa Wheels
1600 Harvard Ave.
Cleveland, OH 44105
(800) 242-9898
www.alcoa.com

American Racing Equipment
19067 S. Reyes Ave.
Rancho Dominguez, CA 90221
(310) 635-7806
www.americanracing.com

Center Line Performance
Wheels
13521 Freeway Dr.
Santa Fe Springs, CA 90670
(310) 921-9637
www.centerlinewheels.com

Cragar Industries
4636 N. 43rd Ave.
Phoenix, AZ 85031
(602) 846-0170
www.cragar.com

Colorado Custom Wheels
363 Jefferson St.
Fort Collins, CO 80524
(303) 224-5750
www.coloradocustom.com

Mangels Custom Wheels
710 Rimpau Avenue, Ste 202
Corona, CA 92879-5725
(800) 909-4335
www.mangels.com

Mickey Thompson Performance
Tires
See contact information under
Tires

Prime Wheel
17705 S. Main St.
Gardena, CA 90248
9310) 516-9126
www.primewheel.com

Progressive
3400 Jefferson St.
Riverside, CA 92504
(909) 785-4700
(800) 726-5335

Ronal Intl.
15692 Computer Lane
Huntington Beach, CA 92649
(800) 899-1212
www.ronalusa.com

TSW Alloy Wheels
25954 Commerce Centre Drive
Lake Forest, CA 92630
(947) 609-0801
www.tswnet.com

Ultra Wheel Co.
6300 Valley View Ave.
Buena Park, CA 90620
(714) 994-1111
www.ultrawheel.com

Weld Racing
933 Mulberry St.
Kansas City, MO 64101
(800) 676-9353
www.weldracing.com

Tire Repairs
Safety Seal
See contact information under
Compressors, tire tools, and tire accessories

Drivetrain and Related
Automatic Transmissions
A-1 Automatic Transmissions
7359 Canoga Avenue
Canoga Park, CA 91303
(818) 884-6222
Low-ratio gearsets, built automatics, and parts

Art Carr Transmissions
10575 Bechler River Ave.
Fountain Valley, CA 92708
(714) 962-6655
Performance-built automatics, converters, and parts

B & M Racing & Performance Products
9142 Independence Ave.
Chatsworth, CA 91311
(818) 882-6422
www.bmracing.com
Built automatics, shifters, and parts

Jet Performance Products
See contact information under
EFI and Carburetor Performance
Built automatics, shifters, and parts

Level 10
188 Route 94
Hamburg, NJ 07933
(765) 364-4560
www.rabestosclutch.com
Built automatics and performance parts

TCI Automotive
1 TCI Drive
Ashland, MS 38603
(601) 244-8972
Performance-built automatics, converters, and parts

Trans Go
2621 Merced Avenue
El Monte, CA 91733
(626) 443-4953
Shift kits and auto trans parts

Axle Assemblies
Boyce Equipment
226 West 20th Street
Ogden, UT 84401
(800) 748-4269
Surplus military axles

Currie Enterprises
1480 N. Tustin Avenue
Anaheim, CA 92807
(714) 528-6957
www.currieenterprises.com
Built axle assemblies to order and drivetrain parts

Dynatrac
7236 Garden Grove Boulevard
Westminster, CA 92683
(714) 898-5228
www.dynatrac.com
Built axle assemblies to order and drivetrain parts

R&P 4WD Parts
11889 S. New Era Rd.
Oregon City, OR 97045
(503) 557-8911
Complete custom axle assemblies, floater kits, and custom adapters

Reider Racing
12351 Universal Drive
Taylor, MI 48180
(734) 946-1330
www.reiderracing.com
Ring and pinions, high-performance differential parts

Axle Shafts and Conversions
Dura Blue
1450 N. Hundley
Anaheim, CA 92806
(714) 632-6803
Custom axle shaft and drivetrain parts

Dutchman Motorsports
PO Box 20505
Portland, OR 97294
(503) 257-6604
www.dutchmanms.com
Custom axle shafts and more

Moser Engineering
102 Performance Drive
Portland, IN 47371
(219) 726-6689
Custom axle shafts and more

Strange Engineering
1611 Church St.
Evanston, IL 60201
(847) 869-7010
Custom axle shafts and drivetrain parts

Randy's Ring and Pinion
11630 Airport Road #300
Everett, WA 98204
(888) 231-2488
www.ring-pinion.com
Performance axle products, axle assemblies, and specialty tools

Summers Brothers
530 S. Mountain Ave.
Ontario, CA 91762
(714) 986-2041
Complete custom axle assemblies, custom axle shafts, and floater kits

Superior Axle and Gear
3954 Whiteside Street
Los Angeles, CA 90063
(323) 268-4151
www.footeaxle.com
Performance axles and more

Warn Industries
12900 S.E. Capps Road
Clackamas, OR 97015
(800) 543-9276
www.warn.com
Alloy axles, full-floater kits

General Drivetrain Parts and Misc.
Dana Spicer
PO Box 1209
Fort Wayne, IN 46801
(216) 483-7174
www.dana.com
Ring and pinion, axles, axle assemblies, and parts

Drivetrain Specialists of Las Vegas
3852 Pioneer Avenue
Las Vegas, NV 89102
(800) 216-1632
Axle, trans, t-case rebuild, and parts

Genuine Gear
801 W. Artesia Boulevard
Compton, CA 90220
(800) 421-1050
www.4WheelParts.com
Ring and pinion, axles, axle assemblies, and parts

Mag-Hytec
14718 Arminta Street
Van Nuys, CA 91402
(818) 786-8325
www.mag-hytec.com
Finned aluminum diff covers

Motive Gear
4200 S. Morgan
Chicago, IL 60609
(800) 934-2727
www.motivegear.com
Ring and pinions and general drivetrain parts

National Drivetrain
3631 S. Halstead Avenue
Chicago, IL 60609
(773) 376-9044
www.natdrivetrain.com
Ring and pinion, axles, and parts

Precision Gear
12351 Universal Drive
Taylor, MI 48180
(734) 946-0524
www.precisiongear.com
Ring and pinion, and parts

Randy's Ring and Pinion
See contact information under
Axle Shafts and Conversions
Ring and pinions, axles, and drivetrain parts

Richmond Gear
PO Box 238
Liberty, SC 29657
(864) 843-9231
www.richmondgear.com
Ring and pinions

Superior Axle and Gear
See contact information under
Axle Shafts and Conversions
Ring and pinions, axles, and drivetrain parts

TA Performance
16167 N. 81st Street
Scottsdale, AZ 85260
(602) 922-6807
Alloy differential and cap reinforcement covers

Tri-County Gear
1143 W. Second St.
Pomona, CA 91766
(909) 623-3373
www.tricountygear.com
Custom axles, gear swaps, trans /t-case swaps, steering mods

U.S. Gear
See contact information under
Diesel
Ring and pinions and drivetrain parts

Locking Hubs, Disconnects
MileMarker
1540 SW 13th Ct.
Pompano Beach, FL 33069
(800) 886-8647
www.milemarker.com
Locking hubs and more

Ramsey Winch
1600 N. Garnett Road
Tulsa, OK 74116
(918) 438-2760
www.ramsey.com
Stainless-steel hubs and more

Superwinch, Inc.
45 Danco Rd.
Putnam, CT 06260
(860) 928-7787
www.superwinch.com
Locking hubs

Warn Industries
See contact information under
Axle Shafts and Conversions
Alloy axles, full-floater kit

Whitey, Inc.
6625 S.W. McEwan Rd.
Lake Oswego, OR 97035
(503) 620-8877
IFS differential Posi-Lok disconnects

Lockers/Limited Slips
ARB
20 South Spokane St.
Seattle, WA 98134
(206) 264-1669
www.arb.com.au
Air lockers and more

Auburn Gear
400 E. Auburn Drive
Auburn, IN 46706
(219) 925-3200
www.auburngear.com
Limited slips

Eaton Posi
26101 Northwestern Highway
Southfield, MI 48037
(248) 354-2700
www.torquecontrol.com
Locking and limited slip differentials

PowerTrax
Dept. 4x4
245 Fisher Ave, Bldg. B-4
Costa Mesa, CA 92626
(800) 578-1020
www.powertrax.com
Locking differentials

TracTech
11445 Stephens Drive
Warren, MI 48090
(800) 328-3850
www.tractech.com
Detroit Locker, TrueTrac, E-Z Locker, Gearless Locker

Manual Transmission and Clutches

Centerforce Clutches
2266 Crosswind Drive
Prescott, AZ 86301
(520) 771-8422
www.centerforce.com
Performance clutches

Hays Clutches
8700 Brookpark Road
Cleveland, OH 44129
(216) 688-8300
www.mrgasket.com
Performance clutches

JB Conversions
Dept 4x4
PO Box 2683
Sulpher, LA 70664-2683
(318) 625-2379
www.jbconversions.com
NV 4500 conversions and more

Overdrives and Splitters

Advance Adapters
See contact information under
Engine Swaps
Ranger II underdrives and more

Gear Vendors
1717 N. Magnolia Avenue
El Cajon, CA 92020
(800) 999-9555
www.gearvendors.com
Over/underdrive units and more

U.S. Gear
See contact information under
Diesel
Over/underdrive units and more

Transfer Case Swaps and Conversions

MileMarker
See contact information under
Locking Hubs, Disconnects
Full-time to part-time t-case conversion kits

4xHeaven
221 W. Fulton Street
Cloversville, NY 12078
(518) 725-1203
Remanufactured transfer cases and parts

Transfer Low-Range Kits

Advance Adapters
See contact information under
Engine Swaps
Atlas Transfer Case

Off-Road Design
See contact information under
Lift Kits and Suspension Hardware
Doubler 4:1 three-speed t-case conversion and more

Tera Manufacturing
7055 S. 700 W.
Midvale, UT 84047
(801) 256-9897
www.teraflx.com
NP-241 4:1 low-range conversions, tailshaft kits

Tailshaft Kits

JB Conversions
See contact information under
Manual Transmission and Clutches
Transfer case tailshaft kits

General Parts Suppliers

4-Wheel Parts Wholesalers
801 West Artesia Blvd.
Compton, CA 90220
(800) 421-1050
www.4wheelparts.com
Mail order plus many locations nationwide

Sam's Off-Road Equipment
4345 S.W. Blvd.
Tulsa, OK 74107
(918) 446-5535
Complete custom axle assemblies, drivetrain and engine swaps

Stage West 4-Wheel Drive Center
79 20 Hwy 82
Glenwood Springs, CO 81601
(800) 240-5227
Custom axle assemblies, fabrication, general drivetrain, swaps

Safety

Fire Extinguishers

Ansul, Inc.
1 Stanton Street
Marinette, WI 54143-2542
(800) TO-ANSUL
Fire-fighting products

Kidde Safety
1394 South Third Street
Mebane, NC 27302
(919) 563-5911
www.keddesafety.com
Fire fighting products

First Aid

Lifeline First Aid
PO Box 14220
Portland, OR 97239-0220
(503) 234-3674
www.bedbolts.net
First aid kits and cargo tie-downs

Towing Equipment

Lindon Hitch
475 North State Street
Lindon, UT 84042
(801) 785-5181
www.equalizerhitch.com
Weight-distributing hitches and anti-sway control

Putnam Hitch Products
211 Industrial Ave
Bronson, MI 49028
(800) 336-4271
www.putnamhitch.com
Hitches, towing accessories, and more

Reese Products
51671 SR 19N
Elkhart, IN 46514
(219) 264-7564
Equalizing hitches, towing accessories, and more

Sure Pull
PO Box 7425
Pine Bluff, AR 71511
(800) 566-5352
www.surepull.com
Hitches, towing accessories, and more

Winching Equipment

Ground Anchors

Pull-Pal
PO Box 639
Carbondale, CO 81623
(800) 541-1817
www.pullpal.com
Foldable, portable ground anchor

Manual Winches, Come-Alongs, and Recovery Gear

MAX
Forrest Tool Company
PO Box 768
Mendocino, CA 95460
(800) 269-6629
Multipurpose ax: seven tools in one

Hi-Lift Jack Company
46 W. Spring Street
Bloomfield, IN 47424-1473
(800) 233-2051
www.hi-lift.com
High-capacity mechanical jacks and more

More Power Puller
Avenir
PO Box 1176
Newark, OH 43055
(800) 626-0095
Two-ton come-along

SamSon Enterprises
PO Box 911
Syracuse, NY 13206
(315) 431-0755
www.quickwinch.com
QuickWinch Manual Winch

Winches and Winch Gear

Master Pull
www.mastcrpull.com
(800) 275-3809
AmSteel blue synthetic winch rope and more

MileMarker
See contact information under
Locking Hubs, Disconnects
Hydraulic winches, recovery Gear, and more

Ramsey Winch
See contact information under
Locking Hubs, Disconnects
Winches. recovery gear, mounts, and more

Superwinch Inc.
45 Danco Rd.
Putnam, CT 06260
(860) 928-7787
www.superwinch.com
Winches, recovery gear, mounts, and more

Warn Industries
See contact information under
Axle Shafts and Conversions
Winches, recovery gear, mounts, and more

4x4 Vehicle Manufacturer Web sites

Chevrolet- www.chevrolet.com
Dodge- www.4dodge.com
Cadillac- www.cadillac.com
Ford- www.ford.com
GMC- www.gmc.com
Honda- www.honda.com
Hummer- www.hummer.com
Infiniti- www.infiniti.com
Jeep- www.jeep.com
Kia- www.kia.com
Land Rover- www.landrover.com
Lexus- www.lexus.com
Lincoln- www.lincoln.com
Mitsubishi-
www.mitsubishicars.com
Nissan- www.nissan-usa.com
Toyota- www.toyota.com

Index

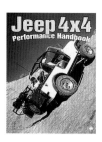

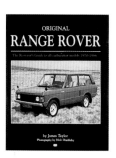

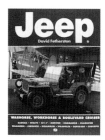